Praise for
The Gentle Traditionalist Returns

Sequels are generally darker than the original, and *The Gentle Traditionalist Returns* is no exception. *The Gentle Traditionalist* was a charming, delightful book which dramatized an encounter between a mysterious Catholic sage and a well-meaning agnostic. I know at least one soul who was led to the Faith by that book's novel and creative exposition of the Catholic Mystery. In this sequel, the Gentle Traditionalist faces not a benevolent agnostic, but a slick and sinister spiritual guru—and the fate of an idealistic young woman hangs in the balance. The personal drama of the main story is mirrored by the backdrop: an Ireland where the forces of secular-liberalism, held at bay for so long by the Catholic Church, are now making spectacular progress. The book is set in the run-up to the 2018 abortion referendum, which sought to remove Ireland's long-held constitutional protection of the unborn child. Although this is a darker book than its predecessor, it would be wrong to assume that it is a depressing read. It builds to an extraordinary conclusion, which left me with a heightened awareness of the spiritual warfare raging all around us, and a renewed eagerness to "fight the good fight." It is not only a compelling story, but a brilliant diagnosis of the spiritual malaise of modern society, written with gentleness, generosity, humour, pathos... and, above all else, love.
—MAOLSHEACHLANN Ó CEALLAIGH, author of *Inspiration from the Saints*

Roger Buck's character, the "Gentle Traditionalist," returns with a vengeance in this stand-alone sequel. In Buck's first book, his protagonist was converted to Catholicism by the charm and arguments of the title character. But said protagonist is now married to a devout Catholic woman; though, happy as their marriage is, a shadow drops across it as the wife's cousin takes up with a self-important New Age teacher. The Gentle Traditionalist re-enters their lives to argue with said Teacher— quite literally for the cousin's soul. Once again, Buck shows his ability to weave together modern religion and politics—and the many defects found therein. Set against the backdrop of modern Ireland's headlong flight from sanity, this book skewers the modern malaise with the kind of sanity we have come to expect from this author.
—CHARLES COULOMBE, author of *A Catholic Quest for the Holy Grail*

Once again, Roger Buck has shown himself to be a prophet in the tradition of Ezekiel; he is the watchman on the wall. Buck's experience as a convert from New Age activism has uniquely fitted him for this vocation. Like Ezekiel, Buck has followed pathways that seem strange, even bizarre. Yet it is these very experiences that invest his writing with an unparalleled and compelling authenticity. It is difficult to escape the conclusion that this man has been raised up by God at this time to warn us of the danger not only at our gates, but already all around us.

—GERARD O'SHEA, author of *Educating in Christ*

Those who were charmed by Roger Buck's previous books—well, prepare to be charmed again, but also warned and given plenty of food for thought. This book strikes a more somber note, but one tuned to the timbre of our times. Read it and tune in.

—THOMAS STORCK, author of *An Economics of Justice and Charity*

The Gentle Traditionalist Returns is a welcome visit from an old friend. Not burdened by the mean-spiritedness of much of what poses as Catholic Traditionalism, Roger Buck's delightful narrative—as the title assures us—gently leads the reader into a new perspective on the Catholic Mystery. An absolutely refreshing read!

—MICHAEL MARTIN, author of *Transfiguration: Notes Toward a Radical Catholic Reimagination of Everything*

The
Gentle
Traditionalist
Returns

THE GENTLE
Traditionalist

CLARIFICATIONS PROVIDED

QUESTIONS ANSWERED

ARGUMENTS ASSERTED

All in the
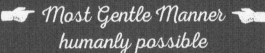
Most Gentle Manner
humanly possible

**(Entirely *Free of Charge*
to all *Genuine Enquirers*)**

ROGER BUCK

The Gentle Traditionalist Returns

*A Catholic Knight's Tale
from Ireland*

✵ Angelico Press

For information, address:
Angelico Press
169 Monitor St.
Brooklyn, NY 11222
angelicopress.com

ISBN 978-1-62138-500-4 (pbk)
ISBN 978-1-62138-501-1 (cloth)
ISBN 978-1-62138-502-8 (ebook)

Cover Design: Michael Schrauzer

This book bears a dual dedication

First to the countless future babies in Ireland who will be killed in their mothers' wombs, owing to the decision in the Irish Referendum of May 25th, 2018 to repeal anti-abortion legislation, the last significant legacy of Catholic law in Ireland.

And second to that great soul who counted the immense human cost of theological, social and economic liberalism, with a heart in pain. Hilaire Belloc, I never knew you, but you nonetheless remain the beloved mentor to whom these pages owe more than words can possibly express.

CONTENTS

A Cautionary Set
of Acknowledgments...

I COMMENCE with an ambiguous debt. The following novel features two New Age characters—one good-natured and naive, the other decidedly less so—that I could never have penned, had I not known countless folk like them, during four decades of experience with the "holistic" scene. (As I explain in the afterword, I was for many years a New Age activist, spending also nearly three years at the Findhorn Foundation in Scotland, which can lay a claim to being *the* seminal centre for the New Age movement.)

This means I have engaged untold people the likes of whom most Catholics never encounter. As I hope this book makes clear, sincere observant Catholics and New Agers are often like "ships in the night" who scarcely register each others' actuality. And even if they do, they may barely be able to believe that people with such different views exist ("How can you possibly *believe* all that jazz?!").

An Irish reader of this manuscript brought this problem home to me: my friend had trouble conceiving the New Age characters' comportment in these pages. Alas, for me, such reactions evidence a frightening lack of awareness among Catholics about the things New Agers *truly* are saying, doing and thinking everywhere—with vast consequence for the Christian culture of the West.

Indeed, as these words are written, Marianne Williamson is an official candidate in the 2020 Democratic primary elections for US president. Marianne Williamson is also a number-one *New York Times* bestselling author of books inspired by *A Course in Miracles*, a key New Age text allegedly dictated by "Jesus," in which "Jesus" appears to undermine the entire edifice of Christianity. Whilst no one need lose sleep at the prospect of a "president from Aquarius," the phenomenon surely demonstrates just how large this massive "tanker in the night" has grown in recent times. It goes without saying that, not so long ago, most Americans could scarcely *imagine* such a presidential candidate, let alone *watch* her in nationally televised debates!

In a sense, then, this book is likewise indebted not only to countless New Agers I have known in real life, but also to New Age authors like Williamson and "Jesus" whom I once esteemed.[1]

That being said, I would stress that most New Agers are *not* consciously out to subvert Christianity. The vast majority are like my good-natured, gullible character: sincere, idealistic, but swept up in modernity and not carefully thinking things through. The more sinister New Ager in this novel is truly a *rarity*, something of a composite of all the worst New Age features rolled into one. Few, if any, New Agers embody all these at once, and it is not without regret that I depict this figure in this manner.

Now to move on to more conventional—and happier!—acknowledgments. First, I thank my beloved Kim, my light, my love, my joy—and a great editor! My other joy, my beautiful daughter Mary, also contributed to this book in an unexpected fashion.

Great love and critical challenges over decades from Georg Nicolaus helped shape this book, as they have all my other writing. Apparently endless kindness from Mark Anderson, likewise over decades, has supported me more than words can say.

Thanks go to my friend Tracy Tucciarone, a fighter for Catholic Tradition at FishEaters on the web (http://fisheaters.com). Her large heart and tireless effort over years are never appreciated enough.

I thank John Riess and James Wetmore of Angelico Press for believing in me. Far more important, though, is their intense commitment to Christ, which has made Angelico such an extra-

---

[1] See the Afterword in this volume for more regarding Williamson and *A Course in Miracles*. My previous book also addresses the *Course* and details my extensive engagement with the New Age movement along with my conversion to the Faith: Roger Buck, *Cor Jesu Sacratissimum: From Secularism and the New Age to Christendom Renewed* (Kettering, OH: Angelico Press, 2016).

ordinary beacon of hope in this darkened time. Similarly, my copy-editor and fellow Angelico author Peter Kwasniewski radiates a clarity that graced this book, as his own books carry luminous graces to many more.

Yet another shining, though very different, Angelico author, Michael Martin, is owed thanks. His influence may not be obvious, but it is profound, working in my depths, giving me hope and élan.

Then, there is my friend Maolsheachlann Ó Ceallaigh, an Irish author whose first book was recently published by Angelico. Not only did he offer invaluable advice and encouragement, his profound love and understanding of Ireland carry a special torch for this country. Long may it flame!

Stephen and Nikita Tyrrell have provided me with inspiration for Ireland of a different sort, as well as illumining comments on my manuscript.

Also Charles A. Coulombe's joyous celebration of the miracles of Christendom, penetrating insight into enduring American Puritanism, and unfailing kindness have blessed me beyond measure.

Another tribute is owed to the Institute of Christ the King Sovereign Priest. Their sacred Latin liturgy and Salesian charity have uplifted me, whilst living in four different countries, France, Spain, England, and Ireland.

I also honour Ireland, especially the rural Ireland I have witnessed whilst inhabiting Counties Clare, Wicklow and Tyrone. I have dwelt amidst nine different peoples in my life, but none have ever touched me as profoundly as the Irish. Of course, the Irish are not without their faults (as neither is any fallen people in this world). But never have I found such kindness, warmth, generosity and piety as in my eight years living here. What I write about the mysterious, Christic Irish in this novel is closely based on real experience that has sometimes left me gaping in astonishment.

And, in alphabetical order, I express my warm gratitude to Manuela Andolina, Nathan Banks, Chris Buck, John and Romany Buck, Kelly Calegar, Michael and Eva Frensch, David House, whilst noting other old friends in the silent appreciation of the heart.

When I am weak, then I am strong.
St Paul to the Corinthians

I

Do Not Despair

WHEN I came to my senses, everything was dim. Outside, wind howled. Heavy rain pelted down on a roof far, far above me. I was lying on a hard, wood floor and my head throbbed. Had someone hit me when my back was turned? I was too groggy to say.

And where was I? It seemed to be the cellar of a once-grand palatial residence. Whatever it was, the wind and rain battered the edifice harder now. I had the sense of shutters and tiles being ripped off, as though everything were being swept away. Far in the distance, thunder pealed. But closer by came whimpering. I could just about discern a small dog cowering beneath a night-stand. Poor, terrified creature, I thought.

Then, above me, further sounds—but more like human whimpering. In the faint light, I scried a spiral staircase. Pushing my aching body up, I staggered towards it and started my ascent.

Then, halfway up the stairs, a door. Behind it, quiet weeping. Should I knock? But sudden anxiety gripped my heart and I trembled. Instead, I stooped, peering through the large keyhole into a room, dimly lit. The elegant figure of a woman in a nightgown was visible, her head bent in sorrow. Between her hands, she fingered a Rosary. Its silver crucifix glinted in the pale light. Words, faltering, came to her lips:

> *Ave Maria, gratia plena,*
> *Dominus tecum.*
> *Benedicta tu in mulieribus,*
> *et benedictus fructus ventris tui, Jesus.*

Then, overcome by grief, she broke down. But clutching the Rosary tighter, she continued:

Sancta Maria, Mater Dei,
ora pro nobis peccatoribus,
nunc et in hora mortis nostrae.
Amen.

Did I dare disturb her grief or interrupt her sacred intercourse? Hesitating, I heard still more human sounds, further up the stairway. Once more, I spiralled upwards. The thunder was distinctly closer now.

At the top of the stairs, heavy folds of velvet blocked my way. Inching the curtains open, I saw three men in shadows. Someone struck a match and lit a candle. A small halo of light fell across a low table in their midst. On it stood an antique telephone with a separate handset and receiver. Piles of papers surrounded it. I could even make out the words on one document. Large capital letters said: DANGER—PLAN B REQUIRED.

One man said, "I told you, Gilbert, the situation is worse than you realise."

The second said, "Another intervention below?"

The third said, "Yes, the danger to the women and all the little ones demands it."

My eyes grew ever more accustomed to the dim light. I could almost make out the first two figures now. I stared in disbelief. For they very much resembled Hilaire Belloc and G. K. Chesterton. Both men appeared in their mid-sixties, as they were in the 1930s, when they spearheaded a Catholic revival in England. And both appeared serious, grim even, which jarred with the mirthful image we have of Chesterton today. But how could they be here in the twenty-first century?! Or was I peering through a portal to the past? Certainly, the antiquated telephone suggested that possibility.

Then, that antique rang! For a brief instant, the third man's hand flashed through the small circle of light, seizing the receiver. In that moment, I saw it clearly. It was large and fleshy, and the middle finger bore a golden ring with an enormous red stone. I had seen that hand before…

"Do not despair," the third man said. "I am coming."

Then, he put the receiver down hard.

Suddenly, a deafening clap of thunder and lighting! For a split-second, the entire room lit up. In that instant, I saw the tall, rotund form of the third man, his hair and beard white as snow. I saw the faded tweed jacket. It was the Gentle Traditionalist.

With a start, I woke up.

II

Anna

IT was 5 A.M. I rose from my bed and stared out the window. Rosy dawn crept through the Limerick streets, slowly transforming their shadows into pale, tentative colour. Limerick, of course, is in Ireland. And it was my new home after moving there from London. Then, I looked at Anna, asleep in her nightgown. Anna is my wife. She's English like me, except in her heart. Anna's heart has always been Irish.

Was she the woman in my dream? Anna suffered, I knew. Maybe, though, I didn't see how much. Was the dream a warning? I brushed the thought aside. Back then, I still couldn't face the truth.

We were happily married, I told myself, blissful newlyweds. Moreover, moving to Ireland was Anna's dream come true. Her father had been Irish, and even as a child, she wanted to leave England for a country she found magical. But Ireland was no longer the magical land of her far-away childhood holidays. Its Catholic culture was being destroyed. Even I could see that. But my heart didn't bleed, like Anna's did.

It took me so long to wake up. I'd loved Anna for the longest time, you see, since I was twenty. That's twelve years ago now. Back then, we were madly in love. Later, she abandoned me. I didn't realise it, but Anna couldn't bear my cynical, over-analytical nature. I was utterly irreligious, then. She felt suffocated by scepticism.

And so she left me for its *polar opposite*: the strange world of New Age spirituality. She still thirsted for magic but, by then, she'd forgotten Catholic Ireland and sought New Age magic instead. First, she went to a Scottish community called Findhorn.

4

Then, she travelled the world, from India to California, hopping from one New Age hotspot to the next.

Then, to my astonishment, she embraced something even stranger to me: Roman Catholicism. At last, she remembered the original, true magic of her ancestral land. She even entered a French convent with the Latin Mass, meaning to be a nun!

I thought I'd lost her forever. But I never stopped loving Anna. And I knew, deep down, she still loved me, too. We kept in close contact all those years. First, she wrote me emails filled with New Age mumbo-jumbo. Apparently, we were entering a "holistic epoch," where "new energies" would "initiate a planetary shift of consciousness." Aargh. That stuff always drove me nuts. But years later, her insufferable jargon changed. Instead, the "awesome power of the Mass" transformed the human heart.

To me, it all sounded like the same nutty stuff. What was her problem with *me*? I really did not get it. We loved each other. I knew it! But she preferred this New Age rubbish to me and then—so I thought—this Catholic "rubbish." How blind I was.

But Anna gave up the convent and came at last to Ireland. I visited her and the mysterious power of Ireland started changing things between us. Or *changing me*. That—along with this ancient Irish geezer who finally showed me what was under my nose the entire time. "Anna may not admit it—even to herself," he said. "But she longs to marry you. I am sure of it. It isn't you she can't bear. It's *your world*."

Then he added: "Your secular world with its new religion. Your world that claims to stand for equality and rights, but crushes anyone who dares to stand for Christian principles. This is how she sees it, I'm afraid. Her world has meaning, grace, beauty—*life*. It feeds her soul. Your world leaves her empty, hungry, cold… Her world—the world of Christendom—built Chartres Cathedral, the Sistine chapel and the Sacré Coeur de Montmartre. Your world builds tower blocks and suburbs and billboards and monotonous offices with cramped little cubicles. Not to mention pornographic television networks. Your world is dedicated to power, profit, a purely materialist metaphysic. Her world is dedicated to HIM…"

HIM, of course, was Jesus Christ. My mind screamed. The old

guy was ridiculous, I told myself. Round the bend barking mad. Still, certain things he said made sense. Anna *yearned* for something my secularism couldn't offer. At first, her only outlet was the New Age. Later, she discovered "the Catholic Mystery" (as she came to call it).

Slowly, I started to listen to the old man, really listen. And, in the course of a single mind-bending day, he turned my thinking—indeed my entire life—upside-down.

That man was the man in my dream. The guy with the ring: Gilbert Tracey, the Gentle Traditionalist. ("Just call me GT," he said.) But almost as soon as he appeared, he mysteriously vanished. I never saw him again. Yet meeting him changed *everything*. It was so extraordinary I wrote an entire book about it!

Anyway, GT not only reconciled me to my lost love, he also helped me peer beyond my rationalist blinkers. It's funny, really. I was Cambridge-educated and considered myself cosmopolitan and sophisticated. I was smugly Left-wing, proud of just how "inclusive" I was. But my liberal education never included the greatest force in Western history: the Catholic Church.

GT, then, opened my eyes to a new world, never glimpsed before: a culture completely marginalised by my "multiculturalism." As Tracey made clear, all I really had was a restrictive ideology trapped in time ("post-1960s," GT called it) and culture (English), which *unconsciously factored out most of humanity.*

Preposterous, I said! But, piece by piece, GT deconstructed my culture-bound views. Partly, he achieved this by traditional arguments, arguments my supposedly brilliant education never prepared me for. But he also used other, more mysterious, means, with that ring of his and its strange red stone. Then, bizarre visitors arrived. One of them even said the ring had relics of "the True Cross, the Holy Blood and fifteen Roman martyrs." Anna now says GT is a saint and a priest returned to earth to rescue us. But before the Gentle Traditionalist returned, that seemed highly unlikely to me...

Still, I can't deny downright weird stuff happened that day. And things didn't stop there. No, Anna agreed to marry me! All these years I'd waited for her... Now, thanks to GT, she not only became my fiancé, but also my teacher. Before, I thought her a religious nut. And sometimes, I still thought she went too far, over-reacting to things. Yet now, in many ways, she seemed wiser and older than me.

With Anna's help, I began questioning my progressive paradigm. Increasingly, I realised religious conservatives were not as ridiculous as I thought. Whereas I was concerned with social justice, they were awake to other issues—issues I was *sound asleep to*. For instance, they saw how our supposedly tolerant, multicultural society wasn't really tolerant *or* multicultural. More like a monoculture, really.

This is what this book is about—how I came to see things differently. How Political Correctness tyrannises people. Or how the media is dominated by a progressive narrative that crushes anything anyone like Anna has to say. Yet my old liberal paradigm wasn't completely false. The Left had won important victories, for example, against things like racist segregation or the capitalist excess of giant corporations and banks. In the past, that led me to embrace Socialism. Then I discovered Catholic thinkers like Belloc and Chesterton, who likewise figured in my strange dream. And they pointed me to Distributism, which resolved that false binary: Capitalism / Socialism.

All this theory may seem unnecessary. I warn you: there'll be *more* digressions like this. They're relevant to my story. But there's more to it. Because this book ISN'T JUST A STORY. It's also analysis and commentary: an examination of *why* the Gentle Traditionalist returned. It also concerns my continuing intellectual and spiritual journey: from Left-wing Progressive to Catholic Knight. Yes, *really*. But I'm getting ahead of myself...

Hardly a year after meeting GT, I did the unthinkable: I became Catholic. Three weeks later, Anna and I married in the Church. In just a few short weeks, then, I experienced five sacraments! Baptism, Confirmation, Communion, Confession, Marriage. That was an intense blast, at least for someone who never experienced the sacraments before.

At least, that's what Anna said. She always talked about the sacraments like that: powerful, potent, mysterious. Since she'd started "absorbing the sacramental graces" (as she put it), her entire psyche, even her body, was changing.

Whoa! Claims like that were too much. Weren't they a tad grandiose? But, as time passed, my doubts receded. Anna encouraged me to attend Mass with her every day, and I noticed something strange: an *interior difference* if I missed Communion. (Once, I had a terrible flu and didn't commune for a week. The difference inside was *palpable*—as though something precious was *subtracted* from my life: noticeably *missing*.)

Also, we went to a Latin Mass, offered by a French institute dedicated to Christ the King. Unlike my wife, I had hardly experienced the new English Mass initiated after Vatican II. I went straight from my old secular life to Tridentine liturgy. Anna called that "a rare privilege" for a convert in this day and age. And day after day, the Latin Mass worked on me, shaping my soul.

Now, in Anna's view, the loss of that Latin Mass carried tragic consequences for the Church. Yes, she admitted, certain priests could and did celebrate the new liturgy with dignity. But they were a minority. Across the world, millions were subjected to a morass of muzak and mediocrity that obscured the Miracle at the Altar. In Anna's view this was slowly, insidiously destroying the Church.

Groan. Surely, it wasn't *that* big a deal was it? Surely, she was over-reacting again! Didn't the Church teach that the Body and Blood of Christ were truly present in the new Mass? Wasn't it a contradiction, then, to consider the old Mass objectively superior to the new?

But Anna responded with an unusual analogy. She likened the new vernacular liturgy to a *sieve*. This strange image reconciled two apparently conflicting claims. For, on the one hand, the Church maintained that Christ was equally present in both Masses. Anna accepted that. But, on the other hand, the New Mass clearly lacked something. That was plain to her. Heck, it was even plain to me! People behaved differently at the new Mass. Their attention wandered all over the place. That was perfectly clear from the few times I went to it. Even the priests sometimes appeared absent-minded and sloppy, at least by comparison to the palpable reverence at the old Mass.

Anna's analogy of the sieve resolved this tension between the two Masses. Yes, Jesus Christ became fully present in every valid

Mass, new or old. But the traditional Mass provided something further, a crucial addition: a *container* that aided and HELD His Presence. That container was created through the sacred language of ecclesiastical Latin and the rubrics, prayers and gestures omitted in the new Mass. The fact that the Tridentine liturgy instilled reverence, *naturally directing people's attention to the Mystery,* amplified its effect. That old container was missing in the new Mass, replaced by something else—something that did not hold or facilitate the proper attention, piety and receptivity to the Mystery at the Altar. Something that *leaked like a sieve.* All the omissions acted as HOLES. That was why the new Mass often, if not always, degenerated into a slovenly affair.

At any rate, it is three years since the Gentle Traditionalist upended my life. At times, I still struggle with scepticism, but I am a changed man. Thanks to His Body and Blood. And Anna. Because all this time, she *prayed for me.* And, by now, I know enough not to doubt prayer. (There's one more factor too—the uncanny, mysterious power of *Ireland.* But we'll get to that later.)

Still, not everything was roses. It's a cliché, but that old Dickens line sums it up: it was the best of times; it was the worst of times.

That dream *was* a warning. There was another side to our newlywed bliss. Anna really suffered. She anguished about the world in ways that startled me. This was new! The old Anna was always harping on about "global transformation." The Age of Aquarius was a-dawning and no one would ever be the same again. *Crazy* stuff.

But I see it now as a defense mechanism: papering over pain. Anna, like most New Agers, was highly sensitive. Aquarius offered an easy escape. It helped people like Anna deny life's harsher realities. "New Agers," she would say, "need their fantasies—because they don't have the sacraments. The sacraments give you strength to face the darkness inside yourself. Without that strength, you crave fantasy, magical positive thinking: 'You create your own reality.' 'You can heal your life.' You can do *any-thing*—all by yourself..."

Anna was beyond that now. But she was still vulnerable. When things hit her, they hit *hard.* And shortly after we moved to Limerick, something unexpected hit very hard indeed. Back in England, her Irish father collapsed with a heart attack—and died. Even though their relationship was never easy, Anna was devastated.

Anna's Irish father was raised Catholic in rural County Cork. But he moved to Liverpool as a young man. And promptly lost the Faith. Anna was born there in 1983 and her childhood was not happy. Her father, often drunk, beat her mother, who eventually ran away with Anna.

Yes, that childhood was grim—but for one major respite: holidays with her paternal grandmother in the lush, green mountains of County Cork. This was *another universe* to Liverpool—a magical one! Outwardly, her grandmother's windswept, hillside village, drenched in the never-ending Irish rain, appeared bleak and uninviting. Inwardly, it *felt* different. Rich warmth suffused the place. The Irish were astonishingly friendly—and pious. Because back in the 1980s, Ireland, especially rural Ireland, remained steeped in Catholicism—a far cry from today's globalised, secular Ireland which, in little over thirty years, has almost entirely replaced the old Catholic culture.

But when Anna had to return to Liverpool, everything was "Godless" again, she said. "I didn't use that word then, of course, but even as a child, I saw how *different* Ireland was. My grandmother took me to Mass—*every day*. Half the village was there! After Mass, they'd prayed the Rosary together. Every house had a picture of the Sacred Heart of Jesus with a red lamp beside it. And the people were *unbelievable*. There was nothing like that in England! I was ten when mum left my dad. She never took me to Ireland. I never saw my grandmother again..."

Thus, Anna forgot mysterious Ireland, with the Mass, the Rosary and the Heart of Jesus bleeding for the world. Her teenage years were cold and grey. And *that*, many years later, explained her attraction to the New Age. Her grandmother had awoken deep spiritual hunger inside her. But the Church was forgotten, indeed *obscured, denied and denounced* by British culture. Nothing in England ever suggested the Catholic Mystery could quench her thirst. And so she turned to lesser "mysteries."

All this, I thought, gave Anna something of an animus towards

English society. To my mind, she criticised England excessively in favour of Catholic Ireland—or what remained of it. That always rankled me. But I started to understand now.

At any rate, her thing about England surfaced after her father's funeral. Anna felt the horror of his boozy, wife-beating life like never before. Obviously, her father had free will. But, to her mind, the faith-destroying English culture couldn't be exonerated from this tragedy.

Something else, too, sliced into her heart: the sight of her extended family, *en masse*, at a dreary, purely secular funeral. "It was all so *Godless*," she wailed. And her family, she said—brothers, nephews, nieces, cousins, etc.—seemed lost. "Their lives have no meaning," she cried. "All they have are material things. Good movies, good food, good clothes, a good laugh. All that matters is finding pleasure—avoiding pain. That's it! *Nothing* else."

And so the old theme of soulless England versus Catholic Ireland rose up. Except this time she added: "And now Ireland's going the same way—copying the English…" This bugged me. I knew Anna's family from way back. I couldn't attend the funeral, but I'd met them again at our wedding. They were kind, decent people. "Aren't you being harsh?" I said. "Your family aren't *that* bad! They're nice people. Maybe you're forgetting to see the positive side sometimes."

How our roles had reversed! Before, I was the grumbling cynic and Anna the upbeat New Ager, forever extolling "positive thinking," however unreal it might be. Anna appeared chastened by my reprimand. "Maybe, maybe you're right," she said. But next day, she corrected herself. And me, too. "I've been asking myself if you were right. Was I over the top? I don't think so. You're right, of course—there's real kindness in my family. There's human goodness everywhere. And, nowadays, we're told that's enough. That people are *nice*. But people are *weak*, too. Weak and broken. I saw my nephews and nieces. They're just like I was, growing up. They have nothing meaningful! Some of them may get addicted to alcohol like my father. Or porn. Or drugs. Or just trapped in lost, empty lives. Yes, some may turn out better. Still, they could have so much MORE than this."

Something about the way she said "more" unnerved me.

Maybe Anna wasn't over-reacting, after all. Maybe, unlike me, her eye was always fixed on greater horizons of human possibility.

"But nobody is allowed to say *this more* even exists!" Anna said. "This is what modernity does to people. Denies them *hope.*"

I felt torn listening to Anna. On the one hand, I respected her like never before. Yet I worried that she demonised things. Demonised the modern world, demonised England—even demonised the Church. Because, inevitably, the modern Church came into this too.

Indeed, the dire state of the Church positively *tortured* Anna. Baptisms, vocations, faith in the Real Presence of Christ were in *free-fall*, she lamented. Much had changed for the worse since the shocking resignation of Pope Benedict XVI in 2013 led to the new papacy of Pope Francis. That new papacy created a new ecclesiastical climate, a more "progressive" one that empowered liberal voices. It also led to what looked like civil war. Utter chaos reigned in the Church. The Church was divided and thereby *crippled*, Anna said.

"We have to *do* something…"

"But what can we do?" I said.

"Anything and everything we can!"

Do something. It hit me, when she said that. Was Anna right? Were things worse than I realised? Was I just *dithering* on the fence? Something else hit me too. My wife's face. There was something there that I hadn't seen before. Something that evoked the memory of the Gentle Traditionalist. I had watched, staggered, as that old man wept, openly wept. And not for his own lot, but *humanity's* lot. "The world is turning insane," he said. There was *gravitas* to his stricken expression, when he said those words: a solemn, suffering beauty. And now, in my wife's eyes, I saw the same thing…

III

Ireland

HAMLET: I've always related to that doubting prince of Denmark. "To be or not to be"—that's a *big one* for me. Anna seemed so sure of herself. Like so many people. But the world, with all its conflicting claims, confused me. However did people achieve such clear certainties, which often seemed so pat and simple?

Now, I *was* listening to Anna. Belloc and Chesterton, too. I assented to the fundamentals of the Faith. But that's not the same as crusading for Christ. And it's tough to be a crusader—or a Catholic Knight, if you will—when you aren't *convinced*. The way the Chesterbelloc was convinced. But I am getting ahead of myself...

At any rate, something else now entered the picture. And it started *speaking* to me. It was Ireland.

Yes, Ireland speaks. For 1,600 years, this island has been continuously steeped in the sacraments. Neither the Dark Ages nor the Reformation ever destroyed the Irish sacramental life. Anna says it's like nowhere else on earth. Maybe there, she's not far wrong.

Because something *blew* me away: our visits to a vanishing world. Anna's ancestral home in rural County Cork is scarcely an hour from Limerick and we visited her extended family there— all sorts of cousins, uncles, aunts. There we witnessed a world virtually extinguished, but not forgotten. Indeed, that world could still be glimpsed, talking to the elderly and very elderly. For they remembered all that Ireland had been...

"Today, everybody's just out for themselves," they would say. And clearly, they recalled a time when Ireland was *different*. Different from anything I had ever known. "If your cow wasn't giving milk, you could always ask your neighbour," one man told me. "Or you'd run out of something else. You'd just go next door! We had nothing back then—but we were happy."

These things jolted me. All my liberal life, I dreamed of a communitarian order, regulated by the State. But these people recalled a rich, communal life—the likes of which I could never imagine!—that didn't need state control. It arose *organically* from their Catholic culture. And they grieved its passing. Now, they witnessed egocentric attitudes that were obviously *new* to them. I protested—because the Irish *still* seemed extraordinarily warm and generous compared to England. "Ah, but it's not like it used to be," they said. They *all* said that.

Moreover, they were genuinely shocked by media reports of violence, crime and drugs. Once, such things were extremely rare in Ireland. No more! My old faith in unlimited cultural progress was shaken.

Their faith, too, startled me. The old folk recalled working the fields. When the Angelus rang, everyone stopped to pray. Passing by the church, they crossed themselves and doffed their caps. One time, we took Anna's ninety-four-year-old great aunt Mary out for a spin. The first thing she did was to pray for our protection. Then, she started the Rosary. But she was hardly unique. In church cemeteries, one saw frail old men clutching beads in gnarled hands and praying by the graves of their "mammy" and "pappy," long departed from this world.

Inevitably, we ended up talking about our own country, England. These old Irish folk couldn't understand my descriptions of the English as largely atheist or agnostic.

"Atheist, what exactly do you mean?" one old farmer asked me.

"They don't believe in God," I said.

The old man couldn't believe his ears. "But how, how do they explain all this?" he said, his hand sweeping across the emerald expanse beyond, sheep grazing in the fields and mountains rising in the distance.

"Science, the Big Bang," I said. "Apparently, it's just a gigantic accident. Atoms came together to form molecules, molecules—somehow—formed living cells. It's like that idea of monkeys on typewriters."

"Monkeys on typewriters?"

"Well, some people think if you handed a million monkeys a million typewriters, for a million years, one of them would eventually produce a Shakespeare play. Genius isn't required—only *chance*. Given all the possible configurations of letters and symbols, something complex and meaningful eventually would emerge. Creation is simply a gigantic accident, something that *just happened* without any purpose or intelligence at all."

His jaw dropped open. "It's easier to believe," I added, "that the entire universe results from a one in a million, trillion *chance* rather than intelligence."

"But what about their dead? What about their graves?" he stammered.

"They don't have graves." I told him about Anna's father's secular funeral, without a Mass, without a prayer. I'll never forget that poor man's bewilderment.

Then, Anna's great aunt Mary died. We attended the wake, held in her little cottage. I almost choked, seeing the old lady in her coffin. An awful memory surfaced: the sight of my dead grandmother—the only corpse I'd ever seen. I was visiting my gran in her care home. An awful place, where she was bitter and miserable. A young nurse let me into her room, but gran was snoring away in her chair. Then, she started to make strange noises. Before I could call anyone, she convulsed, jolted forward and collapsed on the floor.

I cried for help. The next two minutes were the longest two minutes of my life. I was stuck, helpless, looking into the tortured face of my grandmother. When help eventually came, I ran to the bathroom and threw up. That face, twisted in pain...

How different this old Irish lady was to my poor, miserable gran. Lying there, her features emanated serenity, while her hands lightly clasped a tattered Rosary. Undoubtedly, those hands had fingered thousands of mysteries. I noticed other things around the room. Two candles burned at either side of a large crucifix. Beneath was a wooden box, filled with cards. Expressions of condolence, I thought. But Anna read my mind. "They're Mass cards," she corrected me. "The Irish are very serious about praying for their dead." The box was stuffed *full*. Unlike my departed grandmother, this woman would have untold Masses said for her soul.

"We're not in England any more, are we, Anna?"

"No, we're not."

"In the name of the Father and of the Son and of the Holy Spirit." The village priest arrived and the Rosary began. Everyone joined in. But I slipped out, needing to digest all I had seen. I was hungry, too, and copious sandwiches were offered in the kitchen.

A sombre man greeted me there. He turned out to be great aunt Mary's son-in-law. His obvious grief surprised me. Clearly, he cherished his wife's mother. Indeed, he built the cottage we were standing in—a small place for her just beside his own. That was ten years ago, when she lost her husband. Situations like this remain common in Ireland. And nothing like what I knew from England, where nursing homes are the norm.

All this, of course, relates to rural Ireland. The Irish cities are different, more globalised. Still, even there, an unusual communitarian spirit persists. In Limerick, the sheer friendliness of the people bowled me over. I was surprised, too, by charitable drives to help the needy, very different to anything I knew in England.

Limerick even had real piety! A church near our house has a permanent chapel for Eucharistic Adoration (as so many Irish churches do). Anna visited it daily, "drinking His Presence," as she put it. Now, I couldn't feel that Presence as she could. I didn't swoon, as she did. Still, I went. And, besides the quiet stillness in the room, something else hit me: the sheer number of pious city dwellers arriving day in, day out, genuflecting before the monstrance, praying hours on end. Definitely not in England any more...

Some say the new, liberal, globalised Ireland is hardly different from liberal England next door. Not me. The longer I lived in Ireland, the more I realised how unfathomably different Ireland truly was. Not only was there a kind, communitarian spirit to the Irish, not only was there piety, there was something else, too. Something harder to name, ultimately mysterious. Anna suggested words like "soul" and "sensitivity." The English, she pointed out, spent centuries ridiculing the Irish as superstitious, even stupid. But Anna asked: "What if the Irish mind were every bit as intelligent as the English and it just lacked that British bent for pragmatism? What if the Irish sensibility were informed by something more profound and poetic that the more rationalistic English just couldn't see? What if the steady, uninterrupted currents of the Catholic Mystery, working over centuries, transformed the minds and hearts of these people in a way beyond all English comprehension?"

Hamlet-like, I vacillated when she said things like that. One day, I'd be sceptical and say, "I know the sacraments are important, Anna. But how can you be so sure they're *that* important—enough to alter an entire country's nature?"

Next day, I changed completely. "Good Lord, Anna! I see it now. Catholicism *did everything for this country*! Now it's being systematically destroyed by secular values." (Usually, on those days, I'd been reading the great Chesterbelloc. But we'll return to that duo later.) Then, the day after, doubt returned.

Still, the new globalised culture is making powerful inroads, particularly with the young. Even on my more vacillating days, it bothered me. By contrast, it *afflicted* Anna. What happened to Ireland stabbed at her heart. The younger generations of Ireland, bombarded by global media culture, had *no idea* what their grandparents cherished. How many of them would never know the wisdom of tradition, the solace of prayer, the sheer power of the sacraments, Anna asked. How many would *never know* the Catholic Mystery?

Moreover, the young were regularly told their ancestors were idiots. This was the media. It appalled Anna. All you ever heard was how backwards, hidebound, small-minded Catholic Ireland was. Yet Anna was clear that "narrow" Catholic Ireland possessed a breadth of heart and mind and vision that was utterly beyond the tunnel-visioned media.

Really, I couldn't disagree. Of course, the old Ireland, like any country, had problems. Utopia never existed anywhere. Some of these problems were *serious*. There was sick clerical abuse of children, which afflicted a small, terrible portion of the priesthood. Disgustingly, certain clerics covered up the abuse. At the same time, the small numbers involved were comparable to the numbers found among caring professions in secular countries. Yet the media painted this sickness as something *specific* to Catholicism, while it denied all the other good in Irish Catholic culture.[1] Increasingly, the sheer injustice revolted me.

Anna was right. Catholic Ireland *did* have something special, very special. Moreover, Ireland was remarkably free from other problems in the West. And all the while I listened to Anna, the Gentle Traditionalist's words kept ringing in my ears. Like the old folk in Cork, GT, too, remembered Ireland from long ago. His memories, too, opposed all the media said.

"I've been watching all this for a long, long time. Longer than you think," the old man said. "The ever-increasing murder and suicide rates in de-traditionalised Ireland, for example. Or drugs, prostitution, domestic violence, homelessness... These things would have shocked previous generations. But we accept them as 'normal' now. And it's not stopping, but growing..."

"There's more," he said. "The growth curves of mental illness. And the growth curves of children taking drugs to combat mental illness... What about other forms of illness? We see an explosion of sexual perversity, sadomasochism for example. It's pathological. But you're no longer allowed to say that, of course. In the past, these things were seen as sicknesses of the soul. Now they're normalised and accepted as an 'alternative lifestyle'! It's politically incorrect to call them 'sick.' Soon it may be illegal to do so—what with legislation against 'hate crimes' and the like... Moreover, the power of technology is boosting the secular metaphysic like never before. Never before has humanity been bombarded like this—round the clock. Television. Advertising. Pop songs. Jingles. Internet. iPods. And it's going to get worse. Virtual reality is coming, no doubt virtual pornography..."

When GT said that, it was too much for me. *Way* over the top, I thought. Increasingly, though, I no longer felt sure. Hamlet, vacillating, confused, conflicted...

Because GT's words planted a potent seed in my mind. Like never before, I noticed the pernicious effects of media. It was clear

---

[1] This appalling topic is important. But this is not the right place for it. It is, however, addressed in depth in my previous books: *The Gentle Traditionalist: A Catholic Fairy-tale from Ireland* (Kettering, OH: Angelico Press, 2015), 114–22; *Cor Jesu Sacratissimum*, 412–17.

to me now, as it was to Anna, that the media *lied* about Ireland, lied to *millions* of people—as GT said: *around the clock.* These old folk weren't fools. They were some of the best people I ever met in my life! And the Ireland they remembered wasn't a lie.

Well, I digress. Once again, there'll be more digressions like this. Because *there's more to this story than just story.* Madness and media are key to this book. They're key to understanding why the Gentle Traditionalist returned. And they're key to understanding my impending knighthood.

Likewise, they're relevant to something else: Brigid's predicament.

IV

Brigid

BRIGID was another of Anna's relatives from Cork. A cousin—pretty, petite and just turned twenty. She and Anna shared the same grandmother who, long ago, offered my wife a childhood taste of Catholic Ireland.

But Brigid was fifteen years younger than Anna and had never known their grandmother, who died not long after she was born. Meanwhile, by the time Brigid was growing up in the 2000s, Ireland was far more secular than the country Anna remembered from the 1980's. Still, Brigid's youth remained somewhat Catholic, at least. Perfunctorily, her family heard Mass each Sunday. But she heard other things too—including all the media mendacity against Ireland's past.

At any rate, we both liked Brigid. The three of us started hanging out. We went down to Cork; she came up to Limerick. But Anna was appalled at how little Brigid understood the Church, even if she identified as Catholic. When Brigid and Anna discussed the Faith, it was like *two different religions.*

Brigid adored Pope Francis. His famous injunction, "Who am I to judge?," referring to gays, stunned the world—and she loved it. Pope Francis, Anna pointed out, never endorsed gay sex—let alone gay marriage! But that, Brigid insisted, was because "the forces of intolerance" remained too strong in the Church. Pope Francis had to move slowly, but "everyone knew" he was "cool with love"—whatever form it took. He was just beleaguered by "rigid right-wing Cardinals" and so on.

"Everyone knew... cool with love... rigid right-wing Cardinals." Where did Brigid get these interpretations? Had she studied the matter—carefully comparing different Cardinals to arrive at her own independent conclusion? Evidently not. And the all-too-obvious answer hit Anna in the guts. Me, too, actually. Ultimately, it boiled down to the media: the see-all, know-all, tell-all media, the new Super-Pope of the modern age.

One time, Anna challenged Brigid on "gay marriage." "Doesn't a child need a mother and a father?," Anna asked. But her cousin gave a pat answer about two lesbians she knew who were "great mothers."

Anna and I looked at each other. How well we understood Brigid! Not long ago, we would have said the same thing ourselves. Any who disagreed with us would be damned as heartless homophobes. It would never have occurred to us that anyone opposing "gay marriage" could be anything else.

"Brigid," Anna said, "I don't doubt these women are good, kind people. I also know there are terrible 'straight' parents. My father beat my mother. He was awful to me too. My mother ran away. I'm sure there are many gay couples who are better than that. But—"

"I don't see what your problem is, then. Why discriminate against good, loving people? Just because they aren't sexually fulfilled by the opposite gender."

This was painful. To Brigid, our thinking obviously sounded rigid, bigoted, cruel. I understood just how "sensible" her position sounded. Why shouldn't two homosexual people who cared about each other be sexually gratified?

Only now, I saw the problem here: just how utilitarian that argument was. *And nothing else.* For millennia, the wisest people in every religion saw that sodomy, mutual masturbation, and the like were wrong because contrary to the natural order that came from God. And there is *more*: the wise also knew that the world is not simply rational, it is also trans-rational. God encompasses human reason. But, likewise, He transcends human reason. What if sex involved a mystery far beyond anything materialistic logic could account for? What if sex meant *more* than simply pleasuring genitalia? What if, throughout the ages, Catholics always knew these things—until their knowledge was shattered by modern pundits, pop stars and politicians? Could it be the great saints and philosophers of antiquity knew something we didn't?

"Brigid," Anna continued, "this isn't about individuals. It's about a principle that transcends that, a religious principle."

But how the heck would Anna explain a *transcendent, religious principle*? When a lifetime's media conditioning, which endlessly mocked religious reality, filled Brigid's mind to the brim…?

I interjected. I couldn't explain something *precluded* by Brigid's life-long brainwashing. But I could do something else, instead. I could point to people Brigid respected, who held the same views we did. Alas, these couldn't be Catholics. The media rendered anybody but the most progressive Catholics automatically suspicious. But Eastern figures were "legit." The media always painted them as "cool."

So I invoked the Dalai Lama and Mahatma Gandhi. The first spoke out against gay sex and the latter was appalled by *any sex at all outside of procreative purposes.*

Brigid was taken aback. How could such "cool" people be so stupid?

"Geoffrey is right," Anna said. "For millennia, people from all religions—Catholic, Protestant, Buddhist, Hindu, Islamic— always saw something distinctly problematic in de-coupling sex from procreation in the context of committed marriage."

Anna was being gentle. I was more sarcastic: "But now we're supposed to believe they were all idiots or homophobes, filled with hate!"

"All I want to say," Anna said, "is when you have people in all traditions for thousands of years, seeing, sensing, feeling the same thing, when you have sages, saints, mystics agreeing, perhaps there IS something to consider here. That's why it's dangerous dispensing with tradition. People get so trapped in the Zeitgeist."

"Zeitgeist?"

"It's German. Literally: time-spirit. Basically, it means the spirit of the age. But this age doesn't have a monopoly on truth! That's why tradition is important—so people don't get *trapped in time.* Geoffrey was a bit blunt. But he's right. Not everyone who came before you and me was blind or stupid."

Anna paused, before adding, "Sex entails profound transcendent mysteries. The greatest souls of all ages always knew this. And not just religious souls. Many non-religious psychologists and philosophers still maintain that the male and female archetypes are important. Especially for a child growing up, needing both mother and father."

Brigid had no idea what to say. Anna took this as a hopeful sign. Maybe she was getting through, even a little. Still, my wife had no illusions. Brigid's mind, she knew, was bolted shut to the truth—that male and female represented sacred realities and that the more those realities were blurred, bent, distorted, the more suffering was bound to happen.

Seeing the sheer hopelessness of explaining true, sacred sexuality, Anna stuck to her original question: was it right to foster a climate of gay adoption, where millions of children would grow up never knowing who their father or mother was? Was it not possible growing children needed both the male and the female?

"B-but," Brigid said, "don't gay people deserve the joy of children too?"

"Your compassion for gays and lesbians is important," Anna said. "But a child deserves compassion, too—above all, the child. The child is the most vulnerable person here! There's a risk of commodifying children..."

"Commodifying?"

"I mean a child is not a commodity. You can argue people have a right to own *things*—a house or a car, whatever. They may even have a right to destroy them if they like. A little boy or girl is something different. There's no right to mess with a child's psyche!"

Brigid looked bewildered. Anna was actually getting through. Brigid said she'd never heard anything like this *in her life* before. And no, it didn't quite make sense that today's world was all right and yesterday all wrong.

Brigid left. Anna had been magnificent, I thought: kind, considerate, but passionate and intelligent. But my wife was distraught. Why were *we* the only people who ever said such things to her? What on earth were her priests telling her? And why was the media her *sole source of authority*, without reference to the Church?

Exchanges like this helped me see just what had happened to Irish Catholicism. Like never before, they forced me to confront the awesome power of government, business and media elites. The power to destroy an entire culture like Catholic Ireland...

And so I decided to study the situation, to look at Irish history. Researching this, I learned that television only arrived in 1961 via a *single* channel (followed by a second one in 1978). Before the '60s then, people, obviously, didn't watch television in their homes. No, they prayed the Rosary daily. Frequently, they heard Mass daily as well. Confession was a serious thing, too. As late as the early 1970s, a quarter of the Irish population still confessed weekly and many, many more went monthly.[1] By the time Brigid turned teenager, there weren't just one or two television stations, but plenty. The new media acted as a powerful, corrosive solvent. Like battery acid...

Indeed, when television arrived in 1961, a certain visionary already saw what would happen. During the very first Irish television broadcast, Éamon de Valera, then-president of Ireland, issued a prophetic warning:

> Like atomic energy, [television] can be used for incalculable good, but it can also do irreparable harm. Never before was there in the hands of men an instrument so powerful to influence the thoughts and actions of the multitude.... It can lead through demoralization to decadence and disillusion.[2]

It was strange. Éamon de Valera had been not only president of Ireland, but a founding father of the Irish Republic. As an Irish nationalist, he fought in the 1916 Easter Rising that led to Irish independence. And Brigid's family identified strongly with Irish nationalism. They even sent her to an Irish-language school. Yet hardly any Irish culture existed in her home. It was nearly all English and American. British pop music, British soap operas, Hollywood blockbusters, Amazon, Facebook, Google and all the rest. And the little Irish media that *did* exist aped the Anglo-

---

[1] Buck, *Cor Jesu Sacratissimum*, 383.

[2] Quoted in Robert J. Savage, *Irish Television: The Political and Social Origins* (Westport, CT: Praeger Publishers, 1996), xi.

American culture. De Valera must be turning in his grave, Anna said. But that hardly bothered Brigid's family.

At any rate, I came to agree with Anna: the Irish elites had *no idea* what Catholic Ireland had been. They bought into the same secular myths of "progress." They repudiated the principles of 1916. But as Anna pointed out, these elites were raised in the "Anglo-American sandwich" of 1960s and 70s television and pop culture. Which is to say, Ireland was wedged between mighty forces from either side, England to the East and America to the West.

And now the "progressive" tide appears unstoppable. Year after year, it gets worse. In 2015, the new secular Ireland became the first country in the world to approve "same-sex marriage" in a referendum. Maybe nothing else better illustrates the change in Ireland from the 1980s that Anna still remembered. Back then, divorce was illegal in Ireland! That blew my mind when I first heard it. The idea that Ireland could be *so* different from Britain was staggering. (Indeed, in 1986, not even 30 years prior to the "gay marriage" referendum, there had been another referendum—for divorce. But the pro-divorce side *lost*.)

Such an astonishing change in less than thirty years! The media had a *lot* to answer for. Anna, I realised, was not as extreme as I thought. Brigid changed me. I saw she'd been brainwashed. Bombarded from her earliest days. Round the clock. Like GT said. She never stood a chance.

Still, it wasn't just the media. It was hard not to imagine that Pope Francis's famous "Who am I to judge" played its part in the referendum. Certainly, it was quoted everywhere in Ireland at the time. There were also reports of millions of dollars pouring in from progressive groups in America to ensure the Irish voted the way they "should." Moreover, the same sort of thing happened years later with an abortion referendum. But, again, I am getting ahead of myself...

V

A World Turning Mad?

THE day after Brigid left, I found Anna weeping. She pointed to an email from Bobbie-Jo, a conservative Christian friend—Protestant, in fact—from Alabama.

In the past, I rolled my eyes at Bobbie-Jo's beliefs. Her fundamentalism was *way* too much for me. Today, my mind was more open. Her email talked about Political Correctness. Apparently, it was running riot in America. There were Americans who actually believed that saying "God bless you" when someone sneezed was an *act of violence*. They called it a *microaggression*. Shop assistants, too, risked their jobs saying "Merry Christmas," instead of "Happy Holidays." And terms like "hate speech" were applied to people who didn't hate at all. They just refused to be flattened by our "open, tolerant, multicultural" society.

But was this why Anna cried? No. I kept reading. The letter grew ever more disturbing. Bobbie-Jo quoted snippets from the internet. One concerned a young boy—under ten—performing shows as a "drag queen," while his mother looked on proudly. Another young boy, likewise under ten, was given "puberty blockers"—powerful drugs to delay the onset of adolescence—by his lesbian mother so that he could "choose to be a girl" (as Bobbie-Jo put it). "It's terrifying," Anna said. "'Male and female he created them.' This is what happens when you throw that truth away. Children are driven into hell, hell on earth."

Anna got up, saying she needed to pray. I was at a loss for words. By now, you'd think I was completely on-board with her. Yet *still* my "inner Hamlet" vacillated. I remained conflicted about her dark view of humanity. Was she not too fearful, too despairing, too black and white?

But then, the other side rose up in me. I felt like giving Hamlet a boot in the rear. Maybe my problem was that I just didn't care enough. Anna cared. She *cared deeply.* Maybe my heart wasn't as big as hers. Or it was numb, de-sensitised to the madness we both saw around us? Or was I *addicted to sitting on the fence?* All that's true, I think—looking back now.

Of course, no two are the same. We all experience the world in different ways. Lord knows Anna and I were very different! For a start, I was more gregarious, craving stimulation. Also, I'm a news junkie. I need the internet. Anna got that, just like she got so much else. But she herself avoided media. It seemed toxic to her. To an extent, then, we inhabited separate spheres. I meant to engage society. But painfully sensitised in ways I couldn't imagine, Anna was turning inwards. She was a contemplative, praying for the world, but needing retreat from that world, a world which, increasingly, *hurt* her…

And here is the place to say how, just four weeks after we were married, *the world changed.* Future generations may not remember how this *astounded* people of our time—but on 23rd June 2016, Britain voted for Brexit, withdrawal from the European Union. Months later, Donald John Trump beat Hillary Clinton in the American election. It was widely described as the greatest political upset in American history! There was a palpable sense, "this wasn't supposed to happen." Indeed, *Newsweek* even prepared a special edition in advance, with Clinton's beaming face on the cover, beneath the legend "Madam President." 125,000 copies were actually bound and printed—until someone must have made a terrified, frantic phone call: "Stop the presses! Something's happening that's not supposed to happen…"

Like everyone else, I was stunned. And to my shock, I realised I was not disappointed that Clinton lost—as I would have been before. Which is not to say I liked Trump! Clearly, though, my thinking was evolving.

Here I digress again. This book is a record of my journey, a meditation on why the Gentle Traditionalist led me to the Emperor of Christendom. And all this, including my digressions, entails what GT saw so clearly: *the world turning insane,* becoming ever more polarised, ever more hysterical, ever more *abstract and unreal…*

The last is something conservatives appreciate better than progressives. And before GT entered my life, I had been extremely
progressive. You'll get the idea, if I tell you Noam Chomsky was
my hero. But now I was starting to see how much the annihila-
tion of Irish Catholicism owed to the Left.

Obviously, it wasn't just Ireland. The Left opposed the Church
from the start. That start had been 1789, the French Revolution.
The Left was born when the revolutionaries *lined up on the left side*
of the French parliamentary chamber. Not long after, they seized
control of the Church. Soon, they were executing priests and
massacring Catholic laity. Yes, the Left has a long history of crush-
ing the Church at every turn. There's been genocide, including
abortion, and now the "right" to give children puberty drugs and
have their genitals chopped off.

At first, all this was a tough pill to swallow. I valued the Left's
call for economic justice. As far as I could see, gigantic banks and
corporations menaced humanity, indeed, the entire biosphere.
And Chomsky's critique of this perversity still spoke to me, even
if his socialist solutions didn't. (And Chomsky's calling an unborn
child "an organ" now revolted me.)

All this, in time, led me to the great Chesterbelloc. Now, Chesterton and Belloc criticised Socialism and Capitalism equally.
Indeed, they considered Socialism as the *bastard child* of Capitalism.
After all, Socialism only rose in protest to the new capitalist order
pioneered by Britain (and Holland) after the Reformation. Capitalism *and* Socialism, then, were byproducts of Protestantism. But the
Chesterbelloc proposed a Catholic alternative: *Distributism*—a system where wealth would be concentrated neither in the state
(Socialism) nor in gigantic banks and corporations (Capitalism).

We can't go into Distributism now. But you'll see something
else was changing for me: my reading. Before, I was your arche-
typal "*Guardian* reader." (That's a British term. It's even in the
Collins English Dictionary: "a reader of the *Guardian* newspaper,
seen as being typically left-wing, liberal, and politically correct.")
Indeed, *The Guardian* was the only paper I read. I abhorred most
other English papers, like *The Daily Telegraph*, as "fascist rags."
(Just like I automatically rejected conservative evangelicals from
Alabama with names like Bobbie-Jo.)

Now, I tried something *new*: reading both sides! I subscribed to both *Guardian* and *Telegraph*. And I read more on both the radical Left, beyond the mainstream *Guardian* (e.g., Chomsky), and the radical Right, beyond the mainstream *Telegraph* (e.g., the Alt-Right that emerged at this time). Just as Chomsky had some terrible ideas, so, too, did the Alt-Right. It carried with it an ugly new racism, which also reared its head in the new, changed world of 2016. But I meant to listen to *everyone*, including abortionists and racists.

This was a revelation. My long-trusted liberal narrative began to collapse. The liberals, I saw, weren't *listening* to the other side. They suffered from kneejerk reactions, just like mine with Bobbie-Jo. Of course, the conservatives were frequently not listening either. Politics began, then, to look quite different to me. For one, I was astonished how my old Leftist colleagues lionised Clinton. Even a little wider reading made it clear how corrupt a candidate she was: a pawn to the Wall Street banks. But my old friends on the Left couldn't see that. And the very fact I criticised Clinton meant they no longer heard a word I said. For them, all light was concentrated in Clinton, all darkness in Trump. Any sense of perspective was obliterated. A charged binary fever took hold of people. Yes, 2016 seems to me, at any rate, a landmark: *the year the world changed.* Sheer hysteria reigned like I'd never seen before.

Something else made an impact on Anna and me during this time. Brigid went to London for some temporary work. Or so she said, because she never came back. Weeks turned into months and all Anna received were a few strange emails—with phrases like "consciousness shift" and "holistic paradigm." Anna recognised the jargon instantly. She feared Brigid was taking the same New Age route she had done, years ago, at much the same age.

Anna tried ringing, to no avail. When she finally got through, Brigid was mysteriously vague and evasive. However, she perked up when Anna mentioned one thing: Findhorn, the New Age community where Anna once lived. Findhorn—now *that* was something interesting!

"Brigid," Anna said, "I thought Findhorn was great at the time. I would never have moved there if I didn't! But it never gave me anything, anything like the Mass."

"But why can't you have both?" Brigid said, "be Catholic and holistic, too?"

Anna sunk. As though Catholicism were not already holistic, and needed supplementing! What to say? Quoting Scripture or the Catechism would be meaningless to Brigid. She was replete with the New Age ideology Anna knew so well—where all religions were the same and it didn't matter what you were: Catholic, Buddhist, Wiccan, Voodoo. Whatever floats your boat.

Anna tried a personal tack. "I thought that once too. But the more I went to Mass, the more I saw that the Church offered something *completely different* from 'holistic spirituality.' I had to choose *which* spirituality to follow. Christianity—or that other one."

This made no sense whatsoever to Brigid. Anna knew why. After the phone call, she explained it to me. According to the New Age, there was only one timeless, universal "spiritual path." In every era and culture, it always amounted to the *exact same thing* (at least in essence).

"That's why it doesn't matter to New Agers what religion you have or whether you have any religion at all," Anna said. "It's *inconceivable* to them that the Church offers *anything different* to what they already have!"

"I get it," I said. "If you already have direct access to 'universal spirituality'—why bother with anything else?"

"Yes, Geoffrey. But it's not just that! New Agers can't see that anything else *even exists!*"

"I'm not with you. Nothing else exists...?"

"No OTHER form of spirituality. My old New Age friends think *their spirituality is just the same as mine*—I've just added some useless baggage to it. Catholic baggage."

Only now did it sink in. "I see. Catholicism and New Age-ism must share the same 'universal' essence. Because, according to the New Age, there *can't be any other essence*—only the 'one timeless path.'"

"Yes. They think they're just the same as me—except I'm

bogged down by 'Old Age' dogma." Anna was horrified. "She wants to go to Findhorn! Throw away the Church for that."

This bothered me too. In the past, I hated Anna's New Age-ism. It seemed so superficial, anti-rational, filled with facile answers to everything. By now, I realised there was nothing glib to Catholic tradition. Unlike the New Age, it was intellectually and existentially *serious*. It wasn't anti-science, anti-"left-brain," and it didn't say human suffering would soon be washed away by an Age of Aquarius.

This time, I truly understood my wife's pain, I knew what Brigid was losing. And I knew the reasons too. Ireland's new progressive culture paved the way for New Age-ism. Brigid grew up hearing a constant mantra: how *bad, bad, bad* the Church was. Yet, like so many Irish, she experienced a spiritual thirst. Now a brand new "cool spirituality" came along which would *never offend secular values*.

Irish progressivism was preparing for something else, too: abortion. In 2017, a new Irish prime minister promised a referendum next year to repeal Ireland's long-standing legislation against abortion. This referendum stood a chance of success. Irish twenty and thirty-somethings like Brigid were especially likely to vote for a horror their forebears could never have imagined.

So much was coming together now, hitting me at once. And it all turned on just what GT said: the world turning insane. There was the binary madness around Brexit and the American election. There was the madness that children didn't need a mother and a father. Or children becoming drag queens. There was New Age madness that all religions that ever existed were "just the same thing, really." Or that we were all about to experience a "planetary awakening to higher consciousness." Man, people must be truly *desperate* in order to believe this stuff.

By now, it was clear something was very, very wrong with my old progressive paradigm. Yet I remained uncertain what the answers were. And I worried that traditionalists like Anna went too far. Maybe that was the problem: I *worried* too much. Hamlet, indeed.

VI

Belloc

THE music was exquisite, sublime even.

And it was *my* music. I was playing Mozart on my violin.

It sounded incredible. I'd never played music like that before. Indeed, I'd never played *any* music before. I'm tone deaf and can't sing a note—let alone play an instrument.

Yet now I was a soloist in a vast auditorium. And everyone was enraptured by my virtuoso performance.

The hall, however, was getting mysteriously warm. Too warm. I put the violin down to take off my tuxedo and loosened my bow-tie. The audience didn't seem to mind. I was a maestro, after all. What did a little interruption matter?

Again my magnificent music filled the hall. Yet still the hall grew hotter. Suddenly, a stout old man stood up in the audience and screamed "FIRE!"

But no one seemed to care. My rich, resonant refrains were all that mattered.

Then, that stout man bounded onto the stage. He seized my violin! And with a mighty blow, he smashed it over my head!

You'd think that would be painful. Oddly, though, it wasn't. The violin near broke in half. But, apparently, I was impervious to pain. "That's one thick skull you have," the stout man said, handing my ruined instrument back to me. "Sorry about the violin, Nero. But it's time you woke up! The whole house will go up in flames if you don't!"

I stared at the man in disbelief. Only then did I recognise him: it was Belloc! And now, the floorboards beneath my feet buckled and gave way. They were on fire…

Then, I really did wake up.

Nero, he called me, the Roman Emperor who proverbially fiddled while Rome burned. Most dreams are cryptic. This time, the symbolism was hard to miss. Was I fiddling like Nero while the West was on fire? While everything that protected human sanity went up in blazes...?

After that dream, I really had to ask myself that. And before continuing my story of Brigid, Anna and Ireland, I digress one more time about media, madness and Mr Belloc. For Belloc, you see, not only featured in my dreams, he figures later in this tale, the tale of how I became a Catholic Knight...

For Belloc—unlike me—confronted reality head-on. A century ago, he faced the stuff people still can't see today—including the scandalous power of the media. Also, Belloc remembered the time before the media assumed its awesome might of today. Because when Belloc was born in 1870, *the only regular media was the Press.* Even that was relatively new, back then! There was no radio or cinema, much less television. But, during his own lifetime, Belloc witnessed developments that deeply troubled him:

> There had appeared in connection with *this new institution* [my italics], "The Press," a certain factor of the utmost importance. Capitalist . . . in origin and therefore exhibiting all the poisonous vices of Capitalism as its effect flourished from more to more. This factor was *subsidy through advertisement.* . . .
>
> Long before the last third of the nineteenth century a newspaper, if it was of large circulation, was everywhere a venture . . . dependent wholly upon its advertisers. It had ceased to consider its public save as a bait for the advertiser. . . .
>
> In the first place, if advertisement had come to be the standby of a newspaper, the Capitalist owning the sheet would necessarily consider his revenue from advertisement before anything else. He was indeed *compelled* to do so unless he had enormous revenues from other sources. . . . For in this industry the rule is either very great profits or very great and rapid losses. . . . He was *compelled* then to respect his advertisers as his paymasters. To that extent, therefore, his power of giving true news and of printing sound opinion was limited...[1]

---

[1] Hilaire Belloc, *The Free Press: An Essay on the Manipulation of News and Opinion, and How to Counter It* (Chicago: IHS Press, 2008), 33–35.

I still recall when I first read that. It knocked the wind out of me! Which was funny—because, at one level, it was patently obvious. Yet, at another level, no one seemed to notice. Everyone, including myself, was sleepwalking through the *scandal* that giant business elites owned the media, and news inimical to their interests was easily suppressed in favour of

> the news which its owners desire to print and the opinions which they desire to propagate. . . . The strength of a newspaper owner lies in his power . . . to withhold or to publish at will hidden things. . . . The power of the Press is not a direct or open power.[2]

> We see the growth of the Press marked by these characteristics. (1) It falls into the hands of a very few rich men... (2) It is, in their hands, a mere commercial enterprise. (3) It is economically supported by advertisers who can in part control it, but these are of the same Capitalist kind.[3]

> The big daily papers . . . have become essentially "official," that is, insincere and corrupt in their interested support of that plutocratic complex which . . . governs England. [They] are not independent where Power is concerned. They do not really criticise. They serve a clique whom they should expose, and denounce and betray the generality. . . . The result is that the mass of Englishmen have ceased to obtain, or even to expect, information upon the way they are governed.[4]

These words were written back in 1918. But if you substitute "Western world" for "England" and "media" for "press" you have, I think, insight even more relevant today than it was then, because today's situation is the above writ large, beyond Belloc's worst nightmares. Since his time, media has become concentrated into even fewer hands than before. Only a few giant corporations now control the major means of communication. Moreover, today's media is a hundred times more insistent, invasive, blaring, than anything Belloc could ever imagine. It has

[2] Ibid., 39, 44.
[3] Ibid., 37.
[4] Ibid., 51.

transformed into an all-encompassing, all-consuming "surround sound" presence—bombarding people's minds from multiple directions at once. "This Capitalist Press has come at last to warp all judgment,"[5] he said a hundred years ago. But in terms of humanity becoming warped, Belloc had seen nothing yet...

All this helped me understand the schizophrenia I started to see from 2016 on. It also explained a strange new term that emerged about this time—as though a new, sinister force had suddenly entered society: "fake news." Reading history, though, convinced me that "fake news" was nothing novel.

Example: In 1916, America needed British propaganda in order to enter the First World War. That requirement was met when the English press reported fake news of "massive" loss of American lives in the German sinking of the *Lusitania*. There was also the constant media drumbeat as to how bad, bad, bad the Germans were. Which is not that different from the Irish drumbeat today: how bad, bad, bad Catholic Ireland was. *Plus ça change, plus c'est la même chose.*

Slowly, I developed ever more respect for Belloc—a respect Chesterton obviously shared. The latter joined the former's crusade against the plutocratic media. But what was I doing about these things? Nothing... nothing but fiddling!

Let me return to my marriage. Anna and I both felt the dark clouds gathering over Ireland, particularly as 2017 turned to 2018 and the ominous abortion referendum was set for May that year.

Anna, then, prayed ever more intensely that the unborn might be spared. But she also encouraged my quest to understand history. Indeed, she coaxed me to take writing classes and record my insights. Tentatively, I began to blog. Frequently, though, I suffered writer's block. I *still* wasn't sure of myself.

Maybe, reader, you think that's crazy! After all that happened to me with GT, Anna and Ireland, and now Belloc and these dreams! But if you've been radically Left-wing all your life, you don't turn into a Catholic crusader overnight. You don't get to meet the Emperor either—not without a special dispensation.

---

[5] Ibid., 37.

No, more would be needed to penetrate "Nero's thick skull."
And it came in the form of a very different kind of crusader that
Brigid met...

VII

LightShadow

"BRIGID spilled the beans," Anna said, one cold winter morning. It was February, three months before the 2018 referendum. And now, the mystery of Brigid's extended stay in London was explained: her "heart chakra had opened."

She had met a man with a strange name, Gareth LightShadow. That's how he spelled it, both parts capitalised. LightShadow, it turned out, was a rising star in England's New Age scene. And Brigid was besotted with him.

And there was more. Brigid was visiting Ireland—with her beau! LightShadow was touring the country, talking in all the major towns. Brigid wanted us to hear him next Saturday night in Limerick. Then, she suggested they visit us the Sunday afternoon.

"What's he speaking on?" I asked.

"Apparently," Anna said, "the talk is called: *A Love Revolution: Holistic Spirituality for the New Millennium.*"

I groaned. "Do we *have* to go—can't we just see him Sunday?"

Anna looked glum. "I need to, Geoffrey. I want the best possible sense of this guy. I wish you would come, too. Brigid says they're really serious. She thinks they're getting married. She also has something big to tell us."

"What could be bigger than getting married? Unless it's a 'love revolution'…?"

"I don't know. It's all so mysterious. Brigid says LightShadow was a Labour Party activist in London. Then, he moved to San Francisco where a 'peak experience led to an astonishing spiritual transformation.'"

"Oh?"

"Apparently, he was head-butted by a wild zebra on the rampage—"

"A wild zebra...?" I said, reeling. "Rampaging through *San Francisco*?!"

"Er, there seems to be a Safari park just outside. Anyway, he was knocked unconscious for three days. But not before he saw the zebra's black and white *stripes* charging toward him. When he came to, in the hospital, he saw the stripes as 'nature's perfect, seamless integration of darkness and the light.' And so he 'learned to love both sides of reality.' I guess that's why he calls himself LightShadow. Now he teaches 'Zebra consciousness'..."

"Wonderful. I can't wait."

"You'll come then?"

"Wild zebras couldn't hold me back."

And so that weekend, I made my way to meet LightShadow. (Anna was arriving separately, after an appointment elsewhere.) To our disquiet, his talk was hosted on ecclesiastical property—St Columba's Hall, next door to the church. That sent a clear signal that the church was fine with LightShadow's revolution. And when I entered the hall, it hardly felt Catholic. Temporarily, at least, the surroundings were transformed. Crystals were laid in every corner of the room, while a CD played mellow sounds of ocean waves, gently lapping on the shore. Candles burned, and the hall was filled with the scent of incense and aromatherapy oils.

Brigid ran over and gave me a big hug. Then, she took me to meet her man. He was not at all what I imagined. I expected a goofy-looking guy, even a clown in a zebra suit. Maybe my misapprehension holds a lesson—that people like me aren't prepared to see what the New Age truly is. They expect non-stop silliness, without realising New Agers can be seriously ambitious, determined, steely.

LightShadow, it turned out, was all these things. He was also tall and handsome, with piercing blue eyes. The minute I saw him, I didn't like him. He dressed expensively, entirely in black. From the top of his head—black hair pulled back into a neat ponytail—to his shining black Gucci shoes, the guy looked *slick*. And strange. For he wore a jet black cape and a purple amethyst ring. Another amethyst featured in a silver earring. Finally, silver buttons stood out prominently against his black shirt, like little stars in the night, complementing a black and silver Yin-Yang medallion dangling from his neck. The man exuded power, charisma, magnetism.

I was surprised, too, by his age—fifteen years older than Brigid, as it turned out. The petite Brigid seemed young and naive next to his commanding presence. I couldn't help thinking she looked like a little elf captured by a great magician.

LightShadow greeted me with a condescending grin, which I soon saw was a trademark feature of his mien. At last, my wife arrived. "Anna, meet Gareth," Brigid said. But Anna blushed when she saw him. I didn't understand why till she explained later—she'd met this man before. What was more, she'd *kissed* him. It happened at a Findhorn workshop, long before we met. Anna was only eighteen at the time.

One evening, they walked out to the beach by the Findhorn bay. Moonlight glittered on ocean waves. Suddenly, he made a pass at her. Anna didn't resist. She was young and insecure about her looks, even though she was always stunning. Still, she felt fat and this charismatic man flattered her. He was obviously a "kindred spirit" too—a romantic, a New Age dreamer, hardly like the other young men she knew from Liverpool. They lay down on the dunes. He continued his advances…

Nothing like this had ever happened to Anna. Fortunately, she broke it off, saying she wasn't ready. The next day, LightShadow was involved with another woman. But days later, he was after her again, intensely flirtatious, trying to charm her at every angle. But Anna was wary now and nothing came of it. After a fortnight, the workshop finished. They both left and never saw each other again.

"We've met before," Anna said.

LightShadow looked at her quizzically. "Really?"

"Findhorn, 2001. We did the holistic transformation workshop together. We… also went to the beach one night."

"Oh man," Gareth said. "I remember! Hey, you were great at that workshop. I liked what you said there—a lot! What happened after that—did you ever go back to Findhorn?"

"Well, actually, I went to live there for a few years."

"You actually *lived* there—cool!"

Anna felt dazed. She didn't know what to say. She saw how he looked at her. Was it her imagination or was he drawn to her all over again, as the memory of their moonlit passion surfaced in his mind?

"What are you doing in Ireland?"

"Well, I'm married now, to Geoffrey here."

"Oh, cool," he said. But Anna couldn't help thinking he sounded disappointed. "Hey, Bridge" (it was clearly an affectionate nickname) "and I sometimes talk about getting married. I'm not sure we're ready. But maybe someday, we'll be related."

"Maybe," Anna said, struggling to recall something. He had a different name back then. A name that disturbed her. But she couldn't remember...

"You changed your name."

"Yeah, I liked the old one—but it creeps some people out."

"Really? I don't remember."

"Crowley. Yes—as in Aleister. Actually, I'm distantly related to him. My father's second cousin or something. Personally, I don't have a problem with the name. But occasionally I got flak for it. I don't need that. Better to claim my own identity."

"So Gareth Crowley transformed himself into Gareth Light-Shadow," I said.

"Yeah—but Crowley wasn't as bad as people think. Some things he did were amazing. That Tarot deck he designed is sublime."

"Yes, I remember those cards," Anna said and shuddered. But LightShadow didn't notice. He was relaxed, clearly imagining himself amongst fellow-travellers.

"Of course, Crowley had a shadow. Who doesn't? No light without darkness—we all have to embrace our shadow. That's all I'm trying to say."

"By your name, you mean."

"Yeah, my name is a symbol. Symbols are important. But there's more, like this cape..." He opened out the black mantle. Inside, it shimmered a silvery white.

"You see, light on the inside, shadow on the outside. Both one. Both parts of the same whole. You have to surrender to the darkness and the light. Enlightenment. Endarkenment. It's all the same thing, really."

"Uh-huh," I said, "Like Jesus and Hitler, I suppose." Light-Shadow gave me an odd look, but said nothing. He was more interested in Anna, I think. At any rate, LightShadow's weird outfit made sense to me now. The prominent silver buttons on the black shirt. The Yin-Yang medallion. Even his jet black hair had a thin white streak down the centre.

"Really, Crowley wasn't that bad." LightShadow said. "He had an inner light, for sure. And he had to walk his own path."

I felt like screaming. Right now, though, wasn't the time. His talk was just about to start. And I wasn't going to start something I couldn't finish. Still, I didn't like the guy and I especially didn't like how he kept staring at Anna.

"So, Anna, what's *your* path these days?"

"Well, I'm a Catholic now," Anna simply said.

"Oh. Wow. How did *that* happen?" LightShadow was taken aback. His brain could not compute how someone could go from Findhorn and the Tarot to Catholicism.

"It's a long story…" Anna was also struggling, uncomfortable with his gaze.

"Well, that's cool. There are some great Catholics too. Bridge was raised Catholic."

"This isn't England," I said. "Most people here are."

"Yeah, it's true! You can't escape it over here!" he laughed. "Still, it's cool if you want to be a *conscious* Catholic. That's what's needed today, conscious people in every religion. The Church needs consciousness! It needs healing—people to shake things up. I mean, Pope Francis has made a start. But there's a way to go. A *long* way," he laughed, before adding: "I'll catch you later. My talk's starting now."

With that he was off. He interpreted Anna the only way he knew how. No way could Anna be a *real* Catholic, he must have thought. She just meant to "heal" the Church: help it to achieve "higher consciousness."

VIII

A Love Revolution?

BRIGID, Anna and I sat down in the front row. Suddenly, a blast of music startled us: the opening notes of the Marseillaise, the French National Anthem—originally the marching song of the 1789 revolution. Except it wasn't the Marseillaise. Only the first few seconds were. After that, English lyrics started in: "Love, love, love." It was, of course, *All You Need is Love:* the Beatles' smash hit from the so-called 1967 "Summer of Love," which co-opted the first chords of the revolutionary anthem. Was it merely coincidence, I wondered, that this theme song of the 1960s cultural revolution began with the bloody battle hymn of that earlier revolution, which shattered Christendom? At any rate, LightShadow clearly felt that the tune suited his new twenty-first century "Love Revolution."

Moreover, listening to the lyrics, I saw why. Inane lyrics, when you stopped to consider them. "Nothing you can do that can't be done." What on earth was that supposed to mean? Also: "Nowhere you can be, that isn't where you're meant to be." I wondered what John Lennon, who wrote the song, would have said to the Jews in Auschwitz? But, "it's easy. All you need is love, love, love is all you need." I'd never thought much about pop music or its social impact before. But, increasingly, I questioned the effects for humanity bombarded night and day by catchy tunes spouting meaningless words. Or worse than meaningless. I thought of Belloc, who recalled a world before anything like this existed. What would he make of today's civilisation, inundated by the trivial and absurd? A silly question...

The song receded into the background, while a young Irish woman introduced LightShadow. Or Crowley. Or whoever he was. She lavished praise on him as a new, upcoming "spiritual teacher," who we would all remember in days to come. Her implication was clear. LightShadow might not be the next New Age superstar like Eckhart Tolle or Deepak Chopra *yet*—but someday, perhaps someday soon, he could be. She also announced an upcoming three-day workshop in Dublin with a "rare opportunity to work with him directly, in a personal setting." Better snap up the opportunity, while you can, she said—places were going fast. Price: 300 Euros. Finally, she plugged his book—*On Becoming a Zebra: Lessons from the Borderland of Consciousness*. Copies were for sale, which the "spiritual expert" was "happy to autograph."

Grinning, LightShadow began explaining how "all the old barriers to love" were breaking down. In the past, we had elitism, racism, sexism, age-ism, fascism, homophobia and religious fanaticism. Now, everyone was joining hands together in a new "multicultural, multifaceted spiritual reality," which "totally transcended" all bigotry and prejudice. This was the "love revolution"—the dawning Age of Aquarius. From now on, evolution would proceed faster and faster. Everything was "turbo-charged" onwards and upwards.

All this entailed a new "holistic spirituality," which superseded "all dogmas." According to this "New Paradigm Spirituality," all religions expressed the same timeless essence that was always the same in every time and culture. Only externals changed. Hence, religious differences were mostly accidents of culture, relating to "surface stuff": Hindus didn't eat beef, Muslims didn't eat pork. Catholics once avoided meat on Fridays. None of that mattered, according to LightShadow. The key thing was the central points every religion agreed on, "beyond the illusory veil of separation." Things like peace, love, oneness, mindfulness. That, he asserted, was what "the Christ" taught. Moreover, "the Christ consciousness" embraced every perspective. And so all religions, all beliefs, were equally valid. Only "cultural dinosaurs and neanderthals" didn't get that. But not to fear, because today's "holistic revolution" was "conquering minds and hearts everywhere."

Yet all this sounded relatively normal, compared to what followed. For LightShadow increasingly inserted that strange, incomprehensible New Age jargon: things like "gracefully, gently proceeding to a higher matrix of ascending consciousness," or "people's heart chakras beginning to open and rotate in fourth dimensional order."

Now, that's the gist of his talk above, except he also told the story of his "spiritual transformation"—how his "consciousness was first flattened, then profoundly altered by the zebra." (I couldn't help thinking it was the other way round.)

But to make my story perfectly clear, it's necessary, unfortunately, to quote the guy at more length. (Not difficult, as it appeared on YouTube weeks later, rapidly accumulating thousands of views.)

"What the new paradigm is about," LightShadow said, "is *essential* spirituality. What is the true, pure, eternal essence behind every religion?"

"Exterior things change with time," he continued. "Only the timeless 'Now' doesn't change. That's why religions always get stuck in the past. For example, society used to be patriarchal. Naturally, then, you had to be male to get ahead in the religion game. Doesn't matter if you were Buddhist, Muslim or Catholic—the hierarchy was always male. Today, we're transcending that cultural baggage. On higher planes of consciousness, it doesn't matter if priests are women, gay, trans—whatever! Unfortunately, the old mainline religions aren't ready to surrender their control." Then, he looked directly at Anna and said: "Not yet, anyway. They're going to need a big push."

Anna grimaced. She recognised this ideology all too well. Once she had said the same herself. In our own way, we both did. I was an agnostic liberal, she was a New Ager—but we talked about religion just like LightShadow: "cultural baggage," "stuck in the past," "outmoded," "archaic." We didn't realise it then, but Anna's New Age-ism and my Liberalism were cousins. Estranged cousins maybe, but with more in common than either cared to admit. Listening to LightShadow was payback.

"Neither Jesus, nor Buddha, nor Moses was into that junk," the man was saying. "All the great spiritual teachers opposed injustice! They didn't tolerate the status quo! Because every religion always begins with a universal vision. Later on, the authentic inspiration gets warped. The original messenger gets replaced by lesser men every time. (Historically, they're always men.) Religion wouldn't be such a mess, if they only allowed women in. What if we had Oprah for pope?" (Roars of laughter from the audience.) "Really, they should let her have a bash. She certainly couldn't do any worse than your average male hierarch. After all, it's men who usually do the head-tripping, I mean, hair-splitting theology. How many angels can dance on the head of a pin? All that left-brain garbage."

Had LightShadow read a single word of theology in his life? From the evidence on hand, it seemed highly unlikely.

"What's more," he continued, "all those male hierarchs just love a good war! How soon they forget that Confucius, Buddha, Jesus were messengers of peace. Not fundamentalists who traded in violence! That's why you got the Crusades, the Jihads, the Nazis. Don't forget most Nazis considered themselves good Christians. Hitler was actually a Catholic. Undoubtedly, his anti-Semitism came from his own Christian roots. That's why we need 'New Paradigm Spirituality'—something not controlled by theologians and maniacs. (Because that's what happened in the old paradigm. Priests always controlled everything.)"

Horrible. Hardly anyone noticed, I think, the sleight of hand by which LightShadow seamlessly blended priests, fundamentalists, maniacs, Nazis—as though they were all the same thing. Or at least cut from the same cloth.

"But the Middle Ages are *over*! Free spirits can explore life's magic for themselves," LightShadow said. "The change over the last centuries is mind-blowing! Remember, information was so limited before our multicultural society! Or mass media. Or the internet. Spiritual seekers couldn't check out holistic stuff the way they can today! In the past, you had only one option: Your local religion—rigidly controlled by your parish priest, pastor, imam or whoever. Now, there's a vast cafeteria of spiritual options, every one valid for each individual's needs. Cool, huh?"

All this, I guess, sounded convincing. Unfortunately, I doubt any of the audience ever read anything by men like Belloc. Belloc, who recalled a time before media manipulated people—with a power more insistent and invasive than anything ever imagined in the Middle Ages... But nothing LightShadow said suggested the mass media might have any negative sides at all. I doubt the

idea ever crossed his mind. It appeared an unambiguously positive phenomenon to him and he peppered his talk with pop references.

"We are Spirits in the Material World," he declared at one
point, invoking a song by The Police. "Sting gets the big picture!
And he's not alone. There's a sensational new world of movies,
games and music all working together to break down the old
rigid certainties!"

Did it ever occur to LightShadow that the media encouraged
new rigid certainties, such as the ones he parroted? Evidently not.
For him, pop culture, no matter how crass, was a natural ally,
breaking down the bad. For me, it was breaking down a more
wholesome, moral and traditional world—in Ireland as elsewhere—which it thoroughly disparaged.

Unsurprisingly, then, LightShadow's ridicule of orthodox religion continued unabated. "In the new era of higher consciousness, we won't have all this moronic competition. Or asinine in-
fighting between different religions. Instead, we can warmly
embrace every religion—or none. Atheists, agnostics, Christians,
Buddhists—whoever you are, doesn't matter. New Paradigm
Spirituality is all about love and diversity. How can we welcome
everyone? That's what we always ask in the New Paradigm."

Warmly embrace all religions! My mind reeled. How could he
say that with a straight face? I looked around in despair. The
speaker was dynamic, good-looking, unusually self-assured. His
audience lapped up every word he said. Adoring smiles, nods and
chuckles filled the hall. Did no one register the sheer pompous-
ness of the implicit claim here? Namely, that *he*, LightShadow,
understood the true, pure core of all religion—which just happened to be missed for thousands of years by all the "hidebound
male theologians and philosophers" who came before him. Little
or nothing was ever said to back this up. Mostly, his talk was a
string of mere assertions.

"Now some of you may ask: How do we tell what the New
Paradigm is? Actually, it's easy. All you need is love! Anything else
is extraneous. Plus, Old Paradigm Spirituality has serious flaws.
But they're easily identified. If you see any of these things, be suspicious."

"If it's patriarchal—be suspicious."

"If it's homophobic—be suspicious."

"If it's not environmentally friendly—be suspicious."

"If it's against diversity—be suspicious."

Incredible. All he did was wheel out trendy progressive ideology. *That* was his mark of whether something constituted "the real, true core of every religion." I recalled the old canard that the Church of England was the Conservative party at prayer. Maybe the New Age was like that: Progressivism at prayer?

Then, without the least hint of irony, LightShadow finished his litany by actually saying:

"If it's critical of other spiritual paths—be suspicious."

"If it's arrogant—be suspicious."

"If it's shallow—be suspicious."

Mercifully, the talk ended. But not without a climax. Now, I'll never know how he did it. But *somehow* he managed to pack more New Age nuttiness into his final sentence than the rest of the talk put together: "After all, we are all LightShadows together on an effortlessly unfolding journey through the harmonising quantum matrix, which elegantly, ceaselessly and seamlessly integrates light and darkness, creation and negation, fullness and emptiness, selflessness and selfishness, while wholly respecting the right of every individual entity, real or imaginary, to evolve towards his or her own creative, holistic potential, without regard to race, colour, creed or sexual orientation!"

Thunderous applause. LightShadow basked in it, looking supremely satisfied with himself. The floor opened for questions. An American asked about Trump and Brexit. Didn't such things suggest that not everything was bright and rosy, as LightShadow claimed?

"When things are evolving fast, like today, there's always conservative backlash," LightShadow replied. "That's par for the course. Some people can't handle change. Or love. They cling to rigid certainties of the past. Sometimes it's necessary to drag them, kicking and screaming, into the future. But those things are the last hurrah for intolerance, everything opposed to love. People will finally see through the fascists. It's like bursting a boil—they're the puss that needs to come out into the open, before love wins. Wait till 2020, we'll have a woman in the White House yet. Patriarchy is already dead! The fundamentalists, the Nazis—they just don't know it yet."

Amidst all this, one—if only one—faint affirmation of the Church emerged from the audience. One Irishwoman still had a shred of Catholicism left in her. She thought LightShadow went "a bit far" with his crack about Oprah as pope. But LightShadow only warmed to his theme. "Hey, Oprah's not only a great spiritual teacher," he said, "she's also a shrewd manager. She built a media empire—she's the richest woman in America. She proves you can get the bucks *and* get a positive message across. She'd be fantastic as pope or president!" More laughter.

At long last, the torture finished. I chatted with Brigid, while LightShadow autographed copies of his masterpiece. Meanwhile, Anna flipped through its pages. Finally, the man himself joined us, wanting "feedback."

"Well, like Anna, I'm Catholic too—and you just managed to rubbish nearly every Catholic theologian for the last two thousand years as hopelessly male, misogynist, patriarchal, and stuck in the past," I growled. "But, hey, let's embrace diversity. Your perspective is undoubtedly every bit as valid as mine!"

"Wow! You really *are* Catholic, aren't you?" he grinned. "There's no need to get so uptight, man! We can continue this tomorrow. I need to crash now. But I always enjoy dialoguing with people of different perspectives." He gave Brigid an affectionate squeeze and off they went into the night.

My head was starting to hurt. Meanwhile, Anna met someone she recognised—a middle-aged Limerick nun dressed in modern clothes. Anna asked what she was doing there. "Well, I like to keep up with the times," the nun said. "It's important to be open-minded about these things. Ecumenism means learning from everyone. The Church doesn't have the whole truth, you know. That's what Vatican II teaches!"

"Well, I'm not sure any of the actual documents said that…" Anna retorted.

"Oh, the documents, they don't matter! They're just old paper. It's the spirit of the thing that counts—the Spirit of Vatican II!"

"But how can you know what the spirit is if you don't see the record? Then anyone can say whatever they like about the spirit."

"Well, the spirit was openness and freedom—like that young man said up there just now."

"But can't you see," Anna said, "his talk was a non-stop attack on Catholic tradition?"

"Tradition isn't everything, dear." The nun smiled. "It's the spirit that matters. I wonder what Pope Francis would say? I don't think he'd have any problem with it. Who are we to judge, anyway?"

IX

The Gold Exchange

IT was drizzling when we left the hall. By the time we reached home, the drizzle turned to a downpour. Scurrying inside, we sat down in our kitchen. Anna told me of her moonlit tryst with LightShadow and how he still seemed drawn to her, despite Brigid, despite our marriage. My head hurt even more.

"It's incredible," I ranted. "He claims to warmly embrace all perspectives, but ends up slandering every religion except his own! God help us."

"Yes, God help us. That's also what he can't see. We don't need God. All we need is tolerance and mindfulness."

"I wonder why no one ever thought of that before New Agers did? Idiot!"

"Yes, Geoffrey—but your rage won't help…" This was something relatively new in Anna. In the past, she would have shared my fury. But the Catholic Mystery was changing her. And tonight, I saw once more that same stricken beauty in her features. Again, I was reminded of GT weeping for the world.

"I'm sorry. This guy's beyond belief! Absolute certainty he knows everything—his way is best."

"He would say the same about Christians like us."

"Sure. But Christians—even the dumb ones—are grounded in thousands of years of tradition. What's LightShadow got? Zebra-consciousness? Thirty, forty years of New Age crackpots?! People who call themselves 'spiritual teachers'—for no other reason than that's what they call themselves!"

"Try not to rant, Geoffrey. I mean you're right. He doesn't understand much about Christianity, but…"

"He doesn't understand *anything* about Christianity! All he seems to know are dumbed-down media clichés and pop songs.

The Beatles, The Police, Oprah Winfrey—that's who we should listen to. Not Plato, Aristotle or Aquinas—much less Jesus Christ. It's like three thousand years of Western civilisation mean nothing to him. Nothing at all."

Again, our roles reversed. Anna sounded more moderate than me! She aspired to a calmness and charity that was beyond me by that point. Something about this guy riled me! "It's like he's living in this weird bubble of pop-philosophy and pop-culture. And he thinks nobody outside his own bubble knows anything. But New Agers are like that. You were like that..."

"I know. When you're in the bubble, as you put it, it's all very odd. You can't see outside. You're sure everything New Age is good and everything 'Old Age' is bad..."

"Yes, it's just like Liberalism. Progressives have the same contempt for the past."

"But it's an *unconscious* contempt," Anna said. "They don't even realise they're contemptuous."

"Obviously, I was like that too," I said. "But there's something different, more bizarre about this New Age bubble..."

I stared out into the rain, lost in thought. That bit about a bubble wasn't bad, I thought. Still, it didn't go far enough. The edges of a soap bubble were too soft, too clear, too normal to describe the sheer oddness of the New Age. No, another image was needed, something more rigid, opaque—most definitely not normal. Something outlandish. I turned it all over in my mind. And, as I did, the round image of the bubble transformed into a round flying saucer in my mind.

It was almost as if some strange alien craft had landed in the West, filled with beings *who cared absolutely nothing* for the culture beyond. Out-landish indeed.

"No, not a bubble," I exclaimed, "it's like this freakish UFO filled with ideas *completely alien* to Western civilisation. And not only do the aliens reject everything the West has to offer, whether it's Christianity or rational thought—it's all 'left-brain' head-tripping to them—they turn around and say they universally embrace every perspective. What's more, they actually *believe* it!"

"Yes," Anna said, "they honestly, truly believe it—Brigid believes it! She wants to marry him... and it's not just Brigid. It's *millions* like her. That's the *tragedy* here. Forget LightShadow, Geoffrey—think about the audience. All those young people completely sucked into THIS."

"Well, I can't forget about him. He's coming here tomorrow!"

"Try not to be angry, Geoffrey. You see him as a perpetrator. Really, he's a *victim*. Really, *he has no idea*. No idea how *impoverished* he is."

I grunted. The rain outside was heavier now, pelting the roof. A major storm was brewing. Anna continued, "If you've never tasted the Catholic sacraments, you can easily think what he does—all religions are the same. I once believed that was all there was to it, too. Just this basic core spirituality. Be mindful. Be kind. Be tolerant. Listen to your soul. Not much more. *Of course*, the Church doesn't know anything we don't know. *Of course*, the Church is just stupid."

"Of course, aren't we just wonderful!"

"That's how it looks on the outside, gazing in. And that's what New Agers are: Outsiders gazing in. *By definition, they're not religious practitioners.* Gareth's a victim to that mentality. He has a little biography in his book. I read it. He's never practiced any religion—much less Catholicism!"

"Yet he thinks he knows everything about religion! It's unbelievable."

"It's a *tragedy*," Anna repeated. "I need to pray—to get a handle on what just happened." Anna retired to our bedroom to pray. Afterwards, she recorded her thoughts in her journal:

24th February 2018

The talk was horrendous. Geoffrey is livid. I'm angry too. But I can't help feeling we're both missing the real point here. There's something deeper here.

What is it? It's the POVERTY—utter, total destitution. The man has no idea. NO idea.

He could never say these things, if he ever tasted anything else beyond the bubble—as Geoffrey puts it. But he hasn't. Like the materialists, his views of Christianity are all reductionist. Christianity is reduced to human things like sexism or authoritarianism. <u>Nothing else</u>. Obviously, the Church has always had its defects. But he claims the Church is nothing BUT those defects. He can't see that there is anything else to it. And if he could see anything—anything significant—he would just say it was the same thing as the "universal essence" of every religion. It's INCONCEIVABLE to him Catholicism could offer anything more than his "universal vision." Something OTHER.

Of course, that idea is very threatening to him. His whole world would break down, if there WERE something else beyond his "universalism." Just like my world broke down when I finally saw the Church offered something different.

Because I finally tried it. That's the problem: Gareth refuses the only thing that would allow him to see—to actually TRY it. But millions and millions of people won't try it. There's a wall of propaganda: You don't need the Church. You don't need anything else. You just need to be mindful, tolerant, nice.

People are being ripped-off. The New Age started in Protestant England and America. But now the Irish are being robbed too, robbed blind.

If Gareth gave this lecture in Ireland in 1960, no one would have listened. Back then, Irish people knew what they had—treasure. Now they're utterly impoverished.

The Irish once had GOLD. Today, they're trading it for plastic.

X

Thunder

ANNA kissed me good night. I wanted to come to bed, too. But I'd never sleep. I'd just writhe around, keeping her awake. Instead, I collapsed on the sofa. Next to the sofa is an oval mirror and a bookcase. And something very strange was about to happen in that spot...

By now, my mental state matched the weather outside, with howling wind, heavy rain, rolling thunder in the distance. Thoughts jolted me like lightning. I couldn't shake LightShadow from my mind. For all I knew, the presenter was right: he *was* the next New Age megastar, like Eckhart Tolle or Deepak Chopra, selling millions of books. The New Age was big business—much bigger than many Catholics appreciate. Indeed, all kinds of people, Catholic or not, seem completely unaware of this massive phenomenon. This kooky "UFO" doesn't interest them so they easily ignore it. I was just the same.

It was only thanks to Anna that the New Age was even on my radar screen. When she went to Findhorn, I realised she was *not* a solitary eccentric, but part of something gigantic. Still, Anna apart, New Age-ism never bothered me then. It was progressive like I was. New Agers were just a wacky "side-show." Ridiculous, but harmless.

But now, as a Catholic, things looked very different. How asleep I was! But, then, the Church is asleep, too. Indeed, Catholics and New Agers are like ships in the night. For people like LightShadow, we Catholics are irrelevant, "dinosaurs" from a past "Age of Pisces," whom they rarely—if ever—encounter. Yet if, by chance, they *do* run into us, they can scarcely believe we exist. We are "neanderthals" who actually consider Western civilisation worth preserving! On the other hand, Catholics scarcely see New Agers, at least not in all their untold hordes. Nor do we realize the powerful influence of New Age ideas. Because countless people may not consider themselves New Agers, but are nonetheless deeply affected by New Age thinking, as it ripples out through movies, music, internet and other media.

Anna tried to tell me this, repeatedly. "This New Age stuff is changing the world," she said. Yet, until tonight, I remained asleep. Previously I'd just nod my head, with non-committal comments like, "maybe you're right," or "it's not good, is it?"

But tonight, *it was in my face*. Tonight, I saw Brigid adoring this dope. Tonight, I saw the Irish going gaga. Tonight, I saw this weird alien spirituality REPLACING the spirituality of the West.

This was Ireland, of all places! Not California. Not New York. Not England. Yet Catholicism in Ireland was dying. This was what many Irish preferred instead: slick New Age presenters offering a permissive, liberal spirituality. Even—à la Oprah Winfrey—with the bucks as well! The memory of GT flashed into my mind. He called the New Age "Minimum Commitment Spirituality." Tonight, his words appeared more apt than ever.

Belloc's book *The Great Heresies* on the shelf next to me caught my eye. Now, my head was hurting. Still, as yet, it wasn't too bad. And reading calms me at times like this. Not this time though. Because I opened to a long passage that hit me in guts. I won't quote it all, but here are the most relevant bits:

> The Faith is now in the presence not of a particular heresy as in the past—the Arian, the Manichaean, the Albigensian . . . nor is it in the presence of a sort of generalized heresy as it was when it had to meet the Protestant revolution from three to four hundred years ago. The enemy which the Faith now has to meet, and which may be called "The Modern Attack," is a wholesale assault upon the fundamentals of the Faith—upon the very existence of the Faith. And the enemy now advancing against us is increasingly conscious of the fact that there can be no question of neutrality. The forces now opposed to the Faith design to destroy. The battle is henceforward engaged upon a definite line of cleavage, involving the survival or destruction of the Catholic Church. And all—not a portion—of its philosophy.

We know, of course, that the Catholic Church cannot be destroyed. But what we do not know is the extent of the area over which it will survive; its power of revival or the power of the enemy to push it further and further back on to its last defences until it may seem as though the Anti-Christ had come and the final issue was about to be decided. Of such moment is the struggle immediately before the world. . . .

The truth is becoming every day so much more obvious that within a few years it will be universally admitted. I do not entitle the modern attack "anti-Christ"—though in my heart I believe that to be the true term for it: No, I do not give it that name because it would seem for the moment exaggerated. But the name doesn't matter. Whether we call it "The Modern Attack" or "anti-Christ" it is all one; there is a clear issue now joined between the retention of Catholic morals, tradition, and authority on the one side, and the active effort to destroy them on the other. The modern attack will not tolerate us. It will attempt to destroy us. Nor can we tolerate it. . . .

Either the Catholic Church (now rapidly becoming the only place wherein the traditions of civilization are understood and defended) will be reduced by her modern enemies to political impotence, to numerical insignificance, and, so far as public appreciation goes, to silence; or the Catholic Church will, in this case as throughout the past . . . recover and extend her authority, and will rise once more to the leadership of civilization which she made.

I put the book down. Passages like that once struck me as over-blown, paranoid even. No longer. Because Belloc wrote that back in 1938. What I saw tonight told me: *the man was a prophet.* When Belloc wrote those words eighty years ago, his claims *did* seem exaggerated, even extremist. Catholicism remained vibrant, not just in Ireland, but in Southern Europe too—not to mention much of central and Eastern Europe, Latin America and many more places across the planet. But three or four generations later, the "Modern Attack" had decimated Catholic tradition everywhere.

Suddenly it was all coming together. The dreadful state of Ireland. The Irish people abandoning their faith for a "UFO from

Aquarius." And what is more, the only way that UFO could land in Ireland was the fact it was not alone. No. It was part and parcel of something bigger. What Belloc called "the Modern Attack."

The red carpet had been rolled out long ago for the alien ship to land.

There was the "Spirit of Vatican II." There was the new liberal anti-Catholic Irish media. (Although so much of that media wasn't even Irish.) And there was liberal economics. Liberated banks and corporations actively promoted the globalist media destroying the faith.

Another image surfaced in my mind: a multi-headed hydra. One serpent head was materialistic consumerism. Another was the banking that fed on that consumerism and the vast debts it created. Another head was the media the banks supported, with all its politically correct prejudice. Another head involved progressive politicians like Clinton in America or the anti-Catholic politicians Ireland now had—pawns, all, to the banks. And yet another serpent head was LightShadow's New Age spirituality which, implicitly or explicitly, supported all the above. Each head connected to the others. Each head, though separate, reinforced what the other heads were saying. Belloc saw this hydra a century ago when it remained hidden to most eyes. But I could only see it now in 2018!

Outside and inside my mind, the tempest raged. I recalled my dream of Belloc and Chesterton talking together on just a night like this. Belloc had gently admonished his friend about the gravity of the situation. And in real life, Chesterton had been sunnier than Belloc, with a sweeter disposition. Thus, some people thought him softer than Belloc, less radical.

Once I believed that myself. Now, I wasn't so sure. For back in the 1920s and 30s, the great Chesterton poured his *lifeblood* into his own ever-struggling newspaper *G. K.'s Weekly*. He also poured his personal money into it, refusing subsidy through advertisement. Because, like Belloc, he knew the world desperately needed an alternative to corporate media—just as it desperately needed Distributism as an alternative to Socialism or Capitalism. I had seen old copies of *G. K.'s Weekly*, which suggested GKC was every bit as radical as Belloc, every bit as determined to combat the hydra. His passion leapt from every page of that paper—even if his language was usually not as forceful as Belloc's. (Occasionally, though, it was. In one old issue,[1] Chesterton made his vision quite explicit: "Our purpose is revolution. We do not want to tinker with the capitalist system, we want to destroy it.")

Everything came crashing in on me—the UFO, the hydra, the dreams, Belloc, GKC... How different to LightShadow they were. LightShadow celebrated crass mediocrity, the Chesterbelloc championed culture. LightShadow crusaded for liberal modernity, thinking it offered freedom. The Chesterbelloc combated liberal modernity because they saw its tyranny.

And so GKC toiled at his little newspaper—a solitary source of alternative news to the great corporate press. Today, of course, LightShadow would surely say those alternatives were no longer solitary. Indeed, they appeared plentiful on copious sites like YouTube, Facebook, Twitter and all the rest. Information was free, free, free, he would claim.

And, in a certain, limited sense, LightShadow was right, of course. In the last few years, there was a great burst of alternative media. Social media, blogs, forums and the like *did* mean people could air things publicly like never before. Air them across the entire planet! And some of these did fly against the tightly-controlled media.

There *was* hope there! Still, the notion of a new free, independent media appears over-hyped. Dissenting voices are easily overwhelmed by behemoths like Hollywood, Google, Facebook, the major news networks and so on. And this new "free flow of information" hardly stopped LightShadow being a poor parrot of the media himself! That media was more powerful than he ever realized. Moreover, I feared this much-vaunted window of new opportunity might be short-lived. Indeed, in just the last few months, Google's YouTube threatened potentially draconian moves to stamp out anything that deviated from accepted liberal orthodoxy. As someone remarked, YouTube was becoming ThemTube.

---

[1] December 3rd, 1927, quoted in Jay Corrin, *G. K. Chesterton & Hilaire Belloc: The Battle against Modernity* (Athens: Ohio University Press, 1981), 110.

That a vast plurality of perspectives was now available to all was a sorry joke. Disinformation was everywhere on the internet. Government and corporate surveillance meant people were watched in ways beyond anything George Orwell ever imagined. People hid under anonymous aliases on the internet, scared for their jobs and livelihood...

Meanwhile, the monster of Political Correctness marginalised everything that didn't fit the liberal, capitalist mainstream. I thought of poor Pope Benedict. Unless you were an ardent, practicing Catholic, you were likely to have *no idea* what he really stood for. He was the idiot, Pope Francis the great, enlightened one... Millions thought like that. Or rather, *they didn't think*. They parroted what their masters told them.

All this, too, led me to see something unpleasant in myself. Because I still wasn't *serious*. Not like Belloc and Chesterton were serious—as indeed my Anna was. For there they all shared something I did not: *an intensity of conviction that refused vacillation and scepticism.*

I thought of that dream where Belloc smashed that fiddle over my head. And my head didn't hurt. *But my head hurt now.*

But maybe that was good! Because only now I finally, fully got what Anna got. Only now, I felt stabbed to the core, just like she did. I wasn't just nodding my head, mildly agreeing. Or mildly disagreeing. I was no longer numb.

I was in pain, real pain. But I was alive. Not dulled, not deadened.

Now, and only now, I grokked Anna's stricken, wounded heart. Not only did I see what she saw—I FELT it.

Then, it hit me! Scepticism had been my *defence mechanism*. I retreated into safe, analytical distance from the world trauma. And so I never put myself on the line. Belloc's talk of the Anti-Christ, an all-out attack on the Church...Wasn't Belloc over-the-top? I could still hear my inner sceptic scream, like a thousand other sceptics who denounced the man for being polarised, paranoid, erecting "bogeymen" who, they confidently claimed, weren't really there...

But I noticed something. Those same sceptics didn't really *care* what happened to the Church. Not really. Not deeply. Not like the Chesterbelloc cared. Not like Anna cared. What happened to places like Catholic Ireland didn't HURT them. What Capitalism did to the poor as well as culture didn't pierce their hearts, the way it clearly pierced the men behind *G. K.'s Weekly*.

But Chesterton and Belloc put themselves on the line. They fought ceaselessly for the downtrodden, for fairness, for a world ordered to truth rather than lies. This is to say: the truth of Christ. And the mercy of Christ... Compared to them, I was just an armchair dilettante sitting on the fence.

A mighty thunderclap startled me, as if from a trance. Indeed, I almost jumped out of my skin. Then a voice boomed out: "I told you so, Nero. The situation is far worse than you realise."

Nero! The name Belloc called me in my dream! But I wasn't dreaming—I was sure of it! I swivelled around. No one was there. Then, the oval mirror caught my eye. For a split-second, someone appeared in the mirror. It was *not* my own reflection. Belloc stared down at me. His eyes were grim and blazed with fire... Then, he vanished!

That's really how it was. But immediately, I began to feel sceptical. Perhaps I was dreaming. Possibly, without realising, I drifted off for a few seconds, before the thunderclap woke me. Maybe my mind conjured up his image from his book on my lap. ("Hello, doubt, my old friend. I've come to talk to you again.")

Whatever the explanation, I'll never forget the intensity in Belloc's eyes. There was fire there and fire is life. I couldn't help thinking Belloc lived his life far more intensely than I ever do. He was intensely awake to the world, while, comparatively, I remain fast, fast asleep.

I stood up in a daze. My mind reeled. My head split. Overwhelmed, fatigued, I could take no more. I stumbled off to bed and fell fast asleep next to my sad, beautiful wife.

XI

"A Divisive Omniphobic Religious Ritual"

"EVERYBODY'S happy, everybody's laughing…"

Anna recognised the dreamlike Beatles' song from *Abbey Road*, as it echoed round the grand hall. That hall was so immense, it seemed to stretch for miles. Hordes of smiling people thronged around her. Anna stood out distinctly from them. For one thing, she wore her sheer nightgown, which—oddly—did not embarrass her. Yet whatever Anna wore, she could hardly be more different to these people. For Anna invariably dressed in distinctly feminine, albeit modest, attire. Yet no one here wore anything remotely feminine.

Everyone, in fact, men and women, dressed in identical white jumpsuits. Moreover, their height never varied from one person to the next. All appeared an identical five foot six. Their hairstyles were likewise identical—a short pageboy-style cut mid-length at the ear. The effect was distinctly unisex, paradoxically all the more so because the one-piece outfits were tight-fitting. In normal circumstances, then, sexual differentiation would be stark. But circumstances were not normal. For any sexual difference was hardly noticeable at all. Every one, male and female, had the same slight, boyish build—like a horse jockey's.

To her surprise, Anna felt safe in this strange milieu, because her figure was hardly slight or boyish. Normally, she would draw male attention, dressed like this. But no hint of such existed. The men, the women, seemed utterly passionless. Their smiling faces appeared perfectly nice, perfectly bland. To call them "laid back" would be an understatement.

Somehow the vapid, unthreatening environs reminded Anna

of a "New Age gospel" by Eckhart Tolle, *The Power of Now.* Tolle claimed the present moment—freed from every concern for past or future—offered peace beyond all suffering. Beyond passion, too. Tolle even understood Christianity in those terms! Like LightShadow, he claimed you didn't need the Church. You could simply come to him, instead. But having left the New Age, Anna saw just how little the man comprehended Christ. Christ had infinitely embraced human suffering, rather than *circumventing* it. Not only had Tolle understood nothing about Christ, but Anna wondered whether he understood much about being human.

All this, the languid drones in white evoked for her. They were so serene, detached, aloof, beyond all ardour, vivacity and charm. Undeniably, though, she was safe here! No one would ever raise a hand against her. She could strip off her nightgown and no one would raise an eyebrow! Perhaps for Tolle this would be the perfect world of peace: a completely non-violent society. (The fact it was also non-human might escape his attention entirely.)[1]

Moreover, the auditorium remained as anodyne as the people. Walls and furnishings were all the same sheet-white. And that same Beatles' song dreamily reverberated in a loop that never seemed to end: "Everybody's happy, everybody's laughing. Here comes the Sun King..."

At last, relief! Eternal monotony punctured. "Are you here to see the Sun King?" a white clone asked Anna. Desperate to see something different—*anything* different!—Anna nodded eagerly and was beckoned to a narrow door.

The small room she now entered *was* different. Yet its dim, claustrophobic confines offered no respite. Seated on a black throne was a man in a black cape, grinning. He, at least, did not appear "laid back"—but vital and enormously satisfied with himself.

It was LightShadow. "The Universal Awakening has happened, my pet, as we always knew it would. Everything we worked for. Everything we dreamed of has come to pass—exactly as we planned it. Come, shall we dance?"

---

[1] For a discussion on Eckhart Tolle, see Buck, *Cor Jesu Sacratissimum*, 208–14.

No, LightShadow was not in the least passionless. His gaze bore into Anna. For a moment, she stood there frozen, speechless. Then she turned and bolted. Out the door she sprinted, through that immense long hall, through the great crowds, running for her life. No one blinked an eye.

Finally, Anna reached another door. Anna burst through it—into an endless maze of identical corridors. The doors, Anna sensed, led to living quarters, no doubt identical too. The people here dwelt in an enormity of sameness. For the corridors were as sterile, as featureless as the people in the hall. White walls, white doors, white floors, white ceilings, studded with intense white lights. Breathless, Anna ran through endless rivers of neutral, unobjectionable white. No trace of colour would ever disturb these people's lives.

But finally, after running for miles, Anna reached the end of a corridor. There was not another corridor! There was only a locked door, which differed from all the others. A sign on it said: "No Exit." Not knowing what to do, she hurled herself against it. To her astonishment, the door broke open.

Anna was outside! Warm sunlight hit her sweat-soaked body. Stunning colour flooded her starved senses. And beauty! Tall green trees, grasses, flowers and mountains dazzled her at once.

An old track stretched out before her. It led to the ruins of a small medieval English village. And there she found a crumbling edifice that had once been a small gothic Catholic church.

But the door was barred by wire fencing. A plaque read:

! DANGER !
ENTRY FORBIDDEN

*Long ago, before the Universal Awakening, a Divisive,
Omniphobic Religious Ritual was celebrated here.*

♣ ♣

*The religion was repressive and non-inclusive,
inciting hate and other passions.*

♣

**Access restricted to Authorised Researchers only.
2—3—2—3 Second Trimester, 230 A.E.**

Anna did not understand the date system. But, just as she woke, the final initials' meaning came clearly to her mind: Aquarian Era.

She shuddered. What was this dream, which had been so intensely vivid? Could it point to something real? Or even symbolise the English future—at least a potential future?

Like Belloc, Anna knew the Church could never be destroyed. That was Christ's promise to His people. Nonetheless, the Church had almost been extinguished in England before, as it had in other European regions (Scandinavia, for example, now one of the most liberal and atheistic corners of former Christendom). Yes, generation after generation of English people were denied the power of the Mass. Even after the Catholic Emancipation Act of 1829, Catholicism never really recovered in English society. And England's thoroughly Protestant nature steadily degenerated into secularism. (Indeed, what small Catholic presence now existed in Britain was mainly due to massive Irish immigration after the 1840s famine.)

On the whole, the spirit of England had been thoroughly de-Catholicised. Did this dream depict Albion's final destination? Such a fate would hardly be inconsistent with the trajectory of the last centuries.

Eventually, Anna fell back to sleep and was fast asleep, when I awoke—in agony, needing to vomit. My headache had progressed to a full-blown migraine. I don't get those very often. But when I do, they're *bad*. Like iron rods through my skull. Intense nausea. Vision out of focus. Crawling to the toilet to vomit was hell.

Now, it was Saturday and, normally, Saturday mornings Anna and I attend the Latin Mass near our home. Today, though, I had no choice. Anna had to go alone. And she would have to entertain Brigid and her beau alone, too. There's nothing to do but lie in complete darkness at times like these, move as little as possible and wait it out—sometimes two or three days, even.

And so Anna set out for Mass, deeply disquieted by her dream, by LightShadow and the thought of dealing with the man by herself for an entire afternoon. As ever, the Mass brought solace and strength. Still, Anna knew she faced a trial.

XII

"I Guess I Found Something Better"

WHEN LightShadow and Brigid called that afternoon, I heard the doorbell and a few muffled voices. Little else, however, penetrated the blackness of the room and the pounding in my head. Anna, as she later recounted to me, welcomed our visitors into the lounge, explaining I couldn't join them. She also thought Brigid looked less than well.

After the usual pleasantries, Anna cut straight to the point. "You said you had big news for us, Brigid?"

"Oh that," Brigid fumbled, looking distinctly uncomfortable. "I thought I did. But, well, I need to think a bit more first. Talk to Gareth, too."

"Something private between us, I'm afraid." LightShadow looked slightly annoyed. Changing the subject, he, too, cut to the point: "What exactly is it with you and the Church, Anna?"

"I'm not sure I could ever explain it to you."

"Try me! I'm all ears—genuinely interested!"

"Gareth is cool with Christianity," Brigid interjected, trying to help. "I mean, I'm a Christian myself—but a holistic Christian," she added, "Not everybody has to transcend religion! That's what you teach, right, Gareth?"

"Absolutely," LightShadow grinned, "There's nothing wrong with religion if people approach it consciously—with a more universal perspective. In the future, there'll be more and more people like that: holistic Christians, holistic Muslims, holistic Jews, etc. It's a perfectly valid way forward, I think."

"I'm like that, a holistic Catholic," Brigid said. "I still go to Mass sometimes, if it feels appropriate to my needs."

"Right on!" LightShadow said.

But Anna simply said, "I see." Finding words after Brigid's "holistic confession" was hard. Inside her heart was breaking. Ireland had always been so different from England. Its sheer spirituality stood in marked contrast to the materialistic society she grew up in. But now Brigid showed her what Ireland might become. Not as agnostic and utilitarian as England—but "holistic" instead. Its Christianity could be transformed into the substance of her New Age nightmare. Everybody happy, languid, "laid back," *complacent*...

"Whatever you're doing in the Church, Anna, I'm sure it's great," LightShadow said, coaxing her to speak. "It's brilliant you want to do something to heal the Church. That's what Pope Francis wants. What do you think about him?"

Still, the words would not come. In truth, Anna hardly knew how to talk to anybody about Pope Francis—let alone Light-Shadow! She believed in loyalty to the Holy Father and refused to reveal her true feelings regarding him to anyone except me. A limp answer was all she managed, "He's done a few good things, I guess."

"A few good things?! Oh, man. That guy's the best thing the Church has had for two thousand years. Okay, he's still stuck and rigid in certain ways. But compared to everyone else, he's a revolution!"

Brigid looked increasingly uncomfortable. She excused herself for a moment, saying she needed the bathroom. Alone with LightShadow, Anna felt more unnerved than ever. Something about the man made her feel devoured. And without Brigid, his smiling sweetness all but disappeared.

"What's going on, Anna? I really need to know—what's with this Catholic gig?"

"The gig," Anna said slowly, "is real. I lived at Findhorn, as you know. Then, I went to Auroville in India. Like you, I lived in California for a while. I spent years in therapy. I was initiated into Reiki. I practiced astrology. I've been to hundreds of New Age workshops, meetings and gatherings. But I never found anything like the Catholic Church."

LightShadow exploded in expletives I won't repeat here.

"In everything I've experienced, nothing—absolutely nothing!—reaches the core of our being like the Catholic sacraments. No healing, no meditation, no rituals, no exercises, no therapy—I never found anything even remotely like this."

"Oh man. That guy you married has gone to your head!"

"I'm afraid not. I converted him. I would never have married him if he hadn't converted. The Church is the most precious thing I ever found in this world."

LightShadow stared at her, aghast. Only now, the full reality began to dawn on him. Anna was not Catholic because of me. She was not Catholic because she meant "to do something to heal the Church." No, she was Catholic because she actually believed Catholic teaching. And experienced its truth. Incredible!

"I don't know what to say…" He was still at a loss, still protesting reality. "You, *you of all people* ought to know better. You were at Findhorn, man… you even lived there."

"I guess I found something better."

"What on earth is better about *this*? It's completely out of date! It's two thousand years old, for God's sake! Maybe three thousand, with all that Old Testament garbage. It's completely patriarchal, filled with hypocrisy and hate. It's totally morbid. I mean actually *celebrating* some dude being tortured on a cross? How sadistic is that?"

"You really have no idea what you're talking about," was all Anna could say.

"Okay, okay, maybe that's harsh. Normally, I don't talk like that, especially around Bridge. When you've been saddled with that stuff as a child, it's tough to break free. You need to go easy with people like that. But you're different. You lived at Findhorn!" he said, still incredulous. "You have no excuse—you weren't raised Catholic! Or were you?"

"No, I chose it consciously. You could say I had a spiritual transformation." Anna mimicked New Age jargon, managing a sad little smile. "It was like a quantum shift in my awareness…"

"Un–bloody–believable! I mean, I understand less-evolved people still need religion as a security-blanket. But not you! You're more advanced! This is the twenty-first century! How is all that dogma meant to speak to the modern world? It's time to let go of all your precious little doctrines and Rosary beads. It's juvenile. We've moved beyond all your closed-minded fundamentalism now! Grow up, will you? Get a life!"

Anna reeled. This was the man her young cousin hoped to marry...?! But Brigid returned, looking brighter. Instantly, Light-Shadow dropped the tirade and resumed his trademark grin. Brigid snuggled into him. Yet still his gaze penetrated Anna.

Her heart pounded. She could hardly catch her breath properly. It was all too much. That eerie, terrifying dream last night. Brigid's conversion to English New Age-ism. This grinning, supercilious blackguard Brigid loved. Then, that nun who couldn't care less about Catholic tradition. Along with millions of Catholics just like her. A Vatican that hardly seemed any different. Everything came crashing down on Anna at once. She struggled to fight back tears.

"Kyrie eleison," she cried out in her heart.

Then the doorbell rang.

XIII

A Prayer Answered

"I'LL get that!" Anna said, rushing to the door, swinging it open. There on the porch stood a tall, rotund man, holding an umbrella in the Irish rain. His hair and beard were white as snow and he wore a tie and hat with a faded tweed jacket. He appeared old, very old—as though he might have lived a hundred years or more. Despite his age, there was no fatigue about him. Nor was he the least stooped like old men often are. Rather, he brimmed with vitality.

Anna recognised him at once. It was Gilbert Tracey, the Gentle Traditionalist.

"Wh–what are you doing here?"

"Well, we can't take too much more of this nonsense, can we? Not you, nor Brigid either. Your husband lying there like the proverbial wreck of the Hesperus." Tenderly, he stretched out his hand to wipe a tear from her eye. "I'm here to help, of course," he said, handing Anna his hat as he shook the rain from his umbrella, and stepped inside.

I heard that second doorbell ring, but had no idea what was happening. Then, abruptly, the door to my darkened cell opened. Light flooded the room and pain pounded my brain. Instantly, I shut my eyes. But for a split second, I glimpsed the large figure in the doorway next to Anna, a figure I could not make out.

"Geoffrey, I'm sorry—but there's someone to see you."

"Anna, Geoffrey and I need a moment alone," a voice seemed to say. A warm, familiar voice…but I could barely make it out amidst the throbbing, pulsing agony. "We'll both join you shortly. Why don't you make a place for us?"

"Okay," Anna spoke in a daze. "How do I explain who you are—?"

"Oh, just say your dear Uncle Gilbert dropped by for an unexpected visit! You can say I'm a little batty, if you like, but you have to humour the poor chap."

Only then, I recognised that cheery Irish lilt that thoroughly transformed my life! Still, I felt too sick to say a word. Anna mercifully shut the door behind her. Everything was dark again. Only that voice was left beside me, a kind, soothing voice, almost infinitely kind...

"Well, well, well, my good man. Whatever happened to you? We can't have this, can we? Not when your wife needs you more than ever. That fellow out there is no pushover, you know."

"Can't see straight, can't even think," was all I could utter.

"Yes, you were overloaded in a short space of time—overloaded by reality. That creates all kinds of complications, dislocation, even despair. But we can't have that, can we? Too much is at stake. Your wife, her cousin. There's someone else in this equation, too. And millions more like them. We can't have you like this! All hands are needed on deck!"

"But—"

"No protest, my dear fellow. Trust me. Open your eyes!" I obeyed and found myself staring straight into a blazing jewel of fiery red. GT's right arm was extended towards me. And the ring on the middle finger of that enormous fleshy hand pointed directly between my eyes. Was I really staring into the Blood of Christ...a relic of the True Cross...and those of fifteen Roman martyrs...?

"Jesus Christ heals you. Get up from your bed!"

At that instant, all pain, all nausea vanished. I stood up, utterly refreshed, as though nothing had happened at all. Or rather as though something *had* happened, something sweet as honey. As though I had woken from the sweetest night's sleep of my life. I felt not only restored, but rejuvenated.

XIV

A Zebra Meets a Dinosaur

"GEOFFREY'S here—he's feeling better!" Anna said, showing us into the lounge. "And we have an unexpected visitor. Do come in, Uncle Gilbert."

"Yes, Uncle Gilbert," I said. "Meet Brigid and her boyfriend, Gareth LightShadow!"

"Ah yes. Gilbert Tracey at your service. But just call me GT!"

When GT spoke, Brigid was perplexed. She never heard of an "Uncle Gilbert" before. Did GT stem from Anna's English family? Yet the big guy was decidedly *not* English. There was an unmistakeable Irish lilt to his genteel voice and his relaxed, genial manner didn't seem very English either. Still, something about him unsettled her. She snuggled closer into LightShadow, oddly clutching LightShadow's book in her lap.

"That was certainly an interesting talk last night, Mr Light-Shadow," GT said, settling into a chair.

"You were there? I never saw you!" I exclaimed.

"Well, I was hidden away," the old man smiled. "I had my own little perch there, so to speak. My own way of looking in."

Here a lengthy conversation began, much of it between Gareth LightShadow and the Gentle Traditionalist. It was not unlike my own uncanny conversation with GT three years ago, even if it turned out LightShadow was nowhere near as interested in dialogue as he claimed. Indeed, his input was mildly mocking, peppered with put-downs, even while he remained affable and jocular, grinning like that famous cat from Cheshire.

At any rate, I record it in dialogue form, just as I did in my first book about GT.

GT: Your New Age religion certainly has striking beliefs...

GLS: Whoa! My religion? Dude, in case you didn't notice, I don't have a religion!

Brigid: That's right! Gareth is spiritual, but not religious. That's what you teach, isn't it, darling?

GLS: Exactly! And whoever said I was a New Ager? I never even mentioned the term "New Age"!

GT: Well, you evoke a glorious new era, where all sorts of human problems—problems plaguing humanity since the Fall—will suddenly vanish. Or at least be vastly reduced.

GLS: Well, that's progress. That's being an optimist. I happen to believe in human potential. Not like some people!

GT: Indeed. So much so that you subscribe to "an epochal paradigm shift of awesome proportions" wherein "human consciousness will be liberated, expanded and transformed, forever freed from its fixation on morbid patterns of guilt no longer appropriate for a new era." That's from your book. (Page 101, if I recall correctly.)

For a moment, the room fell silent, although Brigid quickly thumbed through the copy on her lap. "He's right!" she gasped.

GT: Alas, to my mind that reads like a thousand other books belonging to... well, I won't say religion—at least for the moment. Maybe we could talk about a New Age *Movement*, instead?

GLS: Frankly, I've got a problem with that, too. You're jumping to conclusions! I'm not into *any* movement, much less New Age. Personally, "New Age" sounds flaky to me.

My mind reeled, hearing that. But it hardly surprised me. Many New Agers were embarrassed by the expression "New Age." At least, that's what Anna said. Once the term was widely—and proudly—embraced. But somewhere along the line, roundabout the 1980s, it became associated with self-indulgent silliness in the public eye. New Agers abandoned it in droves. Suddenly, Anna said, everyone in the New Age was scrambling to say: "I am not a New Ager!"

"Flaky?" I said.

GLS: Well, yeah, a lot of those books are over the top. I don't deny I've read some—

GT: Or plenty?

GLS: Whatever—that still doesn't mean I signed up for a movement. Give me a break! I believe in *freedom*—not movements, not categories. People like us are free spirits. We don't need labels like "New Age."

LightShadow smiled, secure in himself. He was too sure of himself to take GT seriously for an instant. Perhaps, though, he was curious to meet this old "dinosaur" who could quote his book verbatim, even if he was too unenlightened to grasp the message.

"Brigid, Gareth," Anna said, "I'm sure you mean that. But I used to say exactly the same thing. I never wanted to be a New Ager either! But I read New Age books; I listened to New Age music; I went to New Age workshops and festivals. I lived in a New Age community. Most of my friends were similar. And we all said what you say: "Don't categorise us. We aren't New Agers…""

GT: Yes, Anna. There do seem to be people sharing similar features here—reading the same literature, going to the same seminars, thinking the same thoughts. Like they've transcended religion or belong to an "evolutionary shift of consciousness" that will usher in a new age (even if it's not always called that). All that looks like a definite sort of movement to me—*people moving together in the same direction.*

GLS: Okay, okay. Maybe there's a loose kind of movement. *Very* loose. Big deal. You still don't need to call it "New Age."

Brigid: These days, people prefer other names—like "holistic."

GLS: That's better, for sure!

GT: Alas, we have a little problem here. Christianity is holistic too! Christians see God's creation as a whole: the work of a single loving hand. I can't call your philosophy "holistic"—as if mine weren't! Then there's "Mind-Body-Spirit"—as though Christianity did not honour the mind, did not honour the body, did not honour the spirit. I am sorry; these names are *implicitly* condescending.

I'll tell you what... You believe in freedom. Would you grant me freedom to talk about a New Age Movement—one that appears quite definite in my mind? At least for the purposes of our little discussion today?

GLS: Call it whatever you want! It's a free country. Nobody's legislating your delusions.

GT: No... at least, not yet. Moreover, I believe you celebrate diversity. We all have a right to our different perspectives. For you, New Agers are just free, independent spirits. To me, they're enmeshed in a distinct religious system they can't even seem to see. Our viewpoints here are wildly diverse. I hope you can tolerate mine.

GLS: Can do, dude. Diversity is where it's at today. I'm sure you have a perfectly valid perspective to offer.

GT: Why, thank you, my dear fellow. Anyway, my own perspective is that *nobody ever gets away from religion*. In fact, your belief in diversity seems a defining tenet of your own religious system. Dare I say dogma?

GLS: Oh, man! You know what your problem is? Your need for all this "belief" and "dogma" stuff! Religion is so attached to all that garbage. I mean, why even talk about it—unless you need to shove it down people's throats? We don't need your beliefs, anymore.

GT: "We don't need?" Who is this "we," I wonder? Could it be your movement—the one I call "New Age"? I mean, your "we" does seem rather different to my "we." "Your" movement doesn't need "our" beliefs...

GLS: Call it what you like! I just say there's a new freedom of the spirit, freedom from belief. We don't need absolute truth. All that arrogant junk!

GT: So, am I hearing right? Religious belief is a problem for you. Because it inhibits spiritual freedom?

GLS: Right on!

GT: Well, freedom is tremendously important. You know, friend, we're actually agreed on that one.

GLS: Oh man, is that rich! How can people be free with all your legalistic dogma?! Nobody needs that now. People want something universal—something everyone can relate to. Spirituality is dead simple when you boil it down. Be kind. Be tolerant. Treat people as you'd like to be treated. Even Christians have a name for it—the Golden Rule. What's important is what's in your heart. Beliefs only get in the way.

GT: Oh, really?

GLS: Yeah—it's like religion. It's just a means to control people.

GT: "Just?" That's *all* it is?

GLS: Look at history! You see the same thing in every time and culture. It's all so rigid. And not only that. Beliefs are so divisive, man. It's time to get away from that—get out of your head.

GT: I'm sorry, I rather like my head. Vacating it has never particularly appealed to me.

GLS: You should try meditation then. Just enter the silence. You'll find a place beyond all this head-stuff.

GT: Like that Beatles' song, you mean: "Turn off your mind, relax, float downstream."

GLS: Now you're talking! Try it—there's a deep, still place within, where we're all one. No beliefs. No concepts. No division.

"Sure," I grumbled, "Silence thinking—then you have no more concepts. If we have no more concepts, everyone can agree with each other. Great."

"Well," GT countered my irritation, "contemplative silence is

something of tremendous beauty. But that's not to negate thinking. In fact, true silence enhances thinking. Still, we have a problem, Mr LightShadow. You advocate a silent space of 'Oneness'
beyond all beliefs. But I counted at least five, just right there.
There may be even ten or fifteen, if we carefully considered everything you just said."

GLS: Ten—fifteen what?

GT: Why, beliefs of course. I can number them, if you like.
First, religion is "just" about control. Second, religious
beliefs make people rigid. Third, they're obsolete now.
Fourth, it's best to "get out of your head." All this carries,
fifth, the evident belief *you've found something superior to religion.* Before that, you indicated your belief that simplicity is
better than complexity. And there are still more beliefs, I'm
sure. Even dogmas. Like there's no need for priests or hierarchy…

GLS: Get real, dude. These aren't dogmas! Any ordinary,
modern person can see these things! But I'm not sure you
know much about ordinary, modern people…

LightShadow smiled smugly. I was getting riled. The guy obviously hadn't heard a word GT said. And last night's lecture with
all its non-stop sureties still rankled me. "Will you, please, for
once in your life listen?" I roared. "GT's right, you've just listed
one belief after another. Your talk last night was loaded with
plenty more!"

For an instant, LightShadow was caught off guard. GT took
advantage of the moment, saying "My friend Geoffrey may be
hotheaded, but he has a point. Both explicitly and implicitly,
there's *a far more developed set of beliefs* here than you may realise.
Please, I think I could manage a little summary. Could you
indulge an old man for a few minutes?"

"Go on, then. I'm dying to hear this one!" LightShadow
grinned.

"Well, thank you, my dear chap," GT said. "This may take a
moment…" With that, he took a breath, winced and started to
recite a strange credo:

GT: I believe in One, Timeless, Universal Spiritual Reality, which is always fully accessible in every time and culture.

I believe religions are human-made reflections of that Universal Spirit, which necessarily obscure and deflect spiritual seekers from the truth.

I believe in equally embracing the shadow and the light, yin and yang and every other duality which, on closer inspection, dissolves into transcendent Oneness. No true division exists. Beyond the illusory veil of separation, no true, meaningful differences exist. The Inner is the Outer; the Outer is the Inner. Male is female; female is male. I am you. You are Me. And we are all together.

I believe in eternal evolution. We are all just "spirits in the material world," ever reincarnating in different forms, even different planes of existence, to achieve our fullest, highest potential.

I believe in ascended masters who have evolved more highly than us and light the way ahead.

I believe, therefore, in *inevitable progress*. Today's modern age of Aquarius is more evolved than the preceding Age of Pisces. The epoch of prejudice, patriarchy, authority and hierarchy is past. We are all moving onwards and upwards in ever ascending spirals of radiant possibility.

I affirm creativity, optimism and positive thinking over needless guilt, morbid thinking and anxiety for the future. "Don't worry. Be Happy."

I believe in Gnosis: my own personal intuition. I proudly claim my own reality and my own truth. Likewise, I empower everybody else to do the same, forgetting all doctrines, dogmas and head-trips.

I believe in love, tolerance and understanding. With an open heart and mind, I warmly affirm the right of all individuals to freely choose their own spiritual path. No perspective is ever any more real or valid than any other.

In summation, I believe in "whatever works" to achieve health, happiness and personal power, with liberty and justice for all.

"Wow," Brigid gasped. "You really *did* read Gareth's book, didn't you?"

"Indeed, I have. And many more like it," GT sighed.

"That is what you teach, isn't it, Gareth?" Brigid ventured, a little nervously.

"You know," LightShadow grinned, "That's not too shabby! I probably do believe some of those things, like you say."

GT: Only some?

GLS: Okay—most. Maybe even all. Whatever. But here's the thing. I don't need to *define* them like that! That's one thing I'll never understand about you religionists: why explain everything in set doctrines? There's no need for that. You're better off without fixed creeds!

GT: Well, my friend, there's another belief there—that it's better to avoid clear religious definition. Why do you *believe* people are "better off" without creeds?

GLS: Isn't it obvious? It's impossible. You can't cage infinity! The spirit is beyond all human concepts. All those theological definitions are just head-tripping, man. Mental masturbation. Follow your heart—not your head. People need some room to breathe, for God's sake.

GT: Perhaps it is more for *your* sake. Of course, no human words can ever fully capture the Infinite Mysteries of God...

GLS: Right on!

GT: Still, that hardly means people should remain mute—refusing to address spiritual reality. Indeed, refusing to *think* about it! Language is always imperfect, but we can't renounce it. Not unless we'd rather return to being apes—or vegetables.

GT nailed it. I was always irritated by New Age nebulousness. A corollary to GT's credo popped into my mind: "I believe in switching off my mind and making every statement as neutral, vague, fuzzy and empty of meaning as humanly possible..." Then, something Chesterton said wandered into my thoughts—except I couldn't quite recall the words.

"Man can be defined as an animal that makes dogmas," GT said, as if out of nowhere.

"That's Chesterton!" I exclaimed. "I was thinking the very same thing! But there's more to the quote—if only I could remember."

"I can help you there," GT smiled. "He goes on to say that when man

> declines to tie himself to a system, when he says that he has outgrown definitions, when he says that he disbelieves in finality, when, in his own imagination, he sits as God, holding no form of creed but contemplating all, then he is by that very process sinking slowly backwards into the vagueness of the vagrant animals and the unconsciousness of the grass. Trees have no dogmas. Turnips are singularly broad-minded.

Anna and I burst out laughing. LightShadow looked at GT as though he were mad. I doubt he had ever encountered people like us before in his life: Christians who valued thinking.

XV

The Inclusiveness Illusion

"MAN, you are something else," LightShadow said. "Look, no one's talking about giving up language. I just said people need a little breathing room. That's all."

"Or maybe a lot... even an excess," GT mused.

"What's that supposed to mean?"

"Well, we occupy a finite world of limited domains. Sometimes, one sector demands too much space. Inevitably, then, another one gets shortchanged. Given humanity's fallen condition, the potential for tyranny is never absent. Too often, it's disguised as a demand for greater liberty: a cunning conceit. Our contemporary *corporate libertarianism* professes liberty..."

"Corporate libertarianism?" I said, interrupting him.

"I mean our present philosophy of liberating giant banks and corporations as much as humanly possible. That liberation becomes license to crush the little guy. But that's just one example. Hitler's *Lebensraum* would be another. Certainly, the same trajectory appears elsewhere, as well."

For a brief instant, LightShadow seemed lost for words. GT, I think, presented a genuine puzzle to him. He obviously considered religious people simply as idiots. Clearly, though, GT was no idiot. The old man glided articulately from one topic to the next, employing terms and concepts foreign to LightShadow.

GLS: You're going too far. Exaggerating things! You're right: I have beliefs. Everyone does. I just don't codify them in rigid rule books. Once you define everything like that, it marginalises people. It's like an exclusive club. Either you agree—or you're out. We live in a multicultural society today. Whether you like it or not, inclusiveness is not an option any more.

80

GT: Hmm... another belief: Inclusiveness is mandatory now. That certainly sounds like a main tenet here (whether "codified" or not). How did inclusiveness become obligatory, I wonder? And which progressive "pope" decreed it?

GLS: I can't believe it—you're not actually saying you're *against inclusiveness*?

GT: Indeed I am! At least the way that idea is defined today. To me, it seems a nascent totalitarianism, bent on reducing all differences to manageable dimensions.

GLS: Manageable dimensions?

GT: Well, by our new corporate and capitalist oligarchy, I mean.

GLS: Oh my God. You... are... completely unreal.

GT: I'm not God, my friend. But I assure you I am quite real. People who don't subscribe to your ideology can be real too, you know! Let me be frank. That's what I think we have here: an ideology tantamount to religion. And it has *two different wings*—a secular wing (which is materialistic) and a New Age wing (which aspires to be spiritual).

I could see where the old man was headed. All along, GT pointed out precisely what LightShadow meant to deny: that he possessed a clear system of belief. That system made distinct, definite claims about the spiritual nature of reality. In that, it was "tantamount to religion."

On the other hand, secularists had something comparable. I recalled the first time I met GT. I was a committed secularist then. Like LightShadow, I also denied possessing beliefs—in my case secular beliefs. GT called this the "New Secular Religion." Because like the "New Age Religion," it, too, made distinct, definite claims about the nature of reality (although the claims were materialistic rather than spiritual).

Here, then, were the two "wings" GT now referred to: spiritual and materialistic versions of much the same thing. Kissing cousins, you could say.

Like LightShadow, I had resisted everything the old man said. But GT *rendered conscious* the materialistic beliefs that lurked in my unconsciousness. For example, I affirmed euthanasia, like nearly everyone else of a progressive persuasion. But that, GT pointed out, was either because they *believed* there was no afterlife or else, they *believed* it didn't matter. Whichever way you sliced it, *there were beliefs here*, beliefs that were either explicitly materialistic ("there is no afterlife") or implicitly so ("it doesn't matter if there's an afterlife or not; only the present material world matters").

Moreover, GT pointed out something else: This dismissal of life beyond death *generated its own ethics*. Only thus did one arrive at assisting suicide. A similar situation pertained to abortion. A "right to abort" depended on a *belief* about the nature of the foetus.

Thus, little by little, GT revealed the "New Secular Religion" to which I unconsciously adhered. Because all the ethical injunctions of secular society *rested on a definite system of belief*. Yet secularism, like the New Age, denied this. It always claimed to be neutral, open and tolerant. That, GT said, was "why secularism gets away with murder" (and speaking of things like assisted suicide and abortion, it was obvious he meant that quite literally).

Just as GT prodded me to admit that secularism manifested as a materialistic creed with its own moral judgments, he now tried something similar with LightShadow. But LightShadow was not a materialistic sceptic like I had been. So GT went after the other wing instead: the "New Age Religion."

> **GT:** The New Age Religion features all those elements in the creed I recited—oneness, evolution, reincarnation, etc. But there's more. It *also adopts secular beliefs*. So we need to factor them in, too. Abortion, "gay marriage" and of course so-called multiculturalism. Or, like you just said, *there is no other option*, except inclusiveness. That seems to me another New Age dogma: that a diversity of views is always and everywhere a good thing...
>
> **GLS:** Let me get this straight: Are you actually saying diversity is NOT a good thing?
>
> **GT:** Well, not in the sense *you* mean it. Indeed, I am staunchly opposed to it! A culture committed to complete

diversity would be a sorry thing indeed. Completely insane, in fact.

GLS: Un–be–liev–able!

GT: You know, I was in a society like that once. We had a strange debate. The speaker maintained that, according to the latest quantum research, the old Newtonian paradigm was all wrong. Apparently, the *true value* of two plus two was not four, but actually 4.0000000001. And then this other fellow—he was a skinhead—claimed that was wrong. It was 5.6! And finally a little old lady with blue hair and a koala bear chimed in and said it was 132...

GLS: You said this was a *debating* society?!

GT: Well, not exactly. It was more like an asylum, actually. The SDSII it was called—St Dymphna's Society for the Incurably Insane. Anyway, finally, I had to object and say that quantum mechanics was absolutely irrelevant here! And in fact, two plus two really was truly four. I'm afraid the other three didn't take to that very kindly. I'm not sure about the koala bear...

GLS: I see. Tell me, old man—precisely what have you been smoking?

GT: Why nothing, of course (apart from some beautiful frankincense I might have inhaled at Mass). At any rate, you take my point: that little society—even if insane—was positively filled with diversity! One might even call it multicultural. The four of us couldn't agree on the simplest thing! Pluralism isn't always a good thing, you know.

GLS: You're talking about a nuthouse!

GT: Well, some of us feel modern society is more like that than people realise. Alas, there's plenty of evidence to back that up. Mental illness rates in the modern West are off the scale. The number of people taking medication to control anxiety or depression: it's enough to break an old man's heart. It was nothing like that when I was young... you don't hear much about that in "progressive" narratives. That's just an aside. My real point is that *diversity of views isn't always a good thing.* Any form of society needs common standards. That's necessary for freedom.

GLS: Freedom? I think "control" is the word you're looking for...

GT: Well, it's a paradox. But think of traffic lights in a big city. No one could move anywhere unless *everyone agrees* that green means go and red means stop. Diversity there would mean gridlock—or complete chaos.

GLS: Give me a break! You're just talking about practical necessities of everyday life.

GT: Well, admittedly, that's an extremely superficial example. Red and green are arbitrary and shallow. It might just as easily be blue and orange. Of course, the most profound order isn't founded on human conventions—but immutable divine TRUTH. But that's a very major topic. More than we can manage at this time, I think. For now, I'm only suggesting *freedom without order is impossible.* Law is indispensable, even if it's only traffic law...

And so GT stepped back from the brink of his "very major topic" sensing—correctly, I think—he would lose LightShadow completely. Personally, I wish he could have developed his argument further. For, by now, I was clear that any culture—whether secular, Catholic, New Age, whatever—is *inevitably organised around certain propositions*—propositions it holds as sacrosanct.

Yet such propositions are moral only to the extent they reflect divine truth. For example, a society can have laws allowing abortion, based on the lie "a foetus is not a person," or laws forbidding abortion based on the truth. Two vastly different societies result from the truth or not of the matter. And the same goes for other laws, whether those permitting euthanasia, usury, pornography or what have you. Law based on lies leads to slavery. Law based on truth leads to freedom.

But I digress. For now, I must return to the argument GT was developing—that enforcing diversity as an idol leads to no diversity whatsoever.

GLS: Okay. Common standards are necessary sometimes. That's not religion! That's not the same as claiming spiritual dominion over people's lives with all your legalistic rules. "Thou shalt not this; thou shalt not that." I believe in diversity, man—not religion!

GT: But didn't you just tell me I had *no other option*, except to believe what you believe?

GLS: Only fascists like you would disagree with inclusiveness.

GT: Well, there you go. We have three distinct stages: First, a *formulated belief*: diversity is necessarily a good thing (always and everywhere). That leads to the second, an *ethical injunction*—or a *commandment*: "thou shalt be inclusive." Third, *exclusion*: if I don't agree, I'm excluded as a fascist. Or a dinosaur. Or a neanderthal.

I am sorry, my dear fellow, but whether you "codify" them in formal creeds or not, you *still* have copious beliefs— yes, even commandments. And those who agree are "in" and those who disagree are "out." That's one reason I can't sign up for the Inclusiveness Regime. It's based on illusion.

GLS: I suppose you'd rather return to a rigid, robotic society where everyone has to conform, backed up by the Inquisition?

GT: That's an interesting response. I express my view about current claims to diversity, and all I get is sarcasm. Am I allowed a divergent opinion about diversity in our supposedly diversified society? In other words: do I get any "breathing room?"

GLS: Of course, you're perfectly free to believe whatever garbage you like!

GT: Well, thank you. I do believe you mean that, Mr Light-Shadow. (Unfortunately, I'm not so sure about others in the Inclusiveness Regime.) To my mind, the only diversity that regime tolerates is the most superficial kind imaginable. Like cuisine. Certainly, the modern world has a fantastic "pluralism" of things to eat. Go into any big city now and you can order Italian, Mexican, Chinese, Lebanese food— whatever. (You're even allowed to prefer one cuisine to another!) But real, substantial differences aren't allowed to matter. *Truly* disagree with the Inclusiveness Regime and you get stomped on pretty quick.

GLS: You can*not* be serious. I can*not* believe what I'm hearing.

GT: Well, you're not alone, friend. I can't believe the things I'm hearing either. People forced into a flattened, standardised, one-size-fits-all Political Correctness—then told our society is multicultural! People pressured to abandon the religious and ethical beliefs of millennia—or get labelled as "haters"... It's just like that asylum I visited. You know, that New Ager who told me two plus two was 5.6 became pretty violent when I challenged him...

GLS: New Ager? You said he was a skinhead!

GT: Well, yes, it's all a bit confusing, I know. He claimed to be an "anarcho-holist" and called himself "Schrödinger's Rottweiler." Then, he said he'd thump me one when I questioned his new quantum paradigm...

GLS: There you go again with that nuthouse of yours! Can we talk about the real world, please?

GT: Yes, forgive me. I do digress. Things aren't quite as bad as that *yet*. Still, that "nuthouse" seems a sure sign of where our de-traditionalised "real" world is headed... At least, that's how it looks to me. When I couldn't accept Mr. Rottweiler's "paradigm shift," his explicit hostility only revealed the implicit hostility behind our brave, new multicultural society. That's why I don't believe in inclusiveness. It's illusory because it never includes all sorts of people. Scratch the surface of the illusion, you find rage underneath...

GLS: Gee. No wonder. People today get angry about fascism...

"Well, even there we share a mutual concern," GT said. "Multiculturalism as a new form of fascism—that's precisely what troubles me."

A mischievous twinkle appeared in the old man's eye. "Of course, not *everything* about multiculturalism is bad. I mean, our new expanded cuisine means you can now get root beer in Ireland! Yum, yum," he said and smacked his lips.

"Root beer…?" LightShadow said.

"Yes, I used to drink it back at the Alamo! Or was it the O.K. Corral? I can't remember now. I do get muddled sometimes. Anyway, Billy the Kid introduced me to it. Or maybe it was Butch Cassidy…"

Brigid and LightShadow stared at each other in disbelief. (Of course, I felt just the same when I first met GT. Back then, the old man likewise carried on about odd historical characters he could never have met. And he extolled that same sickly sweet fizzy drink, whose mysterious appeal to Americans completely eluded me—and, GT aside, pretty much every other European I ever met.)

"At any rate," GT continued, "until recently, I could never find it this side of the pond. I say it's time for a round! Who would like a glass?"

"But GT, we don't have any root beer!" Anna said.

"Never mind. I always carry a case with me wherever I go!"

"But you didn't arrive with a case—"

"Oh, don't let that bother you! Go to your fridge. You'll find a six pack there, I believe."

Anna went to the refrigerator. To her astonishment, six cans of root beer were there.

"You're right," she called back from the kitchen.

"Like I said—I never leave home without it! That makes one for each of us. And an extra one for me!"

"Er, not me," LightShadow said. "I can't stand the stuff!"

"Nor me either." I said.

GT looked around at our faces, but none of us appeared keen. "Ah, well, I suppose that means they're all for me, then! Pour me a double, would you, Anna?"

Anna returned to the lounge with a big mug of the stuff.

"Ah, delectable!" GT exclaimed and glugged it back. Then, wiping his mouth with a handkerchief, he added: "My tastes may seem a bit strange, I know. At least, in this case, though, I trust our new multicultural society can tolerate me. Alas, it's everything *else* I'm worried about."

"You are a complete trip," LightShadow said. "Look, I don't say everything's perfect. Maybe some people go too far with Political Correctness. Me, I always stand by Voltaire. There's a famous saying attributed to him. I don't suppose you'd know it, though…"

"Ah yes," GT said. "You mean: 'I wholly disapprove of what you say and will defend to the death your right to say it.'"

"Hey, I'm impressed." LightShadow looked surprised. Throughout everything, the man's conceit had been palpable—as though he were a titan who'd stumbled into a den of hopelessly reactionary pygmies. The fact GT recognised Enlightenment thought took him aback.

GT: Funny that, when you think about what happened *after* Voltaire?

GLS: What's that supposed to mean?

GT: Well, Voltaire's philosophy was, par excellence, the inspiration for 1789—the French Revolution, which ended up killing everyone in sight who didn't share its vision of a free, tolerant open society. To this day, people still speak of Voltaire in hushed tones—as though he pioneered freedom. But it rings a bit hollow to me. Maybe, though, you regard the French Revolution as a great point in human evolution? Even an early herald of the new Aquarian consciousness…

GLS: Sure, everyone knows it liberated the people from the Church's power.

"Great," I grunted, "the inclusive French Revolution couldn't include the Church, so it was forced to eliminate Her…"

XVI

On Human Suffering

"1789," GT said, "truly astonishes me. Rather, I should say the cult of 1789..."

"The cult?" Brigid said.

"Well, I don't mean a sect, but rather the ritual celebration—year in, year out. People *commemorating* this unimaginable orgy of cruelty, barbarism, genocide. I mean, the Inclusiveness Regime is more understandable. It's highly repressive, but not so nakedly as the French Revolution. Mostly, the repression still happens at psychological levels (though sometimes people's livelihood—their jobs—are threatened). Still, it's nowhere near as blatant as the bloodshed of revolutionary France."

> **GLS:** Sometimes, stuff happens. Revolutions happen. Tyrants need overthrowing. People get killed—including innocent people caught in the crossfire. It's not pretty, but it's inevitable.

> **GT:** Some would say that sounds callous. Have you any idea of the hundreds of thousands massacred in France alone—let alone the death tolls of the revolutionary wars across Europe in the aftermath?

> **GLS:** I know it sounds bad. But it's the price we pay for progress. Anyway, death may *appear* terrible. But really it's nothing to fear. It's merely transition from one plane of existence to another. The ultimate freedom is being liberated from the body.

> **GT:** Hmm. Reminds me of a quote from a book I know: "I tell you this, at the moment of your death, you will realise the greatest freedom, the greatest peace, the greatest joy, the greatest love you have ever known."

GLS: Yes, exactly! I have to hand it to you—you sure have a thing remembering all these quotes…

GT: Yes, I've been gifted with *eidetic memory*, commonly called photographic memory. If I see a text once, I can still see the image of the words in my mind. Unfortunately, that means I never forget things like that…

With that, GT shuddered. LightShadow looked at him quizzically. "Like what?" he asked.

"Well, the utter trivialisation of death and suffering in New Age texts. That one, by the way, was from *Conversations with God* by Neale Donald Walsch. Book Two, page 56. Would you like to hear what it says on page 36?"

"I would, GT," I piped in, before LightShadow could answer.

Shuddering still, GT continued, "Purportedly, this is the voice of *God*. How Walsch heard 'God' speak to him. Apparently, 'God' says: 'First, understand that death is not an end, but a beginning; not a horror, but a joy. It is not a closing down, but an opening up. The happiest moment of your life will be the moment it ends.'"

"Sounds great to me," LightShadow grinned. "Go on."

"Very well." GT said, "If I must. Further down the page 'God' says: 'The first thing you have to understand—as I've already explained to you—is that Hitler didn't hurt anyone. In a sense, he didn't inflict suffering, he *ended* it.' And then 'God' adds: 'The mistakes Hitler made did no harm or damage to those whose death he caused. Those souls were released from their earthly bondage, like butterflies emerging from a cocoon.' Elsewhere, 'God' tells Walsch Hitler went to Heaven, because no hell exists…"

GT looked almost stricken as he continued. "Those Walsch conversations with 'God'—millions upon millions of people reading them in dozens of languages. Receiving it all as *divine inspiration*. Indeed, you even find these 'conversations with God' in Christian bookshops these days! People everywhere are forgetting what Christianity truly means."

GLS: Okay, I happen to like Walsch. His channellings have done enormous good. Still, no channel is perfect. Maybe Walsch got that one wrong. I'm not saying Hitler never hurt anyone.

GT: Well, I'm glad to hear that, my dear fellow. Still, I'm not just pointing to Walsch—but *a general pattern throughout New Age books*. For example, *A Course in Miracles* discounts all human suffering as unreal. Likewise, Alice Bailey celebrates dropping the bomb on Hiroshima—as the greatest event in untold millennia (greater, apparently, than Christ's coming).[1] Not all New Agers believe such things. And I'm genuinely grateful if you don't. Still, there's this strange *trivialisation of human suffering* throughout New Age literature. Please, I beg you: do not go down that road yourself.

GLS: Oh, man. I need a break.

GT: Well, why don't you take one? The bathroom is upstairs and to the left, I believe…

"Thanks, I will," LightShadow said. Was he surprised GT anticipated his bodily needs? Likewise, GT knew where our toilet was, even though he'd never been here before…

Anna, Brigid and I were left alone with the Gentle Traditionalist. Brigid was completely silent. She had never encountered anything like this before—a Catholic thinker who stood his ground, gently but firmly refusing to pander to popular clichés. A rarity indeed in the modern Church!

Anna, too, was silent, taken up with GT's musings on New Age attitudes to human suffering. She could not help but recall her dream of a detached, passionless, "perfect" world of detached, passionless, "perfect" people who never suffered. She thought, too, of Eckhart Tolle's gospel of transcending pain. But GT broke the silence only to echo her very thoughts…

"This so-called 'transcending suffering' easily leads to *trivialising suffering*," he said. "That's the problem with all this New Age emphasis on detachment, self-control, self-empowerment."

"Or incessant non-stop positivity," I said, "stigmatising any 'negativity.'"

"I know," GT said, dabbing his eyes with a handkerchief. "The

---

[1] In my previous book on the New Age, I focused on this strange, often hidden New Age disregard for human suffering, addressing *A Course in Miracles* as well as Bailey and the bomb: see *Cor Jesu Sacratissimum*, 150–51, 195–96, 201–5.

agony of the Cross—the New Age religion will do anything, *absolutely anything* to avoid that. Even to the point of pretending all human suffering is unreal. There's no time to explain it now. But look into those New Age texts *carefully*, then you'll notice something."

And GT added something barely audible, immensely sad, but filled, nonetheless, with emphatic intensity: "It's all about AVOIDING THE CROSS."

Turning to Brigid, he added, "Please think about that, my child, for your sake and the sake of children you will someday bear." Brigid frowned. But the old man simply continued. "The Irish children, children everywhere, being robbed—robbed by something that pretends to be universal. If only it *were* universal! Instead, it's *subterfuge*: deceit to achieve a goal. There's a hidden, calculated system here *to replace the Cross*. Of course, most are completely unaware of the occult agenda behind all this."

"Occult agenda?" I asked.

"Patience, my good man, patience. We're coming to that. Right now, my point is that our poor Mr LightShadow *truly* believes in his 'universal spirituality.' Just like he *truly* believes in his 'tolerant, inclusive, multicultural' society. Without ever seeing, he's one step away from the jackboots…"

XVII

The Real Ultimate Sacrament

THE Cheshire zebra returned to the room. Or maybe rhino. Because I couldn't help but think the man possessed an unusually thick skin, impervious to anything beyond his own orbit. There seemed little hope, then, for any genuine debate this afternoon. That would presuppose LightShadow was genuinely interested in people with views different to his own.

"I must thank you, Mr LightShadow," GT said.

"Oh?" LightShadow grinned, sitting down again.

> **GT:** Well, at first, I doubted we'd achieve much in our little conversation. Because we couldn't even agree on the simplest things—such as whether a New Age movement even exists! But you've been honest enough to admit some sort of movement here. Moreover, that it has definite beliefs, even if they're not formally defined. Truly, I feel good about these things. If only more people could own up to their own belief systems—systems which necessarily exclude non-believers! My greatest difficulty isn't so much the New Age religion itself, but *the power it assumes by pretending it isn't a religion*. All this hiding away helps no one.

> **GLS:** Hiding away? Who's hiding away? What are you on about now?

> **GT:** Well, only this. As a Catholic, my dogmas and doctrines are *out in the open*. They're plain for everyone to see. Anyone can consult our Catechism and find them, if they want. New Age positions, on the other hand, remain elusive. People can't easily determine where you really stand. Alas, this lack of definition renders New Agers a tremendous cultural advantage. Dare I say an unfair one?

GLS: Unfair?! Tell me another one…

GT: New Age ideology gets space in the public square—space traditional religion doesn't get—precisely because it's never seen as a religion. Secular ideology gets the same. Potent belief systems creep into people's minds—*because they're never identified as belief systems.* These belief systems pretend to be neutral, tolerant and inclusive, when in fact they're anything but!

Instead, they continuously undermine the very things they claim to tolerate. Look at your talk last night. Whether you realise it or not, dear chap, you claim to be inclusive, but, in fact, you're not. You profess to honour all religions, but you repudiate pretty much everything they stand for. You claim to accept Christianity, but you dismiss it, without perhaps ever realising.

GLS: Oh man, that's so arrogant. You don't even know what I think. I don't reject Christianity! Obviously, Christianity has a shadow and I see that. Most people do these days. But I celebrate the Christ-consciousness. I celebrate diversity. Apart from a few shadow aspects, I'm totally cool with all religions. Every perspective is equally valid!

"Oh, come on," Anna burst in. "I heard your talk. I saw your book, too. You may not like the term 'New Ager' but you sound just like I did. I rejected nearly everything Christianity stood for. I didn't believe in the Devil. I didn't believe in the Fall. I certainly didn't believe in original sin. And when you think like that, there's no reason to think Jesus Christ died for that sin!"

"Indeed, Anna," GT said sombrely, "The New Age *renders Christ on the Cross unnecessary.* Or, rather, that is what it very much aims to do."

"Yes," Anna continued, "and, likewise, I rejected priests, dogma, authority. Yet I still said I respected Christianity—like every religion. But I disrespected ninety percent of what the Church stands for."

"Well, well, well—aren't we uptight?" LightShadow smirked. "All that is just an extremely narrow, twisted version of Christianity. The devil, hell, original sin—has it ever occurred to you those are all excellent means to frighten people? That's what this is really about."

"Like I say," said Anna, "that's what I used to think…"

GLS: Before you went over to the dark side, you mean. Sorry, Anna—I really don't get you. You—of all people— should know there are only two types of spiritual seekers on this planet. The real ones seek love. The other lot just want power. Like the priests—they want to control people: regulate their lives, how they feel about their bodies, who they have sex with. Some people get their kicks out of that, you know… Concepts like sin and hell provide all the ammunition they need! Jesus never meant to control people! The real Jesus was all about freedom. He totally rejected the legalism of his own era. That's why the priests had him killed! After that, they twisted his teaching into the same old dogmas.

I wanted to explode. He'd completely dodged Anna's point about dismissing Christianity while pretending to respect it. Better: he completely confirmed her point, without even realising it. I was about to object, when GT's solemn look silenced me.

GT: There seems to be a "real Jesus" here who doesn't believe in dogma…

GLS: Well, obviously. He would be as bad as the Pharisees if he did.

GT: I see. Hmm. I wonder what he would say about "gay marriage"?

GLS: Obviously, he would be totally cool with that. No way Jesus was a homophobe!

GT: Yes—no way. His infinite compassion precludes all fear. What about divorce?

GLS: Well, again, Jesus came to liberate us from the law.

My mind reeled. With LightShadow, it was one cliché after another. I wanted to invoke the Gospel: "Do not think that I have come to abolish the Law or the Prophets; I have not come to abolish them but to fulfil them." I wanted to scream, in fact. But GT's look held me in check.

GT: What about women priests?

GLS: I don't know about your Jesus, but my Jesus wasn't a misogynist!

GT: Ah, I see. "My Jesus and your Jesus." Your Jesus presumably being the real one?

GLS: Well, it's certainly easier to believe in a Jesus who isn't a bigot.

GT: Yes, yes, *easier*. An interesting word, that. And easier to accept, as well. It does seem rather easy that the "real Jesus" just happens *to believe everything you believe*. Dare I say... a bit *too* easy?

GLS: I don't know about you, man, but some of us live in the twenty-first century. This isn't the Middle Ages! Today, there's modern scholarship. Also archaeological discoveries. The Gnostic gospels were only discovered in 1945. The real Jesus can't be covered up any longer.

GT: The real "Jesus." The real Christianity. You're saying it's accessible like never before. I suppose that was the Church's *main function* these last two thousand years—hiding the real truth of Christianity?

GLS: You got it in one, dude!

GT: But now people like you have finally found the real thing...

GLS: Look, it's not rocket science. Today everyone can read the Gospels suppressed by the Church. *The Gospel of Philip* says Jesus kissed Mary Magdalene "on the mouth." The Church buried that one. It couldn't handle the idea Jesus had a lover. Jesus needed love, too!

At last, we can peel away the layers of illusion. Get to what's real.

GT: Yes, yes. How silly of me to forget that. And, of course, there's channelling too. The "real Christ" is still with us and he still talks to people, channelling various books—like *A Course in Miracles*?

GLS: Exactly, there's all kinds of new stuff now. Not just the Gnostic Gospels—but also the great channelled texts of our time. The Christ will not be silenced any more!

GT: No, no, I see. And he talks to New Age channellers, of course. Just not people in the Church, though.

GLS: Well, no doubt he would, if they'd only listen! It's hardly surprising he can't get through. All that dogma is enough to close anyone's mind.

GT: Yes, that makes sense too. The "real Jesus" only speaks to those with open minds and open hearts, ready to warmly embrace every perspective. Just not to us closed-minded dogmatists.

GLS: Well, you're being sarcastic. But at last you're making sense.

GT: Yes, yes. I must watch my sarcasm. It is a sin, to be sure.

GLS: Look, there's something else you're missing. Modern people don't need Gnostic gospels, channelled texts—or *any* books. All that head stuff! Today we find our own personal truth. Have you heard of Rennes-le-Château?

GT: It's in southern France, the Pyrenees, I believe.

GLS: That's right. Some say Jesus is buried there. I went there once to meditate—

Tears appeared in GT's eyes and he murmured quietly: *"Crucifixus etiam pro nobis sub Pontio Pilato, passus et sepultus est, et resurrexit tertia die, secundum Scripturas, et ascendit in caelum, sedet ad dexteram Patris."*

GLS: Could you speak English, please?

GT: Sorry, the Latin is just so beautiful. Essentially, though, I was saying that after He was crucified, He rose again and ascended into Heaven. There was no body to bury, *secundum Scripturas*—according to the Scriptures.

GLS: *Your* scriptures, you mean, imposed on people...

GT: We imposed? Or maybe the early Christians were perfectly capable of separating the gold from the dross? Could it be these Gnostic gospels and suchlike never spoke to the early Church with the same power and authority?

GLS: "Power and authority"?! Listen to you, man. You guys need to focus on love…

GT: Well, yes. One can never love enough. I'm quite the failure there, sinner that I am… Anyway, my friend, please continue. I'd like to hear your "personal experience" at Rennes-le-Château.

GLS: Okay, so I was on this mountain in the Pyrenees. I'd been reading *The Templar Revelation*.

GT: Which is…?

GLS: Well, it inspired Dan Brown to write *The Da Vinci Code*. Anyway, I got tired of reading. So I put the book down and started to meditate. I entered a very still, silent space. All my chakras were perfectly aligned. Suddenly I felt an extraordinary wise presence before me, emitting waves of love and light. It was Jesus—and Mary Magdalene was by his side! Intuitively, I knew they were both buried on that mountain, just as they had been together in life. They were holding hands and smiling at me. They kissed, just like in the *Gospel of Philip*. Then they started making love…

Anna shivered. Memories of a beach long ago mingled with this outrage. I wanted to show the guy the door. LightShadow, I think, enjoyed being provocative. But GT, though plainly disgusted, merely said "Maybe, you can spare us the gory details. Still, I'd like to hear what this vision means to you."

GLS: Absolutely! I knew in a flash—an instantaneous "peak experience"—what all the great Gnostics, all the great spiritual teachers always knew—that Jesus wasn't against sex. The realisation penetrated every cell of my body. It just felt so right. Everything completely resonated.

GT: Yes, I see. Your own personal interpretation of the Gospel and personal experience "completely resonate." That's what matters in the New Age of Aquarius. Personal certitude—not priests and dogma.

GLS: Right on, man! And you know what? It also resonated with that Templar book I mentioned. I had finished Chapter Six, when I put it down. But I never noticed the title of the next chapter. When I opened the book again, it blew my mind! Do you know what Chapter Seven is called?

GT: No. Do tell…

GLS: "Sex: The Ultimate Sacrament!"[1] My mind was totally blown. All the pieces were coming together. Jesus came to establish sacred union, *hieros gamos*—not more patriarchy. But Peter couldn't handle it.

I could take no more. I leaned forward in my chair, inches from LightShadow's face. My voice trembled with rage. "Do… you… have… ANY… idea what a *real* sacrament is?"

"Whoa, man—no need to get so aggressive! I know about your seven sacraments, all controlled by priests. But the *real* sacraments are everywhere. Life is a miracle. Sex is a miracle. Everything's a sacrament. People can get along just fine without your priests, thank you very much."

"You have NO idea what you're talking about," I bellowed. "And for all your talk of dialogue, you clearly aren't interested in anything anyone else says. Is there any point to this so-called dialogue?!"

At that moment, GT made a sudden motion with his right hand. The blood-red ring on his middle finger caught my eye, startling me. My words faltered. My mind whirled. Something distinctly odd started to happen, as I gazed into the ring…

Vertigo, almost nausea and, then, something else hit me. Something utterly uncharacteristic of me—tears welled in my eyes. Instead of rage, I wanted to sob. Strange, immense pity stabbed my heart. Poor LightShadow! Poor, poor man. Anna was right: he was, more than anything, a victim. Not only did he lack any idea of what he was talking about, he was simply one of millions like him. Millions buying books with entire chapters devoted to the

---

[1] Lynn Picknett, Clive Prince, "Sex: The Ultimate Sacrament," in *The Templar Revelation: Secret Guardians of the True Identity of Christ* (London: Corgi, 1998), 198–238.

"ultimate sacrament of sex." Poor, poor humanity. Poor Gareth Crowley. Less idiot than dupe. Duped by his own culture, duped by the destruction of Catholic tradition, now entrenched in England for hundred of years.

Staring into the ring, I strangely started sensing how centuries of history shaped LightShadow. For the de-Catholicisation of Britain carried *consequences* that still shape people today. Britain would never have become the ultra-secular, ultra-liberal land it is now, without this de-Catholicisation. Nor, without the Reformation, would it be such a hotbed for the New Age. (Or better, *seedbed*—the New Age's ultimate seedbed, along with California.) All this contributed to LightShadow's formation.

Then, still more of LightShadow's formative influences were plaintively, hauntingly evoked by the ring. I sensed his early Labour Party activism, inherited from his family. And something else too: a younger Gareth Crowley. A frightened child, hiding in his room, while his Marxist father raged at his bisexual mother, whose affairs with women created constant havoc in the home.

Poor Gareth, poor man, poor boy—he never stood a chance in a house like that! Then I sensed him in San Francisco, years later, in psychotherapy. Such therapy, though, was only needed because a door had been barricaded in his youth. Just as that door was barricaded in his parents' youth before him and his grandparents before that. I sensed a whole line of ancestors going back to the Tudor times of Henry VIII, when the door to the sacraments—the door Christ opened!—was bolted shut by the English Reformation...

At once, the prayer of St Michael the Archangel at Fatima erupted in my heart: "My God, I believe, I adore, I hope, and I love You. I ask pardon for those who do not believe, do not adore, do not hope, and do not love You."

I was on the verge of breaking down, when, once more, the ring caught my eye. Somehow, it steadied me. Now, something else shot through me. Not pity, but wave upon wave of gratitude, sheer gratitude. Like Anna, I had found faith. Against all odds, against all the lies entrenched in secular society. For unlike most of my British compatriots, I now *knew* what a real sacrament was. Something precious, precious beyond words, precious beyond anything LightShadow had ever known. It was *hard* for me to miss communing with Christ that morning. The Eucharist was my daily consolation and desideratum…

Of course, I appreciated lovemaking with my wife, too. But as much as I received from that, it paled into insignificance compared to consuming His Body, His Blood.

Certainly, Holy Communion with Christ lacked the physical intensity of sex. But it possessed something else far more delicate and profound. And as I stared into the ring, I saw how the Eucharist's soft, subtle glow changed *everything*. It irradiated my entire existence now, cleansing me, healing me, day after day after day. This was why Anna and I could feel its absence, even after missing it for a short spell.

I saw, too, how the Eucharist strengthened me to *bear* suffering, rather than "transcend" it. This was why New Agers tried to circumvent life's pain: they never knew the genuine "Ultimate Sacrament." The authors of *The Templar Revelation* could only call sex "the Ultimate Sacrament" because they never experienced the life-enhancing radiance from the Body of Christ. A Body which was not buried on a French mountain, but *transformed*, that it might become present in a hundred thousand Masses around the world every day.

And I recalled what GT said the first time we met—that these hundred thousand Masses daily were like the beating of a Planetary Heart. Every minute of every day, the Mass was celebrated by countless priests across the planet. But books like *The Templar Revelation* and *The Da Vinci Code* robbed people of that. For long moments I sat there, rent with sheer gratitude for all that I received and real horror for all that modernity was denied.

At that point, I heard GT say, "I'm curious, Mr LightShadow. Did you 'experience' whether 'your Jesus' married the poor woman or not?"

> **GLS**: No. That wasn't part of the message—because it's not important. Maybe he secretly married her; maybe he didn't. They loved each other. That's what matters. Love trumps hate.

GT: Love—I wonder if that's what we're really talking about?

GLS: Love, love, love. That's what this is *all* about. The whole enchilada! At least, it is for me. I don't know about you guys...

GT: I'm sorry—but everything seems so bound up with sex here. Love and sex are two different things—alas, sometimes completely different.

GLS: Yawn. You Christians are so *repressed*. People have needs, you know. Surely, Jesus had needs. He was just a man after all...

GT: Just a man?

GLS: Well, an initiate, to be sure—a very advanced man, high on the evolutionary scale.

GT: Whom "the Christ consciousness" entered...?

GLS. Well, yeah. Doesn't mean he didn't have needs.

GT: Jesus was *not* just a man.

GLS: Well, that's what your religion says!

GT: Hmm...as opposed to *your* religion, which decrees he was? I realise you claim not to have a religion. Forgive me, but that claim seems increasingly problematic. Because statements like "Jesus was just a man" remain just that: statements of belief. Moreover, beliefs that *carry enormous consequence*. They lead to other doctrines too. Like marriage isn't important. Fornication is fine because men need love—or sex...

GLS: *Fornication?*

GT: It means—

GLS: I know what the word means! I just never heard anyone use it before! Some of us don't live in the Middle Ages...

GT: Well, my good man, I can't say I'm surprised! Because I see how it all adds up for you. Jesus wasn't a homophobe, so undoubtedly he'd support "gay marriage." You believe in free love, sex without commitment. So the "real Jesus" must too. The "real truth" of Christianity is whatever resonates with your experience. It also resonates with pleasure.

Once more: isn't it convenient how this "real Christianity" *just happens to agree with everything you already believe yourself?* A bit too convenient, if you ask me. Heaven forbid the real Jesus challenge you! Heaven forbid the real Jesus stand in the way of sexual pleasure!

GLS: You know what your problem is? You're so totally *judgmental!* Without the slightest understanding of human needs. Still, you're a funny guy—in a thoroughly twisted, perverse sort of way, I mean…

GT: Well, since I amuse you, perhaps I can continue…

GLS: Sure—go right ahead! Like I said, I'm all for dialogue. Let it all hang out, man.

GT: Dare I say, then, your belief in the "real Jesus" illumines your commitment to inclusiveness? As I said, it's easy to include a Jesus who happens to agree with you. The "real Jesus" is cool with sex without commitment. He can be included, then. Or a "New Age Jesus" imbued with the "Christ consciousness." No problem including him, either. No doubt the "real Mohammed" was a man of peace who can be slotted into the New Age too… Forgive me, but your inclusiveness only seems restricted to a *narrow fringe* of religion you find acceptable. Meanwhile, the ninety-eight per cent of Christians who abominate your free-loving "real Jesus" get written off. And it's similar with ninety-eight per cent of Muslims, etc. We don't fit *your* pattern, so we're fanatics or neanderthals. Hmm. I wonder who is more inclusive—me or you?

GLS: Don't be ridiculous. I'm not promoting medievalism! You exclude everything the modern world has to offer!

GT: Well, not quite everything. But much of it, yes—indeed.

GLS: I'm glad you admit it!

GT: Indeed, I am highly selective and profoundly exclusive. I proudly confess it and encourage you to do the same.

GLS: What the—?

GT: What I mean, friend, is something that is true for you, me and everybody else. *We all exclude the viewpoints we don't agree with.* You exclude an enormous number of views that people held in the past—up to the 1960s, say—and, indeed, that vast numbers *still* hold today. I exclude the modern, liberal ideology of the post-60s elites. Meanwhile, we both include the people who agree with us.

I am sorry, but your inclusiveness sounds a little too easy to me. Re-define Christianity to what you can agree with— then you can include it. Re-define Islam to what you can agree with—then you can include it. Re-define Jesus as advocating post-1960s Western liberal secular and sexual attitudes and—voilà!—you have "the Christ consciousness."

Inclusiveness is easy if you only include that which agrees with you! Respecting, really respecting those who disagree with you, that's where things get tough. And that means not calling them neanderthals…

Brigid shifted uncomfortably. She was shocked by this sudden hostility to the Church. LightShadow always said he was "cool with Christianity," cool with every religion. After all, he celebrated diversity, believed in tolerance and respected every point of view as equally valid. Not once did Brigid think to question that.

Now, an unsettling memory of Father Brady surfaced in her mind. Father Brady was an elderly priest who came to her parish in Cork when she was fourteen. Only a year later, though, he died unexpectedly. Still, she never forgot that frail old man. He was definitely no idiot, but he definitely believed the very things LightShadow regarded idiotic…

Brigid was beginning to think. And, lost in thought, she only caught brief snatches of the conversation. At one point, Light-Shadow was saying "Your judgmentalism is just another means to control people. Get them to feel guilty—so they'll do what you want."

But Father Brady never struck Brigid like that. She remembered him in the confessional. Back then, she still went, every month. Certainly, Father Brady encouraged her to see herself as a sinner. But he never shamed her. She never felt judged by him.

According to Father Brady, we were all in this same broken boat together. He was no better than her and probably worse, he said. He was just a fallen sinner like everyone else. And he, like her, desperately, desperately needed help.

Was this judgmentalism? Brigid didn't think so. LightShadow might call the old priest a closed-minded dogmatist, but Brigid couldn't imagine him dismissing other people the way Gareth did.

Then, GT's voice startled her. "Brigid, you've been very quiet," GT said, "You needn't say anything if you don't want, but I'm genuinely interested what you make of all this."

Brigid fidgeted. "Well, I don't know what to say really. You're probably both right in a way. I think Jesus expressed the Christ consciousness, and Buddha did, too. And everybody else does— at least sometimes. But I don't think priests are as bad as you think, Gareth. Maybe there's a bit more to the Church than you realise. I mean, you've never really been to church, have you?"

Anna and I glanced at each other. We never expected this defense of the Church, half-hearted as it was. Yet, Brigid nailed it: LightShadow, like most New Agers, had never experienced a single religion in his life.

"Well, no. I haven't. But, Bridge—" His tone was softer now, albeit condescending as ever. "You don't need to go to church to know what the priests think. It's obvious they believe this Hell and original sin garbage. You don't need to hear their sermons to know that."

And then, Brigid said something that blew me away: "But Gareth, the Church isn't only about sermons..."

Another memory had crossed her mind. It was Father Brady at the pulpit. "I won't tell you much today," he was saying, "I don't really like long sermons. Oh, they're all right in their way—if the priest has something good to say. Which, quite often, he doesn't. But even if he does, nothing, nothing he ever says will be as important as Our Lord, in His Body, His Blood. That's why we come to church to receive the Body and Blood of the Risen Christ. Nothing I will ever say compares to THAT."

"Okay, you go there, sing some hymns, maybe you say some prayers," LightShadow objected. "But the ideas are in the sermons! That's the key thing."

Then Brigid made me gasp. Anna, too. "Maybe you don't really understand the ideas, Gareth. And, anyway, you don't go to church just to hear sermons! You go there to receive His Body and Blood…"

XVIII

"Deprived of the Universal Remedy"

"BRIGID, I really must congratulate you!" GT exclaimed, utterly delighted. "You've hit the proverbial nail on the head. Our friend here has entirely failed to grasp the heart of Christianity: the direct encounter with Christ in His sacraments. I am sorry to be so blunt, Mr LightShadow, but everything you've said plainly demonstrates your ignorance. You haven't the slightest understanding of Christianity whatsoever."

"Oh, thanks a lot," LightShadow said.

"Well, it's not really your fault. I blame your culture—not you."

"How magnanimous of you."

GT: Forgive me. That sounds condescending, I know. But everything you say of Christianity is a stereotype. Alas, more often than not, those stereotypes proceed from Protestantism. Like assuming the sermon is the key reason for attending church! That's a horrendous mistake. Again it's hardly your fault. It's quite a typical idea in Protestant countries like England or America. Although you mentioned visiting France—

GLS: Well, that was only for a few days.

GT: Ah yes. And if I'm not mistaken, you haven't been anywhere else outside of England, except your time in America? Even Ireland is new to you...

GLS: Well, I spent time in Canada, when I lived in the States.

GT: English or French-speaking Canada?

GLS: British Colombia.

GT: Again, a region thoroughly Protestant in its cultural origins. Apart from a few days, you've spent your entire life in a culturally Protestant context.

GLS: Groan. Next you'll be calling me a Protestant...

GT: Well, no. But there may be a lingering *cultural Protestantism* you're not aware of. At least it's clear to me that whatever little you've absorbed about Christianity is *strongly coloured by the Reformation*. Alas, English folk like yourself tend to forget Protestantism has always been a minority view within Christianity.

GLS: Minority view? Oh, come on. It looks pretty mainstream to me!

GT: Yes—*in the Anglosphere*. Beyond that, it's maybe a third of global Christianity. The other two thirds, mainly Catholic (but also Eastern Orthodox), see things differently. For them, Protestantism remains a five-century detour within two thousand years of Christianity. Moreover, to a large extent, it's confined to speakers of Germanic languages— mainly English and German, but also Scandinavian, etc. I don't mean to knock Protestants. Frequently they put us Catholics to shame! However, English people often think an idea is Christian, when in fact *it's only Protestant*. The majority of Christians don't share it. That's my point.

I couldn't help but recall my first conversation with GT. He explained just the same to me: how much people like me held notions of Christianity that hardly represent the Faith as a whole. For example, I bristled at God "punishing his only Son"—which I took to be the Christian explanation for the Crucifixion. But that, GT explained, had more to do with Calvinism than Catholicism. And so it hardly represented a majority view! He then explained the Mystery of the Crucifixion in a way I'd never heard in my life before.[1]

That, of course, made me wonder *why* I never heard it before!

---

[1] Buck, *Gentle Traditionalist*, 70–74.

Only then did I realise it was because, like LightShadow, *I was English*. Even thoroughly secular English culture remains permeated by Protestant concepts which (subtly) bar the door to Catholicism. I recalled the centuries of barricades I sensed, staring into GT's ring. Walls erected against the Catholic Mystery. And, very strangely, words I once read from Valentin Tomberg flashed through my mind: "The impoverishment of humanity caused by Protestantism . . . consequently humanity is deprived of the effect of the *Universal Remedy.*"[2]

I shivered.

> **GT:** All this is at the very root of the problem—everything we've talked about today.

> **GLS:** *Everything*?! I think you're exaggerating. Again.

> **GT:** Absolutely everything. New Age stereotypes about Christianity remain deeply indebted to Calvinism (and the fundamentalism that proceeds from Calvinism). It's no wonder New Agers are "turned off" by Christianity when they're clueless about the Catholic Mystery. Honestly, *nothing you are saying* would be possible without the historical trajectory started by the Reformation. I could explain, but I'm not sure you have time...

> **GLS:** Go on. Hit me with it. Time is only an illusion, anyway. Time with you *doubly* so.

> **GT:** Very well, then. You've noted, by now, the enormous influence I attach to the Reformation.

> **GLS:** It's hard to miss, dude! Not that I completely disagree. Obviously, it liberated a lot...

> **GT:** There's a striking word: *liberated*. It stems, of course, from the Latin *liber*, meaning free. Which is also the root of our modern word *liberal*. Liberal philosophy today, including New Age-ism, owes a colossal debt to Protestantism. That's why Protestant cultures liberalise more rapidly than the Catholic ones. (Generally speaking, I mean. There are exceptions.)

[2] Anonymous [Valentin Tomberg], *The Wandering Fool: Love and Its Symbols: Early Studies on the Tarot* (San Rafael, CA: LogoSophia Press, 2009), 90.

Still, the "liberations" you champion generally occur first in Protestant cultures. Take abortion, for example, which liberalised earlier in the non-Catholic countries. Places like Holland, Sweden, England are almost always out there in front, leading the pack. Catholic cultures generally remain more conservative. That's why abortion is only stalking Ireland in 2018—more than fifty years since it was first legalised in Britain. And it's still blocked in certain Catholic countries, even today.

GLS: Yeah, they're usually more stuck in the mud. I get that. For once, you're making sense.

GT: Well, thank you, dear chap. Anyway, I hope you see my point about the Anglosphere. Ireland apart, the key Anglosphere countries have not only been Protestant—they've been global pioneers of Liberalism. By that I mean Social Liberalism, but also Economic Liberalism.

GLS: Economic Liberalism?

GT: Well, Capitalism, I mean. People forget the Reformation liberated capitalists, as well, from things like the old restrictions on usury. Capitalism was pioneered across the planet by the Anglosphere. First, the great British empire, now the global hegemony of America. Catholic countries have never been as capitalistic as Protestant ones.

GLS: You're calling Capitalism liberal?!

GT: According to the classical meaning of the word, yes. Liberalism is a current, born above all in the Protestant sphere (but admittedly, aided by the French Revolution, too) which strives to liberate attitudes and actions in different domains.

Luther was a *theological* liberal—he sought to liberate the people from Catholic tradition and the Catholic hierarchy. Abortion, the LGBT movement, and so on, are results of Social Liberalism. And Wall Street thrives on Economic Liberalism, which gives bankers the power to crush people with extortionate usury.

Theological, Social, Economic—these are the main branches of the same liberal tree.

But I'm digressing. My point here is that, apart from a few days in France and now Ireland, you've spent your entire life in the Protestant Anglosphere. That, I maintain, has inevitably coloured *everything you know about Christianity.* It also colours your so-called "New Paradigm Spirituality."

GLS: Groan. Whatever, dude…

GT: Bear with me. Regardless what we call it, you consider this new spirituality as a universal approach that simultaneously embraces and transcends all religions. To me that's poppycock. What appears universal to you looks highly specific to me—indeed highly *particularised.* There are reasons for that. A major one is that New Age-ism emerges from a highly particular setting: the Protestant Anglosphere. Above all, England and America. And it feeds on the Liberalism those countries pioneered in the world. It feeds, too, on the impoverishment of humanity caused by Protestantism…

I sat there stunned. GT employed Tomberg's *exact phrase* that echoed in my mind only moments ago. If that weren't all, he then amplified the effect!

"Excuse me," GT said, turning from LightShadow and leaning towards me for a moment, "I must make a note for Geoffrey here. This *deprivation of the Universal Remedy* explains so much. Not only about abortion or Anglosphere Liberalism, but much else in de-Catholicised Europe. Just think of Locke, Hume, Bentham, Marx, Bultmann and the so-called 'Death of God' theology. Or Adam Smith and John Stuart Mill! How easily could their reductionist philosophies emerge in a truly sacramental culture? How *likely* is it that they'd take *hold* of society, as they have? Think about it, Geoffrey. *Think about it!*"

"I will."

"Good man."

Helena Petrovna Blavatsky, 1831–1891. Russian occultist and world traveller. Claimed to receive training for mission, by Eastern Mahatmas, whilst living in Tibet. Alleged mission involved being sent to America, where she founded Theosophical Society in 1875. Later wrote The Secret Doctrine *(1888).*

XIX

The Anglosphere
and Eastern Esotericism

"THANK you for your patience, Mr LightShadow," GT said. "To return to you, my point is that you, dear chap, are more the product of the Protestant Anglosphere than you may realise. And your very Englishness has more to do with so-called New Age 'universalism' than you readily appreciate. As I said, it doesn't look universal to me, but rather particular. Please, think about that for the moment—all the key New Age texts are in English."

GLS: Well, so is everything else these days. It's the world language!

GT: True, but that's a fairly recent phenomenon. As recently as the nineteenth century, French was the international language of diplomacy. German was perhaps the premier language of science. And I don't mention the nineteenth century for nothing—because today's New Age thinking begins in the nineteenth century.

It's largely due to *Theosophy*, which started then. And Theosophy was very much an English-language phenomenon. You know what I mean—all those esoteric books by Alice Bailey, Annie Besant and everything else drawing from *Helena Petrovna Blavatsky*. Madame Blavatsky's the "grandmother" of today's New Age Movement, I think.

GLS: She was a great leader—not sure about "grandmother" though...

GT: People dispute that point. Still, it's clear to me. So much New Age dogma goes straight back to either Madame Blavatsky or her *direct heir* Alice Bailey. If Blavatsky's the "grandmother" of the New Age, then I think Bailey is its "mother," so to speak.

GLS: Yawn. Whatever. If they pioneered an open-minded, universal perspective, that's good enough for me.

GT: Bear with me. Tell me, do you realise that back before Blavatsky, nobody, but *nobody* in England believed the things you do?

GLS: Nobody? Oh, get real...

Alice Bailey, 1880–1949. English Theosophist, who developed Blavatsky's cosmology. Moved to America in 1907, where she carried out work with her husband Foster, a high degree Freemason.

GT: I assure you—I am *not* exaggerating. Nobody in Victorian England thought of transcending religion to achieve universal oneness. Back then, the idea of being "spiritual but not religious" would have been meaningless. Indeed, bizarre! Nor did the Victorians try to magically re-order reality through positive thinking. And nobody talked about chakras or subtle bodies or even karma and reincarnation. No one ever heard of an Age of Aquarius! Not to mention initiates or ascended masters living on the astral plane. And, most assuredly, no one thought "the Master Jesus" was just an "initiate" who bore "the Christ consciousness." In one form or another, *all that was pioneered by Theosophy.* The thing is, few people these days actually read Theosophy. At least, not the original authors like Blavatsky. Or Alice Bailey. Have you?

GLS: Not really. I prefer modern stuff.

GT: Most New Agers haven't read them. They're not easy authors to read. Still, Theosophy gets translated into more popular, more easily digestible forms by other authors. Sometimes the Blavatsky-Bailey heritage is patent. But often the Theosophical footprint goes unnoticed…

Anna piped in. "You're right, GT. Most New Agers don't see their debt to Theosophy. Hardly anyone at Findhorn read Bailey and Blavatsky. But, although it was tough going, I actually *did* read them. To me, it's obvious their ideas completely shaped Findhorn."

GLS: Whatever. Like I say, I prefer new stuff. But if Blavatsky or Bailey opened things up—good on them!

GT: Well, they opened something up. That much is certain. I wouldn't like to say what, though. Pandora's Box doesn't even come close.

Still, I'm losing my thread. My main point is this: *all this is an Anglophone phenomenon.* And—Ireland aside—the entire Anglosphere is steeped in Protestantism. So the New Age Movement *stems from a specific cultural stream.* It's hardly a universal phenomenon! The early Theosophists were virtually all English or at least English speakers. People like Annie Besant, Charles Leadbeater, Alice Bailey or her American husband, Foster. The same goes for Findhorn— which has wielded such enormous influence. The Findhorn pioneers were English, Canadian, American. Likewise, the authors of your "great channelled texts" like Neale Donald Walsch or Helen Schucman of *A Course in Miracles*—again Americans…

GLS: Aren't you forgetting something? Blavatsky was a Russian!

GT: Yes, she's the exception to the rule. Which proves my point.

GLS: Groan. So your scintillating point is...?

GT: I'm still getting to it. Back in the nineteenth century, Blavatsky was a Russian who spoke seven languages. But she *specifically* chose to write in English. Moreover, she set off for America to found her Theosophical Society *specifically* there! Why English? Why America?

GLS: Beats me, dude. Maybe she didn't like freezing her butt off. Maybe all those Cossacks were a drag.

GT: That hardly explains the books written in English. Nor the fact that Blavatsky claimed *she was trained in Shigatse in Tibet*, by a certain Master Morya—who then sent her *on a mission to America*. Personally, I'm convinced there's more to this than meets the eye...

GLS: Why does that not surprise me?

GT: Yes. Well, anyway, Blavatsky realised the de-traditionalised, once-Protestant, but increasingly secular Anglosphere offered unusual opportunities for her mission. It would be *the world most receptive to her ideas*—ideas which were, in fact, very, very *Eastern*. Hardly universal.

GLS: Oh, man, you crack me up!

GT: History has proved her right, I think. Because other cultures never embraced her Eastern Theosophy the way Anglophones did. Even today, they don't embrace the New Age the same way either. Ask Anna, if you like. She's travelled the world, lived in France...

Anna: That seems right. The rest of the world isn't into New Age stuff like America and England. Ireland is turning the same now—but only recently.

GT: Yes—*because Ireland speaks the same language*. But, in general, Catholic cultures never took to Eastern spirituality like the Anglosphere. Just like they don't take to liberal ideology so easily. Britain, of course, was connected to the East in a special way, because her Empire colonised so much of Asia, above all, *India*... But continental Europe never lapped up Theosophy like the English. Oh sure, there were a few exceptions. Rudolf Steiner in Germany, for example. He was a Theosophist—for a little while. But he recognised that *Christ Crucified changed everything*—the entire universe. So he rejected Theosophy. I think that's why, even today, New Agers still tend to find Steiner's esotericism alien. Generally speaking, they mean to AVOID THE CROSS (and, whatever his failings, Steiner didn't do that).

GLS: Avoid the Cross? Who wouldn't? But I guess you like medieval, masochistic torture instruments. Go figure.

GT: Christians are called to carry the Cross with Our Lord. Here is Christianity's *profound difference* from your "universal spirituality." And why it hardly seems all-embracing to me. That's why I called it "particularised." You might even say *provincial*: it emerges from the provinces of the Protestant Anglosphere. Of course, there is that original Orientalism. Blavatsky introduced an *Eastern esoteric cosmology* into English-speaking culture. Blavatsky was perfectly clear about this, as was Alice Bailey. They both claimed their "esoteric Buddhism" came from the same Tibetan school of masters living in the Himalayas. That's why your universal New Age looks like an English-Eastern condominium to me.

GLS: An English-Eastern *what*...?!

GT: Well, of course, I don't mean what Americans call a condo! I mean the political sense of the word: *joint rulership*. That's what Blavatsky, Bailey and their masters were aiming for...

My mind reeled. Once more, my old sceptic rose up. I could hardly credit what GT was saying. "Ruling the world?!" I said.

"Well, in a *cultural sense*, yes," GT said. "Blavatsky did indeed have a mission. And maybe it *was* given her in Shigatse, just like she claimed. Certainly, she was incredibly well-travelled, not only going to America, but also Egypt, India, the Ukraine and central Asia. She even wound up in Italy—fighting with Garibaldi's armies against Bl. Pius IX and the Papal States. (Which tells you something of her politics...)"

"She was a very strange woman," Anna said.

"Yes," GT said, "and a *formidable* one who changed the world. At any rate, her masters meant to supplant Western notions with Eastern impulses. And they wanted to substitute a syncretistic, supposedly 'universal' spirituality for Christianity. Again, one that avoids the Cross. Today those impulses *have succeeded beyond her wildest dreams*. The Anglosphere is awash with Eastern ideas like never before."

"Okay, but Globalisation makes that inevitable," I said, still sceptical.

"It is more, Geoffrey! Certainly, Globalisation carries Eastern influences that can't be pinned on Theosophy. You only have to look at the craze for things like acupuncture, ayurveda, yoga, Zen, Reiki, shiatsu, feng shui, Tai Chi—the Good Lord only knows what else. Beyond that, though, lies a prodigious, calculated agenda to negate the Cross. It stems from the Theosophical wellspring of the New Age movement. Looking at today's Anglosphere, Blavatsky's masters would be well pleased with all she accomplished for them."

And masters! All this New Age talk of Eastern masters was just so much bunk... wasn't it? But GT implied something more substantial, indeed sinister here. "Surely," I said, "you're not saying these masters are *real?*"

"All I'm saying is Blavatsky and Bailey were *not alone*," GT replied after a long pause. "They certainly did their masters' bidding—whoever those masters were. No, their vast, abstruse cosmology did not result from a febrile imagination. And it carries a puissant ideology that is far too worked out, too coherent, too sophisticated to write off as mere fantasy. Moreover, like Marxism, say, Theosophical ideology has proved incredibly enduring—still going strong after almost 150 years. Unfortunately, unlike Marxism, the ideology is never studied as such. Most academics wouldn't touch it with a barge pole."

Then, winking at me, he added: "Maybe it appears like so much bunk to them."

"Alas," he continued, "it retains potent *concrete effects on people*.

It deserves study like any other system of ideas that powerfully condition masses of people. I can't easily say more. The key point is *a highly Eastern alien ideology* is being seeded in the West..."

LightShadow rolled his eyes. But my mouth gaped open. Yet before I could say another word, I jumped—as suddenly the telephone rang. My instinct was to ignore it. But GT said, "You better answer that. It won't take a moment. The caller has only a thirty second 'window.'"

Whatever GT meant by that, I had no idea. But I picked up the phone.

"Look, Nero," a voice growled in my ear. Nero! That's what Belloc called me! Except, of course, Belloc never called me anything! He died long before I was born!

"What—?" Vertigo almost overwhelmed me.

"Okay, I won't call you Nero anymore. Something finally penetrated your thick skull! Anyway, I must be quick—I only have a thirty second window. But you're on the right track. The Reformation in England felled the forest unlike almost anywhere else in Europe. That allowed Liberalism—Economic, Social, Theological, as GT says—to thrive in Britain. But not only that! It cleared the way for *something else*: a LANDING."

The caller hung up. For long moments, I stood there stupefied, unable to take in anything else happening in the room. Slowly, though, I gathered our party was taking a short break. Anna stepped outside, GT was staring out the window, while Light-Shadow was muttering to Brigid. I couldn't help thinking he wanted to go, but, strangely, Brigid seemed to feel differently.

What on earth just happened? Had GT just opened a thirty second window to another world—just so *Hilaire Belloc* could talk to me?! As he had done from the mirror last night? Was I losing my mind?

In all this, I could not help but recall my first encounter with GT. All kinds of bizarre things occurred, including interruptions from strange, eccentric visitors. At the time, it all seemed completely insane. But later it appeared as though the entire conversation had been *choreographed* in order to open my mind.

And now...? Whatever did the words mean? *A forest felled? A landing?* The first image, however, came clear to me. Apart from the small Scandinavian nations, the Reformation never affected any country as thoroughly as it did Britain. Even large tracts of Germany remained Catholic in tradition. Was that tradition the "forest felled" in Britain? That must be it!

Moreover, the voice on the phone pointed implicitly to how much the forests of tradition continued to thrive elsewhere in Europe—not only in large parts of Germany, but also Eastern and Southern Europe.

That made continental Europe different from England.

Historically, England has always been more liberal than the continent and more capitalist (economically liberal). "Liberated" from Catholicism like nowhere else, Britain forged a mix of Capitalism and Secularism like nowhere else. This she passed onto her American offspring. Certainly, that was what the real Belloc believed. And were he alive today, he would be horrified by the overwhelming growth of the English liberal tree. With all its different branches. Obscuring the sky.

But Belloc—was it really Belloc?!—spoke about a *landing*. Indeed, he bellowed the word down the phone! What on earth was a landing? Then GT's words about an "alien ideology seeded in the West" started ringing in my ears. Along with how the "de-traditionalised, once-Protestant, but increasingly secular Anglo-sphere" offered Blavatsky "unusual opportunities." And something else hit me, too! My strange image of the New Age as a weird spacecraft... Once the forests of tradition were felled in the English-speaking world, the way was cleared not only for Liberalism—but something else, something *other*, to land. Like a UFO? With the New Age, something utterly alien to Western culture had landed in the Anglosphere.

But it was not from outer space. It was from the East. We were being invaded by the East! Was that what Belloc meant?

What was I thinking? Belloc wasn't saying any such thing. That *couldn't* have been him on the phone. Or could it...? Was I going mad? Then, once more, I caught sight of the blood red stone on GT's ring. Somehow, I felt assured. I was not insane and reality was stranger, far stranger, than I ever dared imagine.

XX

A New Provincial Spirituality?

"LET me get this straight," LightShadow said, when our little group re-congregated, "You're saying that because Americans write New Age books and some long-dead English Theosophists took on Eastern philosophy, there's a gigantic plot to take over the world?"

"Well, the West," GT countered.

"Right—the West," LightShadow groaned.

"More or less," GT smiled, "but there's more to the plot than that! At the *very core* of New Age-ism is an extremely specific form of Eastern esotericism. Again: Theosophy. But I repeat: at the core. All sorts of other influences have been added to that original nucleus, since Madame Blavatsky. For example, Western Masonry, gnosticism, psychotherapy, astrology, the 1960s California counterculture that fed into Findhorn. Still, at the very core, the Piggyback globalists—"

"*Piggyback globalists?!*"

"Well, that's a term Malachi Martin used for New Agers.[1] He saw they meant to rule the world. And he was right: a *breathtaking* agenda for a new syncretistic, decidedly non-Christian, 'planetary culture' is evident throughout New Age literature, going straight back to Theosophy."

"Planetary culture, global synthesis," Anna interjected, "those terms are used through out the New Age. And you're right, there's an almost political agenda there to remake the entire world."

---

[1] As well as related groups. See Malachi Martin, *The Keys of This Blood: The Struggle for World Dominion between Pope John Paul II, Mikhail Gorbachev, and the Capitalist West* (New York: Simon & Schuster, 1991), 292–312.

"Globalism by another name," GT said, "And most definitely political, even if that fact is usually hidden. And even if, obviously, New Age leaders lack governmental power to dominate the West. That's why they ride on the backs of those who do. Also, they focus on culture rather than politics (once more, mainly the Anglo-American culture). That way, Martin said, they run piggy-back on the global elites. And because they never protest modern secular values, they remain completely unobjectionable to our globalist masters. New Age spirituality presents absolutely no threat to their corporate goals. (Unlike the Church, needless to say.) And because it masquerades as universal, tolerant and all-embracing, it's never truly seen for what it is."

"An above-top secret, sinister global conspiracy, no doubt," LightShadow snorted.

"Well, again, it only *rides* the global conspiracy! Really, it's more…well, *provincial* was the word I used earlier. But I might say your 'New Paradigm' is quite parochial." Then, with a twinkle in his eye, he added, "Alas, I don't think 'New Parochial Spirituality' has quite the same appeal—even if it's more accurate. I suppose you *could* call a book *The New Parochial Spirituality Promoted by Anglosphere Liberal Elites*. I doubt it would be a hot seller, though."

"You… are… a… complete trip."

"I daresay you've never met anyone quite like me, have you?" GT smiled.

GLS: You can say that again!

GT: Well, maybe you don't get out much. That's my point, friend. Step outside progressive circles, go beyond the Anglosphere—the world starts to look different. You claim to represent modern spirituality for the modern world. But *which* modern world? Modern Africa? Modern Russia? Modern Saudi Arabia? Hardly anyone in those societies would relate to a word you say!

GLS: Oh man, you're the one that doesn't get out. You're totally out of touch with reality! Those people in Russia or Arabia live under repressive regimes. They're either brainwashed or too scared to speak out.

GT: Have you ever seriously asked yourself something? Is it possible *our* society's brainwashed? Or that Westerners are too scared to speak out? As I say, people are frightened for their jobs—their very livelihood—if they defy the Inclusiveness Regime. Plenty of people today won't speak their true mind. Certainly, Brexit and Trump revealed a different reality than our elites were counting on.

GLS: Oh, you're a Trump maniac then. Surprise, surprise!

GT: Well, no. But my real point is that even in England—one of the most progressive countries on earth—liberals were astounded when over half the voters turned out to be Brexit "bigots," or at least "backwards." Indeed, the number of folk who really, truly buy the progressive narrative, even in the Anglosphere, is limited. Certainly, the elites do—those running the universities, media, government offices, etc. But probably less than thirty percent of the populace are genuine true believers. The rest are either unsure or too intimidated to speak frankly. And the further you go from the Anglosphere (or northwestern Europe, which is culturally similar), that percentage of true believers gets even smaller! Southern Catholic Europe is definitely different from Protestant Northern Europe. Eastern Europe differs even more. Look at Poland or Hungary.

GLS: Ugh. No thanks!

GT: Well, maybe that's why these places easily get forgotten. Or what about cultures further East? Kazakhstan? Iran? India? All sorts of people *don't actually like* liberal secularism! They vastly prefer their traditional religious cultures to the *deracinated, soulless abstractions* of modernity. That's why your "universal spirituality" remains more provincial than you realise! It's a limited strand within humanity as a whole.

GLS: Not as limited as your thinking, dude! Or your Church.

GT: Well, Catholicism certainly represents a broader section of humanity than the Anglosphere (along with northwestern Europe). It's also *informed* by a far broader section. There have been great saints and theologians from Europe,

North America, South America, Africa, the Middle East, the Far East. You do know what the word "catholic" means, don't you?

GLS: Oh my God. You're not actually going to tell me it means "universal," are you?

GT: Well, again, I'm not God. Just his bumbling fool. But yes, that's right. That *is* what I'm going to tell you.

GLS: You actually have the *gall* to tell me your precious, rigid, narrow-minded, homophobic, misogynistic, demonising, inquisitorial church is *universal*! With all your *atrocities*?!

Brigid jumped, startled by this sudden, vehement tirade. Light-Shadow's reassurances that he was "cool" with her religion sounded more hollow than ever.

"Well, in terms of its human side, our Church is terribly fallen." GT said those words sombrely, as if filled with sorrow. "We Catholics have committed our share of atrocities. *Nostra culpa. Nostra maxima culpa.*"

"Thank God for some sense—at last!"

"Alas, when you know history, you see the same is true for every other great community of people, religious or non-religious," GT said. "In our tragic, broken condition, *every* great human collective ends up with blood on its hands. Given what human beings are, given everything they're capable of, given the long centuries of time—there are always tragic, terrible acts. That is the nature of the Fall. As I say, doesn't matter whether it's a religious collective or not. Look at the revolutionary forces in France, Russia or China. Look at the British Empire or the American Empire. You will find atrocities."

"Yes," I said. "Secular propaganda always glosses over that!"

"True," GT said. "The Catholic collective is repeatedly shamed by self-righteous secular organs. It's the same in any propaganda war. Still, that hardly excuses us from the sins Catholics have committed, including the way certain Catholic priests abused the young, above all teenage boys."

"Yeah, I didn't even mention that one!" LightShadow said. "I'm glad you admit it."

"Catholicism, genuine Catholicism, is all about confession. We actively aspire to confess sin (though God knows we fail!). And there *is* terrible sin here. What some of these boys suffered is beyond belief!"

Tears formed in the old man's eyes and he continued. "It's difficult to discuss this properly. Catholics must see—better: FEEL!—what has happened here. They must *feel* the pain of those who underwent agony. At the same time, we cannot forget other factors. The incredible sexualisation of society since the Sixties. The Liberalism promoted by the homosexual culture. The fact that sex crimes in all sectors of the modern West are *way* up. The fact that all caring professions suffer this appalling thing. I discussed all this with Geoffrey, last time."

"I remember," I said.[2]

"Many people are very angry with the Church," GT said. "That's understandable. But you have to ask why, so often, *the same people are not angry with* OTHER *cultural groups*: the pornographers, the bankers, the liberalisers. Indeed, people often select *one specific collective* for anger. How easily many Europeans, for example, target 'evil Americans'! How easily they forget *all* great communities have sin on their hands. Whether it's Catholics, Americans, Jews, whatever..."

"They easily forget sin altogether!" Anna said.

"Indeed," GT said, "In modern society, there's a radical *underestimate of sin, evil, the Fall*. Enlightenment philosophers like Rousseau convinced people that human beings are much more innocent than they really are. If you unconsciously expect people in the Church to be free from evil—you're bound to be disappointed. Indeed, angry! The same is true of any other great collective. If you *unconsciously* think Catholics, Americans, Jews, whoever, should be free from evil, you'll be livid when they're not! Again, evil exists in every collective. Harness millions of fallen souls to *any* single enterprise and the Devil notices! He will find his way in, I promise you. In the Church it started with Judas. And we've had countless Judases since. People who betrayed Christ."

---

[2] Buck, *Gentle Traditionalist*, 114–22.

With that, he took out his handkerchief, drying his eyes. "Right now, though, that's not my point. I am not saying Christians are sinless. Far from it! I merely maintain Catholicism is less provincial than your 'universal' New Age."

He paused and added, "It's also *not provincial in time*."

GLS: What the [expletive deleted] is that supposed to mean?

GT: Well, it's like what I said earlier about religious leaders of the past. To you, they *all sound like people today*. Mohammed was a man of peace. Jesus believed in free love, "gay marriage" and more. *That* Jesus approximates to a narrow window of time. Very narrow: maybe fifty years. 1968 or so till today. Your "Christ consciousness," so-called, is *culture-bound*—highly conditioned by your own time, your own society.

GLS: As opposed to your medievalism?!

GT: Well, the medieval era is an important stage in Catholic tradition. But it's *just one stage*. Catholic tradition covers 3,000 years—not just modern media culture! It begins with the Old Testament, becomes infinitely enriched by the Gospel, takes in Greek thinking with the Patristic era, develops through the so-called "Dark Ages." *Then* comes the medieval era. Finally, the tradition significantly develops in modern times, as well. That, my dear fellow, is the whole point to Tradition—respecting three thousand years of Divine Revelation and dedicated human effort to engage that Revelation. Three thousand years of prayer, thought, study, sacrifice—indeed blood, sweat and tears. But all that, I know, is just three thousand years of encrusted patriarchal baggage to you.

GLS: It speaks for itself. All I see is three thousand years of intolerance, bigotry and war...

I looked at LightShadow closely. As ever, he appeared so utterly, superciliously sure of himself. Why did the Gentle Traditionalist persist in this futile "debate"? Only later would I realise his true agenda had almost nothing to do with our ambassador from Aquarius.

GT: Many of the "post-1968" generations feel just the *same* thing. But I worry they're not thinking things through. There's a real danger of simply parroting the Zeitgeist. Again: that's what I meant by "provincial in time." People don't realise just how much their "thinking" is informed by the "post-1968" media narrative. Anything much before "1968" is *automatically* suspicious.

GLS: Man, you haven't heard a word I said! I'm talking timeless, universal truths here. Just be kind, tolerant, mindful. Even basic things like don't steal or kill—just like your Ten Commandments. There's a simple common core everyone can relate to—Buddhists, Christians, Muslims, atheists—everybody!

GT: Sorry, my friend, if I sound obtuse to your message. I *have* tried to listen carefully. I see your idealism—a genuine hunger for a better world.

GLS: Okay, thanks, I guess.

GT: Moreover, we *do* agree on some matters. Genuine tolerance is a beautiful thing. And, yes, your movement maintains a certain limited continuity with the Ten Commandments. New Agers would look pretty odd if they advocated slander, stealing or killing (unless it's abortion, of course). New Age-ism, like Liberalism, possesses a certain *moral minimalism*. Sometimes I call that "Minimum Commitment Spirituality." Still, my question is why would anyone be satisfied with that? Why would you even *want* a moral minimalism?

GLS: Maybe some of us don't want to bossed abound by religion anymore!

GT: Well, quite. And once again, we're straight back to the cultural attitudes of the last fifty years. Before the 1960s, people believed in obedience. And THAT certainly belongs to any "common core" of world religions! Whether it is the obedience of the Hindu chela to the guru, the Jewish hassidim to the tzadekim or the Catholic faithful to the pope, spiritual obedience ought to feature in a "common core" to all religions. Why is that conspicuously absent from your "timeless, universal spirituality"?

GLS: I've been telling you, dude. Evolution. We've evolved beyond that, now.

GT: Or perhaps you've become enchanted by the Zeitgeist?

"Or perhaps," I grumbled, "a harmonic convergence with the essence of random zebraness."

"There, there, Geoffrey. Mr LightShadow does mean well..." As he said that, I saw his ring once more. And the sense shot through me that GT was being *literal* about enchantment. There actually *was* an unholy spirit—*Geist*—working through this age that bewitched people. It was not LightShadow's fault. Not entirely, at any rate. Indeed, the ring brought a pang of conscience. I felt chastened. LightShadow, I needed to actively recall, was a victim to so, so much. Sneering at him meant my heart was closed.

GT: Still, Mr LightShadow, I must say your "universalism" actually dispenses with most of the Ten Commandments. "Obey the Lord thy God!" Or the commandments forbidding blasphemy? Why, those don't fit the Zeitgeist at all! Keeping the Sabbath holy? Well, that one's hardly convenient for modern Capitalism! "Thou shalt not covet thy neighbour's wife?" We have an entire pornography industry built on that today...

GLS: Whoa! Nobody's advocating porn! As usual, you're taking things way too far.

GT: No, I'm sure you aren't upholding pornography. Would you agree, then, it should be banned?

GLS: Obviously, no! I believe in free speech and you may not know this, dude, but there's a price we have to pay for free speech.

GT: Forgive me. Once more, *I hear the Zeitgeist speaking*. People before the Sixties believed in free speech, too, but they didn't include degrading women in that. Right up to the 1950s, free speech advocates everywhere remained firmly opposed to pornography. *Only very recently* did people start saying free speech necessarily includes the grossest obscenities. Alas, if we eliminated pornography, it would hardly be good for the economy—even, if millions of men would be spared the most powerful sexual temptations that have ever existed. And millions of women would be spared the toxicity pornography generates in their relationships. The demands of Liberalism, including Economic Liberalism, are destroying natural human sexuality.

GLS: You mean destroying your sexual repression and guilt trips, man.

GT: Back to our diversity of views again! Still, maybe you'll see my point about liberal economics. "Sex sells," as they say. At any rate, the banks don't complain and the banks power the culture. There's something else, Mr Light-Shadow. The commandment not to covet thy neighbour's wife pertains to more than just pornography. Chastity requires an intimate interior discipline of attention regarding any man's wife.

For the first time, LightShadow appeared unnerved by GT. He realised the old man was perfectly aware of his unhealthy fascination with Anna.

"Once more, I digress," GT said. "My real point is the *narrow provincialism* of New Age spirituality. Provincial in time: bound to the Zeitgeist. And provincial in space: Eastern in origin, but promoted above all from Britain and California…"

XXI

Economic Liberalism and the New Age

FOR a few moments, the room fell silent. Brigid looked at Light-Shadow strangely. Finally, GT sighed and said: "You see why the destruction of tradition troubles me. One so easily gets enslaved to the present moment. All this 'Power of Now' stuff is dangerous, if you ask me. It's also arrogant. Thousands of years of human insight, human enquiry, human intellectual and spiritual endeavour—not to mention Divine Revelation—thrown to the winds. And why? Because it didn't jive with the Baby Boomers after the 'Summer of Love'?"

"Oh, man," LightShadow said, "your version of reality is like Disneyland—on acid. *Bad* acid."

GT: Forgive me, I did put that simplistically, crudely even. It's hard to capture complex realities in conversations like this. Still, we can't close our eyes to the Boomers, especially after they grew up and took power in the 80s and 90s.

GLS: And rocked your tiny world.

GT: I won't deny their sheer power. Alas, they gained access to the greatest communications technology ever developed by man. Never before in human history have elites had power like this: round the clock radio, television, now internet. Never before has so much human energy been marshalled for something as meaningless—and dangerous—as an advertising jingle. Look at the technology drilling those jingles into people's brains. Look at the academy. People go to university now—to get a degree in *advertising*. To learn how to manipulate people's minds. It's a scandal. But nobody blinks an eyelid, anymore.

GLS: Uh huh. Anyway, I'm into spirituality—not Capitalism!

Argh. And LightShadow's 300 euro workshop fee? And all his slick New Age marketing? I almost exploded. But, once again, the blood-red ring caught my eye. And again, I realised LightShadow was a victim, parroting precisely the forces GT now evoked.

GT: Perhaps, you'll concede, then, an advantage to the "backward" medieval mind. Capitalism was beyond the pale in the Middle Ages! That's because usury—the main propellant of Capitalism—remained forbidden in Christendom. Usury and Capitalism are both Protestant innovations. And no medieval university would ever award degrees for something as trivial and cunning as advertising... But I digress. My main point is the immense destruction of tradition. These Boomers, as they're called, SUFFERED that destruction like no generation before them. Their deracinated anomie led to Capitalism taking over like never before in the 1980s.

GLS: *Deracinated anomie?* I think I'll take my chances with that one, rather than your ideas—whatever it is!

GT: Well, I mean the soullessness that stems from abandoning our roots, traditions, ethics. Oh, I know the hippies rejected Capitalism. Funny their generation gave rise to the greatest concentration of wealth and the most powerful capitalists the world has ever known. Far beyond Calvin's wildest dreams. I am sorry, but your "holistic revolution" doesn't look that different to me. All those books about gaining wealth, abundance, "prosperity consciousness," "you deserve to have it all..." Not to mention those enormous therapy and seminar fees! Meanwhile, the Catholic Church offers the Eucharist—the most profound grace on earth—entirely free of charge. Your "holistic revolution," though, comes with a price tag...

I noticed how GT operated. He didn't directly attack LightShadow's expensive Dublin workshop—the way I might. Nonetheless, he illumined the chasm between the New Age and the Church. The Church was meant for everyone, including the poorest of the poor. But the New Age remained a middle class phenomenon: strictly for those who could afford it.

"But all this isn't surprising," GT continued, "if my thesis is true: *the New Age depends on the historical Protestant trajectory which formed the Anglosphere.* Again, your 'holistic revolution' owes a lot to Luther and Calvin. As does the Enlightenment, Secularism, Liberalism, including Economic Liberalism—all these things followed in the footsteps of the Reformation. It was the Protestant reformers who first *took the axe to the forests of tradition.*"

I listened, mesmerised. GT knew exactly what Belloc told me on the phone! "Without that preliminary clearing away of traditional structures," GT looked at me knowingly, before continuing, "your 'holistic revolution' wouldn't stand a chance!"

GLS: Maybe Luther couldn't handle your control-freakery! He just didn't go far enough in dumping religion.

GT: Well, opinions differ. At any rate, Capitalism thrived in the new "free" climate he initiated. The capitalist revolution started in Protestant Holland and England when usury was established there and modern banking began. I don't suppose you ever read Belloc or Chesterton?

GLS: Never even heard of them! Let me guess, your favourite religious crackpots?

GT: Friends, dear friends... Anyway, they're very clear on Capitalism. It's no coincidence the two greatest Protestant powers of recent centuries—Britain and America—were also the two greatest commercial powers. In both empires, Catholic tradition was suppressed, by one means or another, as ever greater Liberalism took hold. And now, even spirituality becomes a BUSINESS. People paying out money for "enlightenment." Again, something unthinkable in the Middle Ages...

GLS: Oh, yeah—what about the Church selling those indulgences? That's what set Luther off!

GT: Sadly, you have a real point there, my dear fellow. The Church on earth is far from perfect—

GLS: I'll say!

GT: We have all sinned greatly against Our Lord. I do not deny it.

GT said those words sombrely, as if filled with pain. "Still, as grievous as that episode is, it is—in the big picture of things—an exception. The Church has worked for centuries feeding the poor, clothing the naked and offering the greatest gift of all: the holy sacraments. All without any charge whatsoever. We're talking about phenomenal charity to billions of souls."

"For two thousand years," I added.

LightShadow laughed. "You guys are hysterical! And all that Vatican wealth?"

"Is something of a delusion, I think," GT replied. "I sadly confess to the tragic sale of indulgences. However, the Vatican wealth story is largely obfuscation, propaganda. True, the Vatican *guards* priceless art and treasures of humanity. But no one uses that wealth for themselves. The people working in the Vatican, including the pope, are poorly paid, certainly by corporate standards today. The Vatican makes do on a small operating budget—something like that of a middle-sized university. From that, she pours out help to the entire world. But I'm losing my thread. Where was I...?"

"You were talking about how the New Age is inherently liberal, as well as capitalist," I reminded him. By this point, Light-Shadow was switching off completely, if indeed he ever paid any attention at all. But I was eager to hear more.

GT: Yes, again, because New Age-ism emerges from a *Protestant cultural matrix*. That renders it both socially and economically liberal. Like I say, the two go hand in hand.

Think of London and New York. They're not only two of the most liberal places on earth, they've long been world "capitals" of Capitalism. London was quite literally the capital of the British Empire, an empire built on financial power. (Somehow other European powers were never quite as good at Capitalism as the British.) And now we have the American empire, built on Wall Street in New York. (Of course, there are other major financial centres, too, like Frankfurt and Tokyo. Still, it's interesting they're not in

Catholic countries.) At any rate, no one doubts the power of Wall Street. And London remains the main banking centre of Europe.

My point is it's no coincidence that London and New York are two of the most liberal cities on earth—with astonishing cultural clout. New York, of course, is home to the world's mightiest publishing empire, including the supreme *New York Times*. And don't forget the sheer cultural force of Hollywood in California! People are riveted by the great liberal Anglophone centres of power.

GLS: As opposed to riveted by the power of Rome, I suppose?

GT: Well, Rome is filled with human beings—fallen creatures—like everywhere else. For all its sins, though, Rome retains the power of its Providential Assignment. St. Peter—the rock on which Christ founded His Church—was the first pope or bishop of Rome. I suspect that's why Dan Brown tries so hard to destroy him.

GLS: Sure, and my pet gerbil works nightshift for the KGB... Dude, if I didn't realise you were a medieval fruitcake, I might think you were paranoid!

GT: I can't ignore the politics here—hidden politics. For anyone with eyes to see, it's obvious Brown has a Masonic agenda closely allied to the liberal Anglo-American establishment.

GLS: Theosophists! Freemasons! Is your entire universe populated by bogeymen out to destroy your precious Church?!

GT: The Church, of course, always has powerful enemies. Anything truly good in this world always does. When Dan Brown wrote his "masterpiece," it was amazing how the New York publishing industry went into overdrive. That book got the best publicity money could buy. Then, right away there was a Hollywood movie with a major star. And not surprisingly, Brown was also promoted by your pope-in-waiting...

GLS: My pope-in-waiting?

GT: Oh, sorry. Popess, I should say. Oprah, her with the big vision and the big, big bucks...

Anyway, these are relatively minor examples of what I mean. Really, the good ordinary Brits and Americans seldom realise how things look outside the Anglosphere. But *other* nations do. They can't help noticing just how often the great banks and corporations behind the Globalist Project are *American*. Maybe you've heard the acronym: GAFA—any idea what it means?

GLS: Let's see. Goofballs and Fanatics Anonymous?

GT: Alas, no. It's a French designation: Google—Apple—Facebook—Amazon. Of course, GAFA doesn't even begin to cover it. There are the Wall Street banks, Disney and the rest of Hollywood, Bill Gates' Microsoft, Ted Turner's CNN, Rupert Murdoch's News Corporation, even Hugh Hefner's Playboy empire. (That one's smaller than the others. Still, it's had a disproportionately powerful effect in breaking down the old Christian restraints on pornography.)

GLS: All these evil Americans!

GT: *Au contraire!* The American people have always struck me as having a fundamental decency. You still find real wholesomeness there, particularly in the so-called Red States. A refreshing difference from tired European cynicism!

Still, the world is increasingly controlled by a limited number of mighty banks and corporations. A disproportionate number of those *are* American. The major world oil companies are also American or British. Think of the sheer power of that commodity and all the wars waged for it. And even though the British Empire crumbled ages ago, English financial and political elites continue their "special relationship" with their corresponding elites on the American East coast.

Don't forget British cultural heft, either. Look at the immense power of British Positivist philosophy over the centuries: Bacon, Locke, Hume, Mill, Russell, etc.—so different from Continental philosophy. Then, there's pop cul-

ture, too: "Cool Britannia" and the British invasion beginning with The Beatles, the Rolling Stones, Led Zeppelin,
Bowie, Elton John—the list goes on. Who listens to French
or Italian tunes?

GLS: Who can compete with Zeppelin or Bowie!

GT: Yes, well, I think there's more to it than that—may I
continue?

GLS: Go on, man. I'm taking copious notes.

GT: Thank you. Anyway, there are hidden strains here, too.
Like I say, the New Age Movement owes a tremendous debt
to Britain, what with the English Theosophists, the Findhorn powerhouse in Scotland and more. Masonry originated in Britain, too, above all Scotland.

The last few centuries haven't been so much dominated
by Rome—but London and now New York! As you said,
English is the world language today. That fact has everything to do with the Capitalism of first the British Empire,
now the American one. Generally speaking, non-English
culture has never been quite as successful at things like business, banking, marketing, mass production and entertain-
ment, pop music...

Oh, once in a while a non-English band surfaces on the
world scene. There was once a German band called
Kraftwerk, I believe. There's another one now, called Tokyo
Hotel. They both had some international success, if I
understand such things correctly. Of course, their songs are
in English...

Forgive me, but Rome never had power like this! All
these pop songs, all this marketing, boring into the heads of
the youngest children. Babies even.

GLS: Better check under the bed—quick! There could be
Brits hiding there! Complete and utter Anglophobia...

GT: It's not Englishness I have in mind, but DE-SACRA-
MENTALISATION. Since Henry VIII, English-speaking
culture inevitably carries a subtle disregard for *the Church's
central mystery* to the rest of the planet. With the British
Empire, that's perfectly obvious. But we see the same with

American culture, which owes so much to the New England Puritans and the elite Anglophile Northeast Coast establishment that dominates the country.

GLS: Oh, man. This is completely paranoid. America is a melting pot of all kinds of cultures. Have you ever been there? There are Italian Americans, African Americans, Asian Americans—some are even Catholic!

GT: This I know. Certainly, America is a much more Catholic country than England. But *I'm talking about the elites.* Think of the names of American presidents—they hardly reflect that melting pot. Okay, there are some recent exceptions: Obama, Kennedy, Eisenhower. But hardly any others. Presidential names are overwhelmingly Anglo-Saxon in origin: Washington, Jefferson, Lincoln, Wilson, Truman, Johnson, Carter, Clinton, Bush—to name only a few.

GLS: Aha! The plot thickens. The conspiracy theory just gets deeper…

GT: Right now, I'm only suggesting a *continuity of culture.* (We can talk about conspiracy later, if you like.) There is clear cultural continuity here: a continued bias against Catholicism. The original Puritan prejudice carried over into liberalism. Still, a subtly Calvinist DNA remains, so to speak.[1]

GLS: Wow! That's some persecution complex you have. A real victim mentality. You could use some therapy, dude— *major* therapy!

GT: Well, unlike you, my friend, I'm not English. I don't belong to the culturally Protestant Anglosphere that's run the world the last three hundred years. British and Americans often forget *they're situated in that context from the moment they're born.* That's why it's hard to see how much the New Age is an Anglo-American movement. But the Brits and Yanks should try to see what their culture looks

---

[1] For an acute in-depth treatment of these matters, see Charles A. Coulombe, *Puritan's Empire* (Arcadia, CA: Tumblar House, 2008).

like *from the outside*. You remember Chapter Eleven of your book, I think. What's it called?

GLS: Groan. "Creative Visualisation"—but I hardly see the relevance…

GT: Well, try to creatively visualise *belonging to a culture other than your own*—one foreign to this Protestant heritage. Then, imagine what it's like to see your culture destroyed. That's why we had the 1916 revolution in Ireland. Back then, it was perfectly obvious the Anglo-Protestant culture was hostile to Irish Catholic aspirations.

"Yes," Anna said, "Ireland was far more interested in Christian spirituality then. Not British liberalism, economic or otherwise."

GT turned to my wife. "Tell me something, Anna. What do you think the Irish patriots of 1916 would make of today's globalised Ireland (dare I say Anglicised Ireland)?"

But the question was too much for Anna. No words came, only tears in her eyes.

Brigid stared at Anna, distinctly uncomfortable. A distant memory was triggered. Brigid was a small child, sitting by a fireside with a wiry old man, smoking a pipe. That man was her great grandfather, Tom O'Neill. Born in 1900, Tom lived to an advanced age. And as a young man, he fought for Ireland's freedom, during the 1916 Easter Rising. He remained a hero to her family and Brigid could remember him, sitting by the warm fire of the hearth. She remembered too, something else above that hearth: a faded picture of the Sacred Heart of Jesus with a red lamp, ever burning, beside it. Next to it were small portraits of Patrick Pearse and Éamon de Valera, leaders of the Rising. Pearse had been executed by the British immediately after the Rising, but de Valera, his follower, survived, becoming, in time, the founding father of the Irish Republic.

Fighting back her tears, Anna finally found words to respond to GT's query. "They couldn't stop turning in their graves."

"Yes," GT said. "Men like that could never be taken in by fake multiculturalism, today's globalised goo that pretends to be pluralist. For them, the reality of cultural division was clear."

LightShadow stared at GT open-mouthed. Throughout our

conversation, he had, I think, regarded GT as a curious creature from a past era. Intriguing perhaps—but as irrelevant as the dodo. Still, GT clearly had an effect on Brigid and LightShadow clearly didn't like it. GT was finally getting under his skin. At last, he was starting to explode. "Cultural division!" LightShadow's voice was raised now.

XXII

It Takes Two...

"DIVISION, division, division! That's all I ever hear from you. I don't know much about Ireland in 1916—but obviously there was war. People got killed—that's all your precious divisiveness leads to! People want unity these days, not separation! That's the real reason your outmoded religion is dying. People are fed up being divided. Can't we all just get along?"

Had LightShadow *already* forgotten how he celebrated *other* wars—like the French Revolutionary ones—when their aims suited his progressive agenda? But a war to establish Ireland as a different society from secular England—a Catholic society? That was obviously different! The man's inconsistencies made my blood boil. The Irish war, as tragic as it was, involved nothing like the bloodshed of revolutionary France or even the American Revolution. I wanted to scream. But what was the point?

Nothing the Gentle Traditionalist said penetrated our visitor in the slightest. The man was impervious. He truly believed he stood for a free, multicultural society with a universal spirituality. And nothing would ever make him question his dogmas for an instant. He would undoubtedly pontificate again on dialogue and diversity during his expensive Dublin workshop next week, saying every perspective was equally valid...

And once again, I saw the blood red ring. It was uncanny—but I could not shake the image of little Gareth Crowley cowering in his bedroom, covering his ears while his parents raged. Years later, I sensed him again, stoned out of his mind, headphones on, Pink Floyd cranked up loud. He had learned to cultivate imperviousness by any means available...

Once more, I wanted to weep. Still, I couldn't see why GT

wasted so much time on this "dialogue." Only slowly did I see he wasn't doing it for LightShadow's sake—but for Brigid's.

"War is a terrible thing," GT said, slowly, painfully. "I won't deny these lines of division carry costs. Often appalling costs. And I know, Mr LightShadow, that you genuinely seek to love…"

"All you need is love, man. That's what this is all about. That's *all* I'm saying. Not all your divisive concepts…"

"Alas, separation—division as you put it—is necessary to truly love. That means risking divisiveness, even violence. The New Secular Religion tries to avoid that by enforcing a sham 'multiculturalism.' But the New Age Religion has a different strategy."

"You mean monism," Anna said.

"Precisely: the idea we're all one and all separation is ultimately an illusion."

"Right on, dude!"

"Well, I'm hardly surprised monism enthuses you. Monism is another key to New Age-ism. It's part and parcel of the Theosophical and Eastern philosophy that undergirds your so-called 'Universal Spirituality.' It's hardly part of Christianity, though."

"What a surprise…" LightShadow groaned.

"Alas, the problem with monism is that, subtly, it denies love. Love, real love means allowing the other person *autonomy*. To be their own unique person, separate and *divided from myself*. It means setting people *free*."

"Letting them do things you may not like and still loving them," Anna said.

"Yes. It's easy to love yourself," GT said. "It's also easy to love someone who just happens to agree with everything you believe. Who isn't *divided from you*. But love—real love—requires something else."

"It takes two to tango," Anna said, "It takes two to really, truly love."

"Yes, Anna. Loving someone where *true* freedom exists—which means the potential for *true* division—that's where love gets tough! That's why Christianity avoids the easy answers of the New Age."[1]

---

[1] For more on New Age monism, see Buck, *Cor Jesu Sacratissimum*, 204–8.

LightShadow rolled his eyes, but said nothing. For the first time, GT looked weary. But for Brigid's sake, for our sake and the sake of the future, he was not ready to stop. Instead, he meant to plunge ahead with a final summary of his argument.

XXIII

Tragedy and Hope

THE Cheshire zebra had lost his zest. Not only was the grin long gone by now, but I had the impression he wanted to escape. Only Brigid's fascination with GT kept him put.

"I know you intend the best, Mr LightShadow," GT said. "But New Age denial of genuine divisions is no answer. The same goes for the compulsory inclusiveness of Political Correctness. To be blunt: You've fallen for a lie. This 'inclusive universalism' you genuinely aspire to is built on a lie. And *anything founded on a lie* is bound to go wrong. With dreadful costs. Some of those costs are already evident. Others we can't begin to conceive…"

"What I can't conceive is why you need all this paranoia, all these bogeymen, all these straw men…"

> GT: I am sorry to be so blunt. But, I repeat, there's a fundamental lie here. Our globalist order is built on this lie. It claims to be neutral, tolerant, multicultural. But it has a tight, narrow agenda, which will not tolerate any other agenda. New Age spirituality would seem to be Globalism's "spiritual handmaiden." And its claim to be free of dogma simply renders it more effective.
>
> Look at the giants of the new Globalist order—Google, Apple, Facebook, Amazon—they're fine with your New Age spirituality. *Doesn't trouble them one bit*! But it's hardly fine with Catholic and Christian tradition! We traditionalists are excluded from public debate. Increasingly we're either censored or concerned about running afoul of so-called "hate crimes." Not because we truly hate! But because we refuse to substitute the New Secular Religion for our own.

GLS: Or maybe you refuse to grow out of outdated ways, once they've been exposed for what they really are.

GT: We face a choice, then: "update" our religion, join your "holistic revolution," become "holistic Christians." Water down the very core of Christianity so it agrees with the New Age (and the New World Order)—or face persecution. To us, the lie is clear. You mean to include us by destroying us. Anna, you once watched that Hollywood show *Star Trek*, I believe. Wasn't there an alien race of robotic beings on that...?

Anna: The Borg?

GT: That was it. What was it they said? Ah, I remember now..."Resistance is futile. You will be assimilated." Science fiction often mirrors people's fears of the future, even if the fear isn't conscious. Today, there's widespread anxiety of being swallowed up by a global machine. Indeed, becoming the machine ourselves! Certainly, I feel it myself. Modern civilisation seems ever more like the Borg. More mechanical, controlling, technocratic... But I digress. My real point is this new "spiritual handmaiden" to Globalism. How easily it supports the technocracy, the plutocratic elites. New Agers just "go with the flow." They never feel persecuted like Traditionalists do.

GLS: You're so morbid. No one's out to destroy you. There's no need for all this polarising "us versus them" stuff...

GT: Yes, even the notion of "us versus them" is shamed now. As though you *must* be paranoid for even suspecting you aren't included in the Inclusiveness Regime. There's a certain sleight of hand there. Meanwhile, we're told Christianity is being superseded by a new paradigm. That's another sleight of hand, if the truth is that all of this is being *socially engineered*. What I said about *The Da Vinci Code* publicity machine is just one small example of what I mean.

GLS: Look at you! You're so threatened, man. It was just one book...

GT: And film.

GLS: A boring movie—hardly anyone liked it.

GT: Sometimes the Powers That Be fail. Even with a major Hollywood star and a major director and an American Memorial Day weekend opening…

GLS: The Powers That Be?!

GT: Well, it's extremely hard to precisely pinpoint the exact players here. Different threads cross over. On the one hand, we have the globalist elites. These are inspired by Western Masonry more than many see. And Masonry, as I said, is British in origin. To this day, there is a powerful Masonic thrust to the Anglo-American establishment—operating out of the major financial centres of Wall Street and London. But also elite universities like Oxford and Yale with its "Skull and Bones" society, and so on…

GLS: Better hang on, folks! We just crossed over…into the Twilight Zone (do-dee-do-dee-do-dee-do)!

GT: Things aren't that black and white, of course. There are non-Masonic threads, too. Sometimes they converge. For example, Blavatsky pioneered Eastern Theosophy. But she joined a Masonic order in America. Then, Alice Bailey developed her Theosophy—but her husband, who fostered her work, was a 32nd-degree Mason. These were all people intent on wiping out traditional Christianity.

GLS: Oh, man. The wheels in your head are amazing. It's all so intricate. Like some crazy cuckoo clock! It takes you to cloud cuckoo land—but the thing still ticks. I'll give you that.

GT: Why, thank you, my dear fellow. If you see *any* of these connections, I'm truly grateful. I hope you at least grasp why I find this "universalism" tough to swallow. Because I see a very particular spirituality. Eastern and Masonic, you might say, *but more Eastern, than anything*. And it means to COLONISE the West. Moreover, in the Anglosphere at least, its success is astonishing! Blavatsky was nakedly honest about her hatred for Christianity. With Bailey, it was more subtle. She pretended, like the New Age she pioneered, to "include" Christianity in a grand new synthesis of all the worlds' religion.[1]

All this hit Anna hard. Many Catholics would dismiss GT as paranoid. But, unlike them, she understood the New Age. Unlike them, *she knew Theosophy first hand*. And she knew Blavatsky and Bailey meant to pioneer precisely what GT said: a global spiritual "synthesis" that would render Christianity obsolete.

But only now did she see how much their dream was already realised.

She remembered the Catholic Ireland she knew as a girl. She wanted to weep. Everything appeared so hopeless. This new "universal" spirituality incessantly and insidiously promoted by the Powers That Be was more potent than anyone realised. For GT was perfectly right about things like the American media establishment pumping up *The Da Vinci Code*, and much more besides.

Travelling in America, Anna saw New Age ideas everywhere. There were television talk show hosts—not simply Oprah—interviewing so-called "spiritual teachers." "Spiritual experts" were all over the airwaves and they were *not* Christian. Four or five decades ago, America would have turned to Protestant leaders like Billy Graham or even the Catholic archbishops of New York. Today, its network-approved spiritual leaders spouted Blavatsky-ite ideology.

Elsewhere, things remained different. Anna's life in France made that clear. Daffy New Age-isms were not nearly so present in French media, for example. But in the Anglosphere, the New Age was now mainstream—so mainstream, in fact, that people hardly recognised it as New Age any more! Aquarius was the new "spiritual air" of the Anglosphere. It even had its own English acronym now: SBNR—Spiritual But Not Religious. Even Ireland—of all places!—was utterly transformed. And the steady drip-by-drip erosion emanating from the media centres of London, New York and Los Angeles factored mightily in that transformation.

---

[1] See Afterword for more detail.

Anna could hardly hold back the tears. At that point, GT subtly shifted his right arm. The ring came directly into her line of vision. And in the blood-red depths of the stone, she started to sense things...

First came the unshakeable impression of immense mountains. She had seen these mountains before, in India, far in the distance. Now, they rose up in her mind again, closer up, higher than ever—the Himalayas! She recalled how Theosophists like Blavatsky and Bailey always claimed they were guided by Himalayan masters, initiated into occult secrets of the East. She recalled, too, an erstwhile Theosophist, Rudolf Steiner, who claimed these Eastern occultists were real, but they were two thousand years out of date. They lacked the least understanding of Christ crucified on Calvary, which changed everything...

Now, she saw before her an ancient Tibetan sage with *no idea* that his pre-Christian spiritual orientation had been transcended, when the world was transformed on Calvary. And yet this Tibetan believed his pre-Christianity could help the Occident! This Tibetan was so very sure the West was benighted—terribly in need of enlightenment from the East. And he found Anglophone emissaries, who also wanted to "help the world" through a redundant Eastern Occultism without Christ.

Anna shuddered. Why was she seeing this? She could not say for sure. But perhaps keys to understanding were being provided. Understanding LightShadow. Understanding Findhorn and her former life there. Understanding the New Age scene she witnessed in America. Understanding, too, the aloof, detached, happy, smiling, frequently even goofy "spirit of Aquarius." That spirit that was so out of touch with human suffering, as well as human evil...

Yet the Christic grace of the sacraments confronted Christians with these realities. The Fall into sin, the forces of iniquity, the need for redemption. And now the blood-red ring drew her attention to darkness, to demons. Abruptly, she was startled by a sociopath! It was Adolf Hitler—Hitler in the 1930s at the height of his power, leading millions into psychosis.

Anna reeled with vertigo. Why, why, why was she seeing Hitler—of all people? Was it because the Nazis manifested the evil

New Agers could not handle? Yes, but there were further reasons...

For, without warning, the ring shot her forward in time! Just a few short years later to a German bunker in 1945. There lay Hitler's body. He had just committed suicide. Once, his dream of conquering a continent, exterminating an entire people, appeared on the brink of success. A little while later and it turned to dust. The collective delirium ended. Germany, once the sworn enemy of France and England, became their friend. Peace was finally achieved in Europe. But at what cost! Millions had been bombed or slaughtered in battle, millions more were tortured and killed in concentration camps. And the "lucky" millions who escaped lived in agonised fear and misery for years.

Another dark wave appeared to Anna. This time, she saw Lenin and Stalin. She watched while the Eastern wing of the Church was destroyed, as Communism swept across Eurasia. Yet this wave, too, had finished. Churches and monasteries were being reestablished across the vast steppes of Russia. Children were once again taught the Faith. Even abortion, introduced by the Communists, was increasingly restricted. Once, it was commonplace for Russian women to have several abortions over a lifetime. Now, these atrocities receded.

Another demagogue appeared that Anna didn't recognise. A female from the future, crying out for "puberty blockers"—that children might "choose their sexual identity." Millions cheered her on. But, in time, the woman grew deranged for all to see. And, like the Nazis and Stalinists before, her followers at long last realised their complicity in a moral monstrosity. Sanity returned. But not before countless innocents had been mutilated beyond repair, while their young, unformed minds were solemnly informed that gender was a choice, not a God-given natural thing.

Anna gazed into the ring. In ordinary reality, that gaze lasted, perhaps, five minutes. But time itself seemed to stretch out for her, as past, present and future unfolded before her eyes. From long ago, the Tower of Babel rose up in her mind and the words of the Psalmist reverberated:

The LORD thundered from Heaven;
the voice of the Most High resounded.
He shot his arrows and scattered the enemies,
great bolts of lightning and routed them.

At once, Anna realised she was seeing the *same pattern* repeated throughout history. For, over and over, the broken, fallen nature of man rebelled against God's law. And time and again, men constructed new towers of their own making. But the towers always fell to the ground, while the men who built them fell into despair and madness.

And it was the same even in the Church. Anna saw bishops and cardinals huddled together. They, too, raised towers of their own making. Or else, they collaborated—wittingly or unwittingly—with the "masons" building the spires of the New World Order. The chaos in the Church was not simply human folly. No, deliberate forces over decades conspired to build the tower of a new, alternative "church" easily adaptable to the Powers That Be.

Anna almost broke down. It was all too much to bear. But then she saw the Church's current trajectory could not last. It was only another tower with the same fate as all the rest.

Indeed, Anna saw, it was merely the latest of many such endeavours in ecclesiastical history. Centuries ago, Arius, who denied Christ's divinity, built a tower. Although little remembered today, the fourth-century Arian heresy nearly carried the Church away with it. Finally, though, the Arian tower collapsed. Now, only dust remained of that grandiose effort to construct an "alternative Christianity."

There was Cornelius Jansen, fixated on human depravity. In the seventeenth century, his dour teachings bred a heresy like Calvinism, stressing human unworthiness to receive the sacraments. Millions of Catholics were cheated of Christ's Body and Blood. Jansenism infected the Church for centuries. Indeed, one could still feel its effects in certain quarters today. But, again, the Jansenist tower could not stand against the truth of God.

Towers raised up; towers fallen. Yet, through it all, Anna made out another monumental edifice, different from all others. The only real tower there was. A tower constantly attacked, yet constantly efficacious, in spite of filth, corruption and everything else.

It was, of course, the Sacramental Reality of the Church. Anna saw it now as the Cross on Calvary towering above the world. Through it, a vast ocean of mercy poured forth. Humanity scarcely realised it, but without its constant, cleansing tide, the world would be lost. It was the Eucharist: the Body and Blood of Christ cascading through the Heart of the Church and the Heart of the World.

At that moment, words from that morning's Mass rang out in Anna's mind:

> *Supplices te rogamus, omnipotens Deus: iube hæc perferri per manus sancti Angeli tui in sublime altare tuum, in conspectu divinæ maiestatis tuæ; ut, quotquot ex hac altaris participatione sacrosanctum Fílii tui Corpus et Sanguinem sumpserimus. . . .*

> Humbly we beseech Thee, Almighty God, command that these our offerings be carried by the hands of Thy holy Angel to Thine Altar on high, in the presence of Thy divine Majesty, that as many of us as shall, by partaking at this Altar, receive the most sacred Body and Blood of Thy Son. . . .

The most sacred Body and Blood of Thy Son. All at once, Anna knew she could bear anything. And this was why. She felt, viscerally felt, the divine substance of that morning's Blood, still pumping through her own veins. The *Sacrosanctum Corpus et Sanguis* was her strength, her only real strength.

Staring into the same Blood in the ring stone, Anna saw more deeply how the Mass protected not only herself, but the world. For it summoned Christ to earth! Yet with a jolt, she realised the old Mass summoned something else, as well: it called on Angels! Further Latin echoed through her mind:

> *Per intercessionem beati Michaelis Archangeli, stantis a dextris altaris incensi, et omnium electorum suorum.* (Through the intercession of Blessed Michael the Archangel, standing at the right hand of the altar of incense, and of all His elect.)

St Michael, the host of Angels, the Body and Blood of the living God pouring from the altar: Anna was offered hope, the only real hope. For months, she almost despaired of everything she saw happening in her family, in Ireland, in a world inflamed with rising hysteria.

Yet Anna's dark vision was not wholly wrong. Hitler, Lenin, Stalin, puberty blockers, the new racism... Again and again, hell erupted on earth. But Christ, His Angels and His Saints carried the Cross of the world. They never gave up.

Heaven and hell, hope and horror teetered back and forth in her as the ring divulged more. Another immeasurable tragedy: Anna realised the new Mass omitted the invocation of St Michael. And all God's elect. Just like it omitted so much else.

Now, Anna saw that her analogy of the New Mass as a sieve was apt. Yes, Christ's Body and Blood remained present in this new Mass, celebrated a hundred thousand times a day. The beating Planetary Heart, the Mass, was still there. But the old Mass carried more graces. Secondary graces, yes, but hardly insignificant ones— particularly when multiplied a hundred thousand times a day!

Now, *grace was squandered*. Christ's Church was weakened. Angels wept.

Fear, once more, clutched her heart. Everything depended on the Mass being properly received and integrated. She saw Archbishop Bugnini, architect of the new Mass, before the pope mysteriously stripped him of his duties, banishing him to ecclesiastical "Siberia." Bugnini was gone, but Bugninism lived on.

But Anna saw that Bugninism, too, would pass. Even now, the Liturgy was being slowly, steadily restored. Amidst the "Spirit of Vatican II"—that strange, self-assured euphoria—the old Mass had been almost abolished. Through the courage and perseverance of a few good priests and bishops, the Latin Mass held on. And there was something else: Anna saw Angels standing behind these men, inspiring their efforts. And when Pope Benedict XVI liberated the Latin liturgy, the Angels rejoiced. Now, thousands of young priests were turning to the old Mass, often to their elders' chagrin.

Angels wept. Angels rejoiced. But through it all, they never lost hope. The Angels saw the Christic power of redemption steadily at work in the human heart. They would never give up. Yet Angels also remain conscious of realities we mortals cannot bear. But now Anna saw the darkness Angels see—their separated brethren: *fallen Angels*. Terrifying, demonic forces were pitted against humanity. Stalinism, Hitlerism, Bugninism, the new gender ideology destroying children: all were *fruits of collaboration*. Collaboration between the tempters and the tempted: fallen Angels and fallen humanity.

At that moment, Anna recalled GT's invocation of *Star Trek*. The robotic, relentless Borg mirrored a terrifying reality. Day and night, demons worked, tempting humanity with might, automated, technocratic might. Decade after decade, humanity became ever more efficient, synthetic, mechanical, powerful.

"Ye shall be as gods," the Serpent-Tempter in the Garden had promised. *And the Serpent did not lie.* Godlike power was steadily being delivered into human hands. Whether it was the power to access endless information with a few mouse clicks, the power of government surveillance of a trillion electronic communications or the power to construct the most effective killing machines ever invented, humanity now possessed power once unimaginable.

But this power was godlike rather than Godly. Godly power was moral. And while morality could inspire the new technology—for instance, the medical will to heal—very often it didn't. Unprecedented power now existed to deluge the human psyche in pornography, violent video games and life-degrading trivia. Mind-altering chemicals also existed like never before—legal and illegal. Some were even prescribed to children.

Fallen Angels rejoiced.

Once, Christian law, particularly in Catholic culture, restricted the portrayal of gratuitous sex and violence in the media. But now the young, males especially, were immersed in it for hours, days, months, years on end. Capitalism didn't care about these young men, nor did New Agers generally pay much attention either.

But Anna saw how Catholic Ireland once protected her young, even while secular England mocked her. Yet this Irish "repression" was rooted in Christian aspiration to a *maximum* moral commitment. Were the results prudish and overbearing? Sometimes, perhaps. Were young people, from their earliest years, protected from fallen Angels? Oh, yes.

But now Minimum Commitment Spirituality arrived full force in Ireland. It was "cool" with all sorts of perversity, including killing babies. Anna remembered the upcoming abortion referendum and started to convulse. She was almost choking, overwhelmed by the sense, even smell, of sulphur.

Yet again the Blood from the Ring rescued her. It called out to the same Blood still present in her organism from that morning. The Blood soothed and steadied her. Thank God, thank God for the Precious Blood. The Precious Body. That was her only hope. It was humanity's only hope. Clearly, that was why Anna was granted this vision, swinging back and forth between polarities. Angels and fallen Angels. God and godlike power. Christ and Anti-Christ. Tragedy and Hope.

XXIV

A Voice from the Past

SLOWLY, Anna's attention returned to the room. At first, it was almost impossible to focus. Still, she saw, in a way she could hardly fathom, that Brigid was in greater trouble than she realised. But GT *did* realise. And he was now addressing the situation. "Brigid, you and your family, I believe, stem from a long line of Irish patriots. Men like Pearse and de Valera. Do you realise what your forebears would think about our new Church-hating, Anglo-Eastern spirituality? After all they suffered and died for? Honestly, what would they make of our new globalised Ireland?"

"Honestly?" Brigid faltered a moment, then admitted, "They wouldn't like it…"

"Allow me, then, to interject a few words which inspired your forefathers. They were written in Ireland in the distant past. And, if you'll excuse me, I'd like to utter them in the original language."

"You speak Irish?!" As I say, Brigid had attended Irish school and was startled.

"Muise, go deimhin, tá, ach seo Laidin agus ní h-ea Gaeilge!" GT said. (Unsurprisingly, no one besides Brigid understood this. Only later I learned its meaning: "Of course I do, but this isn't Irish, it's Latin!") With that GT started to recite ancient words no one could comprehend. But he did so with such profound, reverent intensity that the effect, at least for Anna and me, was spellbinding:

Patricius peccator indoctus scilicet Hiberione constitutus episcopum me esse fateor. Certissime reor a Deo accepi id quod sum. Inter barbaras itaque gentes habito proselitus et profuga ob amorem Dei. Testis est ille si ita est. Non quod obtabam tam dure et tam aspere aliquid ex ore meo effondere, sed cogor zelo Dei et veritatis Christi excitavit, pro dilectione proximorum atque filiorum, pro quibus tradidi patriam et parentes et animam meam usque ad mortem. Si dignus sum vivo Deo meo docere gentes etsi contemnor aliquibus.

Dominus aperuit sensum incredulitatis meae . . . rememorarem delicta mea et ut converterem toto corde ad Dominum Deum meum, qui respexit humilitatem meam et misertus est adolescentiae et ignorantiae meae et custodivit me antequam scirem eum et antequam saperem vel distinguerem inter bonum et malum et munivit me et consolatus est me ut pater filium.

Tamen etsi in multis imperfectus sum opto fratribus et cognatis meis scire qualitatem meam, ut possint perspicere votum animae meae. Non ignoro testimonium Domini mei. . . . Verbum otiosum quod locuti fuerint homines reddent pro eo rationem in die iudicii. Unde autem vehementer debueram cum timore et tremore metuere hanc sententiam in die illa ubi nemo se poterit subtrahere vel abscondere, sed omnes omnino reddituri sumus rationem etiam minimorum peccatorum ante tribunal Domini Christi.

"I'm sorry," Brigid said at last. "I can't understand Latin and I don't see what it has to do with Ireland!"

"Well, those are the authentic words of a Roman citizen who, long ago, brought the Gospel to Hibernia (which, of course, is what the Romans called Ireland, meaning 'land of eternal winter' and etymologically related to our word *hibernation*). It was around 450 *Anno Domini*, just as the Empire was collapsing and the Dark Ages began to descend. Naturally, Roman citizens wrote in Latin. And Patricius was a Roman. Of course, you know him as St. Patrick. This is what he said in English":

I, Patrick, a sinner and unlearned, have been appointed a bishop in Ireland, and from God I have received that which I am. I dwell among strangers as a proselyte and a fugitive for the love of God. He is my witness that it is so. It is not my wish to utter such hard and stern words, but I am urged by zeal for God and the truth of Christ, who has raised me up for the love of my neighbours and children, for whom I have abandoned my country and parents, and would give my soul unto death, if I were worthy. I have vowed to my God to teach these people, though I should be despised by them. . . .

The Lord brought me to a sense of my unbelief, that I might...call my sins to remembrance, and turn with all my heart to the Lord my God, who regarded my low estate, and, taking pity on my youth and ignorance, guarded me, before I understood anything, or had learned to distinguish between good and evil, and strengthened and comforted me as a Father does his son. . . .

Although I am imperfect in many things, I wish my brethren and relatives to know my disposition, that they may be able perceive the desire of my soul. I am not ignorant of the testimony of my Lord. . . . "Every idle word that men shall speak, they shall give account thereof in the day of judgment." Therefore, I ought, in great fear and trembling, to dread this sentence on that day when no one shall be able to withdraw or hide himself, but all must give an account even of the least sins before the judgment-seat of Christ the Lord.[1]

"Whoa! Now, I know why they call it the Dark Ages!" LightShadow said. But Brigid looked troubled.

"All that talk about sin, fear and dread does seem rather incompatible with 'happy-go-lucky' New Age spirituality, doesn't it?" GT said, before addressing Brigid directly. "Tell me, my child, do you *truly* believe St Patrick came to Ireland to teach the *same* 'timeless, universal spirituality' our Mr LightShadow espouses?"

"I don't know what to think..."

"Forgive me, child, but I will be very bold with you. I do not speak lightly about New Age spirituality as a calculated *replacement for Christianity*. Born in the East, nurtured in the Protestant Anglosphere, that replacement is now marketed to the millions by the likes of Oprah Winfrey, Dan Brown and Neale Donald Walsch. Now, our Mr LightShadow may not realise it, but his talk

---

[1] GT quotes from St Patrick's *Epistle to Coroticus* (first paragraph) and his *Confession* (final two paragraphs).

makes a mockery of everything the Irish stood for these last 1,600 years, since Patricius first testified to the *saving power of the Cross*. It likewise mocks the Easter Rising, when men like Pearse and de Valera rose up against the British colonisation of Ireland. But today that colonisation has returned by another means—cultural imperialism."

And turning to Anna, he added, "Yes, dear Anna, Éamon de Valera and Patrick Pearse *are* weeping. I can personally attest to that."

"Personally attest to that"!—whatever did he mean? Could GT be speaking literally?! Could he actually know the hearts and minds of the Irish revolutionaries looking down on a re-colonised Ireland today? In a flash, my dream of Belloc, Chesterton and him together...my split-second vision of Belloc in that mirror...that telephone call...all came flooding back. Perhaps GT truly *did* know the spurned, slandered Catholic fathers of the Irish Republic...

"Your culture, like so many cultures today, is being assimilated. But resistance is *not* futile!," GT declared. "The spiritual power of what Ireland IS still exists *beneath* the morass of lies and propaganda. That power is gold—the gold of Christ, which will *never* decay. Ireland is nothing without that Christian gold St. Patrick brought from the Roman Empire. But there are those who want the Irish to sell their patrimony, trading in their gold for..."

"Plastic!" The word burst involuntarily from Anna's lips.

XXV

The Unravelling

"PLASTIC," GT said, "is not a bad word. Certainly, it evokes something synthetic and easily pliable—adapted for almost everything under the sun. And New Age ideology certainly has its uses. Sometimes it's even used to justify massacre."

"Massacre?" LightShadow stared at GT.

"Well, I was thinking about abortion," GT said. "Massacring the millions."

"What the [expletive deleted] are you blathering about now?" For the first time LightShadow appeared genuinely threatened. "Abortion isn't massacre. Because it's not killing. A foetus is a foetus. Not a child. It's a collection of cells! Come on Brigid, let's go. I've had enough of this idiot."

But Brigid was white as a sheet. She'd vomited in the toilet earlier and now, for the first time, felt a little movement inside her. A kick inside. She held her stomach and started to cry.

Neither Anna nor I had the slightest idea what was happening. But Anna laid her hand on Brigid's shoulder while GT looked LightShadow straight in the eye. "Idiots like me," he said, "are concerned about *genuine* inclusiveness. What about the person in Brigid's womb? Does your baby get included?"

Brigid was sobbing uncontrollably now. Then she started to scream. "It's not just a collection of cells! A collection of cells doesn't kick! I can't do it, Gareth. I won't do it!"

GT stooped very close to her. "Won't do what, my child?"

"He wants me to do a ritual, a special ritual...a magical ritual."

"I see. A ritual for what?"

"You tell him, Gareth. I was going to go along with it. Now I can't even say the word!"

"You will never understand this with all your medieval mumbo-jumbo. Yes, Brigid is pregnant," LightShadow said icily.

"I see," GT said.

"That just means a soul—on its own timeless plane of existence—seeks to incarnate into the physical world," LightShadow said. "However, we aren't ready for a child right now. That's what the ritual is for: to contact the soul on the astral plane. In deep meditation, we gently explain to that soul we're not ready to be parents yet. So it can't incarnate now. But if someday we are, we will surely welcome that soul again in a warm, loving embrace."

This was too much for me. "Warm, loving embrace—you hypocrite!" I roared.

"I said you wouldn't understand. But this is all about love. And dialogue."

"*Dialogue!*"

"Ritual facilitates dialogue between different souls on different planes of existence. Souls are eternal beings, filled with infinite wisdom. They understand things your narrow-minded religion never gets. From the astral plane, they wait for the right, perfect moment to incarnate. If Brigid and I still want a child later, the same soul will return."

"I see," GT simply said. "What does this ritual involve?"

"Like I said, meditation. We enter into silence. We contact the soul on its own plane of existence. We tell the soul we're not ready to be parents yet."

"It's not just that!" Brigid cried.

"Well, there's a bit more. Just some occult techniques from an old nineteenth-century grimoire my father had."

"Tell him about the herbs!" Brigid screamed.

"Okay, okay, the ritual requires herbs."

"Abortifacient herbs, I suppose," GT prodded him. "Perhaps a Crowley family tradition...?"

"Whatever!—this is the modern world, you relic! We don't believe in your council of 553!"

"What—" I said, reeling.

"It's a New Age cliché," Anna explained. "That's the council New Agers claim 'suppressed' the teaching of reincarnation. Just like they say the Church 'suppressed' the 'truth' about Jesus kissing Mary Magdalene. They *truly* believe the Church taught rein-carnation before 553—until ecclesiastical 'control freaks' clamped down. I used to believe it myself, before I looked into it."

"That isn't true...?" Brigid appeared bewildered.

"No," Anna said, burying her head in her hands, hardly able to believe her ears. Brigid had been *that* close to killing her own baby.

"The Church, of course, never taught reincarnation," GT said. "Now, there *was* a council in 553—the second council of Constan-tinople—but it says nothing about reincarnation. Not one word. There *is* a sentence, though, condemning Origen's doctrine of the pre-existence of the soul before conception. New Agers blow that one sentence out of all proportion. They don't even realise Origen himself refuted reincarnation. At any rate, you see why the Church was so concerned about Origen teaching pre-exist-ence. Our Mr LightShadow's little ritual demonstrates the dan-ger here. How easily such a notion is used to justify abortion. And other things, besides..."

"What I want to know," I growled, "is what happens if the rit-ual doesn't work."

"Well, it usually works. I've done it before. It's worked every time."

"Every time!" Brigid exploded. "You said you did it only once before! With your first girlfriend... who else have you done it with?"

"Well, there was this other time. But she wasn't my girlfriend, I swear. She was this guy's wife. Something went a bit wr... Look, I promise I'll explain it all to you. Every last bit. But not here. This is an extremely hostile space. I need a safe space to talk about this properly. Let's get out of here."

"If you won't tell him, I'll tell him! If you're so sure about this 'contacting the soul in meditation' business, why don't you have the guts to say what happens if the ritual doesn't work?"

LightShadow clearly didn't like this challenge to his courage. He drew himself up, haughtily. "If that's the way you see it, I'm perfectly happy to say. First, it's necessary to be firm about your intentions in this ritual. You must be one hundred percent clear the soul cannot incarnate at this time. You tell the soul *exactly that* in meditation. You clearly state you are prepared to back up your intention by terminating the pregnancy, if need be. But it shouldn't be necessary. Like I said, the other times I did it, it always worked."

"Wonderful," GT said. "You start with a hypothetical soul on the astral plane, you then argue this soul consciously agrees to your own egocentric agendas, and you arrive at a moral justification for murdering babies."

LightShadow glowered. "It... is... not... murder. You only call it that because your Catholic dogma can't handle the tr—"

"Well, it's hardly just Catholic dogma. Protestants, Hindus, Muslims, Buddhists have all condemned abortion for hundreds and hundreds of years. Pretty much like everyone else did, until your new post-1960s religion arrived on the scene."

"Stop interrupting me! Will you let me finish?"

"Yes. I apologise for interrupting. Finish your thought."

"Your archaic details aren't important here. From a modern, holistic perspective, we know the soul incarnates. Buddhists, Hindus, most of the world's religions know that, too. Even the Greeks knew that. Only your Church suppressed that great universal truth. Moreover, the modern, holistic perspective is backed up by the modern, scientific perspective. Modern people are perfectly clear that a foetus is not a person. You're the ones who murdered people—massacring millions. Look at the Native Americans! We are not massacring anyone. A foetus is a foetus. Not a real person."

For tense moments, I waited, hoping GT would demolish his pseudo-scientific claims, along with his pretensions to be "holistic." But GT chose a different route. "I won't deny Europeans went out and massacred aboriginals," he said. "I won't deny many who did so even called themselves Christian. The motives, though, weren't Christian—they were land grabs, gold grabs, power grabs. We are fallen creatures, *very* fallen. Once again: original sin is radically underestimated. Blaming Christianity for European colonial crimes *results from that underestimation*. Great collectives everywhere commit atrocities. Communist Russia probably slaughtered more than the European colonists. Communist China certainly slaughtered even more than Russia. But do you know what? The Europeans who went to the New World said essentially the same thing you're saying: *the killing doesn't matter—because it doesn't involve 'real people.'* Now our modern, liberal post-60s world is doing just the same—slaughtering the millions because they're not 'real people.' It's the same old excuse. It's very easy to kill people when you won't admit they're people."

And looking him straight in the eye, he added: "Apparently, it's even easy to kill your own baby." Then turning to Brigid, he said, "But you're not going to let him do it, are you, my child?"

Brigid broke down, sobbing uncontrollably. "No, no I'm not."

"I don't know about you, Bridge. But I've had it with these dinosaurs. I'm heading back to the hotel—"

"Well, I'm not coming. I'm keeping my baby—our baby. I need to stay here, where things are sane…"

"I see. Well, I'm off then. I trust we can talk about this later, like modern, rational people." With that he made for the door. But just as he was about to exit, he turned slowly around.

Proudly, imperiously, LightShadow fired his final shot. "Congratulations, old man. You appear to have won a little victory. But this is only one small battle—not the war. And *you've already lost the war.* There's a revolution going on—a holistic revolution—and your kind has been overthrown. A hundred years from today no one will remember that pathetic geezers like you even existed. In England, today, hardly anyone like you still exists. Same thing in America, apart from 'fly-over' country. But in New York, LA, San Francisco, Seattle—all the big cultural centres, where it really matters—you're *toast.* Even in a Catholic backwater like Ireland, people are waking up, freed from the chains of superstition and fanaticism. You saw my talk last night. The young want freedom, universalism, diversity. They don't want narrow-minded bigotry. You're toast. Do you hear me? *Toast!* You're going to lose your precious referendum in Ireland! We are going to *wipe you out.*"

"Well, thank you for your honesty," GT said. "I have to say I prefer it to your warm embrace of my religion…"

"You poor schmuck," he said and slammed the door behind him.

XXVI

"Keep your Head in Hell"

"RESISTANCE is futile," I said. "You will be assimilated."

But no one responded. Brigid collapsed into Anna's lap and cried and cried. Anna caressed her head, weeping softly to herself. GT, I sensed, prayed intensely.

For a long time, no one said a word. Brigid needed this emotional release, silently held in loving care and prayer. Exhausted at last, she began to calm down. GT rose, took out a handkerchief and tenderly wiped away her tears.

"You are going to be all right, my child. You and your baby. You will be looked after. These two love you and will see to it. You will have my protection too."

Brigid could not help but notice the large red stone on his ring. It glowed mysteriously against the darkening room, lit only by the rain-soaked, late-afternoon light from the window. Somehow the glow brought comfort and peace amidst the lengthening shadows. Her head still on Anna's lap, consoled by the love and warmth around her, she gradually drifted into deep sleep.

"Mr LightShadow was not wrong, my children," GT said at last. "We have won but a small victory in a far greater battle. He is also right we may lose this upcoming referendum in Ireland. To me, it looks like a matter of too little, too late. Too many in the Irish Church have been asleep, frightened, hesitant—or *filled with doubt*. Like Hamlet…"

Gentle as GT was, I felt reproached for my vacillation.

Geoffrey: You obviously mean me, GT. And you're right. I've been asleep. Stupid. I'm a complete idiot!

GT: Well, Geoffrey, I won't deny your Anna has been rather less sleepy than yourself. Still, the situation here is bigger than just you. Countless laymen are asleep. And priests and bishops, too. Indeed, compared to most of the bishops, you're rather remarkable, my good man.

Anna: He's right! The Irish Church is like a wet fish, Geoffrey! But, GT, you cannot be saying we will lose...

GT: I make no prophecy. But I do say: do not despair! God loses countless battles, but He will not lose the War.

Geoffrey: *Countless* battles?

GT: Of course! If God loses this referendum, it will hardly be the first. Just think of that great election of 1932. That was an incredible victory for evil—alas, one of many...

Geoffrey: 1932?

GT: The year Hitler was elected—democratically elected. (Seventeen million Germans can't be wrong, you know.) Forgive my sarcasm. One should not make light of something so appalling. Still, 1932 demonstrates amply how God *does* lose. And how people can democratically opt for evil... In truth, God loses countless battles—because he grants us freedom as separate, autonomous creatures to deny him. Again, we Christians are not monists! And that is why we pray: "Thy will be done on earth as it is in Heaven." Because so often here on earth, *God's will is not done.*

I stress this because the world situation is grave, more so than mortals see. Fallen angels have power to work, like never before, through the media, through the new technology. Your dream pointed to the danger, dear Anna.

Anna: My dream...?

GT: That one with the Church reduced to a small ruin...

Anna: How did you know my dream? You're not saying it could be real?

GT: It is a genuine possibility, certainly.

Anna: But nobody was even going to Mass in that dream. The Church was wiped out.

GT: Well, in such a future, if it happens, the Church will not die. There will be secret cells of resistance, as there once were in Ireland. Still, the Church *could* be wiped out of *visible* existence in vast tracts of Western society. It's not like it hasn't happened before! Think of northern Europe after the Reformation, Ireland, Scotland, England, Scandinavia. People were denied the holy sacraments for generations. And don't forget Africa…

Anna: North Africa, you mean?

GT: Yes—once part of the Christian Roman Empire. As was most of the Middle East. Before the last Emperor fell in A.D. 476, Christian civilisation surrounded the Mediterranean. Most of that is Islamic now. For a while, Christianity continued in Constantinople, second city of the old Empire. Today, it's Istanbul in Turkey! There, as elsewhere to the East and South of the Mediterranean, the Church was all but extinguished. She even disappeared from most of Spain for hundreds of years, until that land was reconquered for Christianity. The terrible truth is *people can be stripped of the sacraments for centuries on end*. This *can* happen again in Europe. And America. I tell you: the situation today is grim. What was it that great American Cardinal said…

Geoffrey: Cardinal George, you mean?

GT: The very man. He predicted he would die in his bed, his successor would die in prison and *his* successor would die a martyr. He was no fool, you know. The man was *awake*, awake to the real danger we face.

Geoffrey: You're right. I've been asleep, completely *asleep*…

GT: Waking up isn't easy. The danger, at first, appears so subtle. And it comes on *slowly*. Christianity is steadily, insidiously replaced by a set of secular propositions held as sacred dogma. But no one owns up to the fact. As I said to you last time: *that's why secularism gets away with murder*. Alas, we may see that *literally* in the abortion referendum. The once-Christian faith of the Irish youth is now being steadily replaced by… that *other faith*.

Geoffrey: The last time we met, you called that the "New Secular Religion." I couldn't see its hidden dogmas.

GT: Yes, that's what you needed back then. But with Brigid, it was necessary to focus on its "kissing cousin" instead, the "New Age Religion." Really, they're two wings of the same phenomenon. You can use different names, if you want. Say, for example: *Secular Materialism* versus *Secular Spiritualism*.

Geoffrey: That's a handy distinction! I might use it in my blog.

GT: Please do. You are maturing as a writer, Geoffrey. Catholic writers are needed today! Writers who will *stand for the truth*: that our society is neither tolerant, nor multicultural. Instead, people are increasingly restricted to two choices: either materialistic secularism or else a vague, Eastern spirituality, which avoids the Cross.

Crudely speaking, these two choices originated from two different corners in West and East. The first owes it origins, above all, to Masonry, the second to the flood of Asian spirituality, largely Indo-Tibetan. Again, Madame Blavatsky and Alice Bailey play a particular role here. Their Indo-Tibetan Theosophy is at the root of today's New Age, *far* more than most people realise. Its power is hidden—but ENORMOUS.

Geoffrey: How stupid I've been! In the past, I would have called you facile, simplistic…

GT: That's because you were right. It *is* simplistic! Blaming everything on "Masons" and "Theosophists" goes too far. I would *place the terms in quotes*, remembering they're only rough and ready approximations for occult groupings that are exceedingly hard to pinpoint. At any rate, forces from both West and East have achieved mighty triumphs from the time of the French Revolution. And "Masonic" materialism and "Theosophical" spiritualism are advancing across the Anglo-American world like never before. That fact is not unconnected to Freemasonry which came over from Britain. The powerful elites in the American East Coast Establishment, Wall Street, the Ivy League, are heavily indebted to the traditions of the British lodges.

Again, it's not ordinary, "middle America" I'm speaking

of. Even today *that* America retains Christian impulses far beyond the norm in England.

No, it's the American "coastal powerhouses" that lead the world. The progressive narratives embedded in Hollywood—even Walt Disney now!—all bankrolled by the Wall Street financial institutions.

Geoffrey: Yes, that connection is clear: Social Liberalism depends on Economic Liberalism, and vice versa. Capitalism needs Liberalism. All my life I was fighting the former while supporting the latter. I'm a fool!

GT: Don't be so hard on yourself, my good man. You had to overcome a lifetime's conditioning. And you've succeeded! Not everyone can do that. Most people never will. Look at our poor Gareth Crowley.

Anna: Poor man...

GT: He's victim to a culture he barely comprehends. Not so long ago that culture was still Christian, the American side at least. But powerful forces are now rapidly eroding even American Christianity. Look at the New Age themes in Hollywood blockbusters like *The Matrix*. The protagonist becomes all-powerful after he realises the world is illusory. Look how many more films there are like it with ideas of enlightenment, waking up from illusion—or Maya.

Look at Oprah Winfrey and her media empire. For decades, she's beamed a "gospel" of "inner peace, prosperity and personal empowerment" into millions of American homes. She's championed spirituality over religion. She's reinterpreted Christianity in her terms, while lacing her new gospel with Eastern concepts, such as karma and reincarnation.

Anna: She's on in England. Ireland, too.

GT: Indeed! *Across the Anglosphere.* She promotes people like Eckhart Tolle, Deepak Chopra, Dan Brown, Marianne Williamson (chief spokesperson for *A Course in Miracles*), and their books become bestsellers in America, England, Canada, and elsewhere. She's just one example among numerous American celebrities.

I see Shirley MacLaine is still at it. Would you like to hear something from her latest book?

"Sure," I said, feeling all the more ashamed of myself. GT closed his eyes, no doubt accessing the quote from his photographic memory:

> What if most Holocaust victims were balancing their karma from ages before, when they were... the Crusaders who murdered millions in the name of Christianity?[1]

"You see, the same old themes: Eastern karma. Anti-Christianity. And the sheer heartlessness of it all."

Anna: And now it's come to Ireland.

GT: Even thirty years ago, no one could have believed this. But Ireland, of course, is particularly vulnerable to New Age spirituality.

Anna: Because she speaks the same language...

GT: Alas, yes. But there is more. The Irish possess an unusual spiritual, poetic sensitivity, as you know. Of course, it's not just the Irish! Everywhere you find people sensitive to religious reality, people who will never sink into complete materialism. That's why The Powers That Be promote New Age spirituality. Certain people cannot be diverted to materialism. It's necessary, then, to divert them to spiritualism instead. A spirituality that *avoids the Cross*. Anything, anything but Christ and His Church...

Really, this is what unites the Western "Masons" and Eastern "Theosophists": abhorrence for Christianity and abhorrence for a society based on Christianity—or Christendom. Many materialistic "Masons" think the spiritual "Theosophists" stark raving mad. But they're easily tolerated—because they support the destruction of Christian principles. In other words, secular materialists indulge the secular spiritualists because *they never rock the boat*. They easily sign up

---

[1] Shirley MacLaine, *What If...: A Lifetime of Questions, Speculations, Reasonable Guesses, and a Few Things I Know for Sure* (New York: Atria Paperback, 2014), 240–41.

for abortion, the LGBT agenda, "puberty blockers," et cetera. They are allies in the war against Christendom.

Anna wept. "It's bad isn't it, really, really bad?" The tears in her eyes stabbed at my heart. I looked at GT, half-expecting he might say something sympathetic, comforting, hopeful. But he appeared more grave than ever.

GT: There are words from a great Eastern saint of the Church, Silouan the Athonite. I recommend you ponder them in your heart.

Anna: Tell me, please!

GT: "Keep your head in hell and do not despair."

Geoffrey: Keep your head in hell...?!

GT: Real Christianity does not enter into New Age flights of fancy, my good man. Carrying the Cross means *confronting reality*, not phony positive thinking. And hell is part of reality, including hell on earth. (Remember Our Lady of Fatima revealed hell, even to *children*...)

Anna buried her head in her hands. But I was furious. Angry as hell. Livid beyond belief—*at myself.*

XXVII

The Sword of the Emperor

"I CAN'T believe how stupid I've been," I cried. "What an *idiot* I am! You've been saying this for years, Anna. And even though I'm Catholic now, I still *wallow* in doubt…"

"Don't be so hard on yourself, Geoffrey. As GT says, you've had to throw off a lifetime of conditioning…," Anna said.

"Three years is three years. I can't go on like this!"

"Indeed, there is no time to waste. Every day, every month the situation worsens. This abortion referendum is hardly the final thing the 'Masons' have in mind…"

This was too much for Anna. "Brigid was wanting to abort… Media brainwashing is *so* intensive! All over Ireland, women will be tempted to kill their babies if this referendum succeeds."

GT said nothing. Still, his grim look spoke volumes, as though his eyes probed my soul with an insistent question: "What are you going to *do*, Geoffrey? Here are the consequences of Liberalism. Spiritual Liberalism. Social Liberalism. Economic Liberalism. Ireland has come to *this*. And it's not going away. What are you going to DO?"

At last, a dam began to crumble and to crack. As I say, until now, Anna and I played out different roles in our marriage. Me faltering, sceptical, ever-indecisive. Her determined, certain, committed. But she could not keep up that commitment now, not by herself, not without me. I could not keep letting her down, *letting God down*. And now, again, our roles reversed. Just as she began to drop, something started to rise in me. Rise and *burst*. The walls of worry and indecision disintegrated. Words exploded: "I'm a fool! A fool, totally blind to reality! I can't go on like this. I *won't* go on like this. We have to do something, Anna. And, with God at our side, we will!"

Anna look at me, astonished. Indeed, I astonished myself. "That sounds like a vow, Geoffrey," GT said.

"I believe it is," I said, scarcely able to believe the words erupting from my lips. Or rather, *my heart*. "It is a vow!" I cried. "I'm finished wallowing, wasting time. With God at my side, I will work, with all my might, to defend Christ's Church and Christendom!"

To my dying days, I will never understand what happened then. All at once, these words were *there*. Not just words, but FIRE. A fire never felt before. Before, that is, LightShadow came. Before I saw the Irish trading Christian gold for plastic. Before I saw how—precisely due to this "plastification" of their culture— they might actually start killing babies.

"Yes, with God you can and will do many things. And not only God. Little do you know it, *there are others at your side*. Your Guardian Angel and another, watching your efforts."

"Watching my efforts?"

"Yes, because the last three years haven't been wasted," GT said. "You've been questioning yourself—hard. *Working* to undo your conditioning. You've also been studying, *working* to understand what really happened to Catholic Ireland. Then there's your blog. All that effort counts. All that, plus the Holy Eucharist. You've been communing every single day, haven't you?"

"Well, except when I'm ill."

"That's why you're ready to break free from the matrix. To employ the contemporary vernacular: it's time you took the *Red Pill*, Geoffrey. Because your efforts have not gone unnoticed. Someone has not only been watching you, but preparing you…"

"Preparing me for *what*?"

But GT gave no answer. He didn't need to. For suddenly, before me, a small, spiralling wisp of golden smoke appeared. Anna and I stared at it, astonished. No fire produced that glittering smoke of gold, yet it steadily grew before our eyes—until, at last, it assumed a billowing form, perhaps three feet across. There, directly before me, in my own lounge, *hung a cloud*.

And now something equally strange slowly emerged from the auric cloud. A sword—pointing straight at me! Holding that blade was a large, strong hand, gloved and bejewelled. That hand, of course, was attached to an arm that also started to emerge. And then… no more.

All I could see in front of me was an arm with a sword, pointed to my heart.

"You have an appointment with Providence, Geoffrey. That is why Blessed Charlemagne has come."

"Blessed Charlemagne?"

"Well, yes," GT said, "the Holy Church has not yet recognised his full sainthood—that's why he's only been declared Blessed."

"That's *not* what I'm asking! What the heck is Blessed Charlemagne doing in my living room?! And why is it only his arm?"

"Well, he's here to bestow something on you, should you wish it. And really, only his arm is necessary for that. He's very busy, you know! I take it you've noticed the sword?"

There are no words for this moment. Dumbfounded doesn't even come close. The Emperor of Christendom, crowned in Rome by Pope Leo III on Christmas day in the year 800 *Anno Domini*, had dropped in to pay me a visit?!

Or, rather, his arm had.

"Dear Geoffrey, you still suffer doubt, I know. Faith is ever a struggle. You worry, too, that you're not worthy of this mission…"

Mission?

"But you have taken a vow. The Emperor has heard that vow. Alas, he cannot speak today—but he has authorised me, a priest of his Church, to speak in his name, while I conduct the ceremony."

So GT *was* a priest! Just as Anna always maintained. And there was to be a ceremony… to knight me… for a mission.

"Do you recall your vow just now?"

Normally, my mind would be screaming in disbelief and doubt. But all I felt was the conviction of my vow. Spontaneously, I fell to my knees before the sword. I repeated the oath: "With God at my side, I will work, with all my might, to defend Christ's Church and Christendom."

"Hear, God, we beseech Thee with our prayer," GT started to recite words from centuries ago, words that lost none of their relevance today. "And, with the right hand of Thy majesty, deign to bless this sword, wherewith Thy servant desires to be girded, that it may be the defense and protection of churches, of widows, orphans, and all who serve God, against the onslaught of Pagans; and that it may be powerful, and a fear to all deceivers, through Jesus Christ, Our Lord. Amen."

And with that, Blessed Charlemagne slowly started to move his arm, tapping first my right shoulder with the flat edge of the sword and then the left. As he did so, something surged into me. It was fire.

"On behalf of the Emperor, Blessed Charlemagne, I am authorised to speak. Arise, Sir Geoffrey Peter Luxworthy!"

I rose to my feet in a stupor, while the cloud, the arm, the sword slowly disappeared. Yet bewildered as I was, I felt something new. Fire blazing in my heart.

Anna, however, was different. She was no less astonished than me. Yet she remained afflicted. I was filled with wonder; she could not shake the horror she had witnessed. How close Brigid came to abortion with that ritual, those herbs. How countless women in Ireland were now like her and worse. Anna could not forget these things. That, I started to see, was because she was stronger than I ever imagined. Tenderly, the old man turned his gaze towards her.

> GT: Do not despair, Anna. God will triumph in the end, triumph over this era of abortion, greed, materialism, capitalist injustice to the poor and the destruction of the environment. The question is how long: will it take only a little while—or will it take centuries?

> Anna: Only a little while? You are saying the world situation could be reversed any time soon?

> GT: Yes. Look at history. Horrors like Nazism and Stalinism had astonishing success—in time, they vanished like the mist! Look at the Reformation. The Church took decades to wake up to its danger. For those who were awake, every minute was agony. They felt like you: surrounded by Catholics who didn't care. So much of the Church was supine, spineless. Then, as now. This has happened repeatedly throughout history. But the Church always awoke! She reformed herself and started fighting back.

"And it will do again!" I said with a passion that startled even me. Anna looked at me dumbfounded.

"Indeed, yes," GT said, "because, increasingly, Western society offers only two options: secular materialism and secular spiritualism. That cannot continue."

"Because it is not God's will!"

"No, indeed," GT said.

"It is not His will that the West become thoroughly de-Christianised," I cried out. "It is not His will that Christianity shrivel and die!" Anna's eyes were now bulging out of their sockets.

"No, although *that* is precisely what many would have you believe. *That* is the object of triumphalist secular talk of a post-Christian Age. Or the triumphalist Age of Aquarius. To portray Christianity's collapse as inevitable. This ideology is devious! These forces *want* Christians to believe their cause is hopeless. They mean to engineer *a self-fulfilling prophecy*: that we believe *their narrative* of inevitable decline. That way, we'll despair and give up. Tragically, it's working. Many fall for this ideology, hook, line and sinker..."

XXVIII

Making Catholicism Visible

"RESISTANCE is not futile!" GT said. "That is why the Emperor knighted you, you and many more. Even at this dark hour, unusual opportunities exist."

"You must tell me, GT," I said. All the while, my wife's pained eyes bored into me. So, too, did the sense of her silent strength.

GT: I will try, briefly. Alas, my own window of time is closing. Soon, I must take my leave. Still, I can give you *hints*—but only those. Investigate them, flesh the details out yourself. Clarify the situation for others. Therein lies your mission...

Geoffrey: Yes, my calling. At last I feel it.

GT: It is no accident you discovered Belloc and Chesterton. They weren't just great writers, they were reporters, working on a newspaper. They knew the media of their time was filled with "fake news" just like today. They understood, too, the hidden, plutocratic forces behind it. You, among others, are called to the same work now. But, unlike them, you have opportunities they could only dream of.

Geoffrey: The internet, you mean.

GT: Precisely. Remember those knights of the Counter-Reformation: the Jesuits! They had the foresight to employ the great new technology of their day: the printing press. Today's knights of Christ must use the internet. But soberly, prayerfully, inspired by the Eucharist.

Anna: It's so easy to rant on the web...

GT: Indeed. And many do well to avoid it. Prayer, including the supreme prayer of the Mass, is the most important thing. Still, the Knights of Christ cannot ignore things like Facebook, YouTube, Twitter. Precious opportunities exist to reach people *deprived* of Christianity! The Eucharistic Miracle happens daily, maybe a block from their homes. Yet they have *no* idea... The NSR and the NAR have stripped them, *robbed them.*

Geoffrey: NSR and NAR?

GT: Well, New Secular Religion and New Age Religion. Different names for the same creeds again: Secular Materialism and Secular Spiritualism.

The first, Secular Materialism, is the greatest danger of our age, particularly for males, who are more often bound to dense, rigid rationalism. But for more sensitive people, including many women, the New Age Religion is a potent diversion from Christ. It was *intended* that way. More spiritually sensitive people: they're slowly becoming Easternised, without seeing it. At least in the Anglosphere.

Anna shuddered, recalling her vision of the Himalayas and all the Theosophy she had ever read.

"That acronym, SBNR," GT continued, "people don't see EBNC would be more accurate."

Geoffrey: EBNC?

GT: Eastern But Not Conscious. Conscious, that is, of what SBNR almost always means: a vaguely Eastern spirituality, much like New Age-ism is vaguely Eastern. Or I could even say EOWC. Eastern Occultism Without Christ.

Geoffrey: What?! I don't understand.

GT: Anna will explain. Again, these are just indicators for research. The world is fast asleep to this! Clandestine forces seek to Easternise the West—under people's noses.

Anna: I see what you're getting at. I was EBNC as a New Ager. With no idea my spirituality was essentially Eastern...

GT: Yes, *essentially.* Part of the problem is people don't see the essence here. They think Eastern means practicing yoga or Zen. But we're talking about something more subtle.

Today, for instance, the Christian quest for salvation is increasingly replaced by the quest for enlightenment, mindfulness or self-knowledge. Christian understanding of evil and sin is replaced by the Eastern notion of error and ignorance. And Christian love is replaced by monism, oneness…

Geoffrey: We're all one in the cosmic goo…

GT: Alas, yes. There's also a growing belief reality is illusory, like the Eastern concept of Maya. Syncretism is likewise more Eastern than Western.

It's these *ideas*, non-Christian ideas, indeed pre-Christian ideas, that most concern me. The practices are less common. Most Westerners aren't about to start chanting the likes of Hare Krishna! Little do they realise the spirituality they subscribe to increasingly resembles the Orient's…

Really, I ask myself if it's 1517 all over again!

Geoffrey: You mean Luther, posting his ninety-five theses to the Wittenberg church door…

GT: Yes, the Church was slow to notice. Just like now. By the time she woke up, northern Europe was devastated. Five hundred years later, we still feel that devastation…the world deprived of the Universal Remedy. Future historians may well see a shift comparable to the Reformation—yet scarcely anyone appreciates this today! Of course, the ninety-five theses were explicit: there for everyone to see. Luther, at least, was *honest* about what he wanted. The occultists behind the NAR are different: hidden, stealthy, deceptive…

Geoffrey: You're not going to explain that, are you?

GT: Too little time, my friend. But I've given you the clues. Blavatsky, Bailey, "Masons," "Theosophists" (always bearing in mind I place the last two terms in quotes, as it were).

What's more important now are the unusual, unexpected opportunities I mentioned before. Because the NAR and NSR aren't working out according to plan. Their New World Order is threatened—not quite "in the bag" as they once believed. "GAFA," so to speak, is on the defensive.

Geoffrey: You're talking things like Brexit, Trump.

GT: Also, this insane new cold war. The lodges of the West are not happy with Mr Putin. Putin is no angel. But there are forces in Eastern Europe, including Christian forces, which resist the tyranny of the Western Lodges.

Geoffrey: Putin and Trump both trouble me.

GT: You're not alone! I'm not advocating them. I'm merely indicating an *unexpected spirit of resistance* to contemporary anomie. That *spirit* is important—even if its *manifestations* are inevitably fallen and chaotic. Because people can feel there's something insincere, sterile, fake about... how did I put it earlier? Oh, yes—the "deracinated, soulless abstractions of modernity." People are starving for something rooted, organic, earthy, *real*. They rebel against unreality.

Anna: Like making gender abstract...

GT: Yes, detached from the body. That, of course, goes back to the radical feminism that also denies nature. It tries to make men and women not simply equal, but *interchangeable*.

Anna: My dream... that terrible dream.

GT: Precisely. An empty, abstract world looms—without colour, without difference, without meaning.

Anna: In a sense, the abortion issue involves abstractions.

GT: As I told Mr LightShadow, it's easier to kill babies if you deny they're real people... Liberal secularism is built on abstractions. Denying what is real, healthy, natural. And, of course, deeper religious realities. But many people reject sterile, soulless abstractions. They prefer to be real flesh-and-blood men and women. Not interchangeable units.

Alas, the New World Order is bent on uniformity! Hell-bent, I should say. It's good for Capitalism—we make better cogs in the machine that way. The more standardised we become, the cheaper, more efficient we are...

Anna: Many women would like to stay at home, raise their children.

GT: Capitalism doesn't like that one either. Nor does it care what happens to all those tiny children deprived of mothering. But people are starting to see. There's an unexpected reaction to unreality. Alas, that reaction is fallen, chaotic. You've been reading about the Alt-Right, Geoffrey...

Geoffrey: How did you know?! Oh, forget it...

The old man smiled. I knew, by now, questions like this were futile. It was strange, though, how GT knew things like Anna's dream or even my reading matter. And how he weaved these things together into meaningful patterns.

GT: The Alt-Right is a reaction to abstraction. Alas, it's too often thoroughly materialistic. Focussed on chemicals like melanin...

Geoffrey: Skin pigmentation, you mean.

GT: Yes. Sickening materialism of the crudest, cruellest kind. However, millions fall into this, because they *hunger for something concrete, organic, earthy.* You know, Chesterton and Belloc saw Socialism as the bastard child of Capitalism. I think this new racism is the bastard child of Liberalism.

GT was still weaving the different threads of my life together! Or perhaps the threads were already more meaningfully woven than I realised. And GT simply revealed that fact. At that point, the old man stood up, saying he needed to stretch. Perhaps, though, he had another reason. For GT now positioned himself directly in front of the mirror...

GT: That's why Chesterton and Belloc remain so relevant! They saw that Capitalism not only destroyed the poor, *it destroyed culture.* Distributism means restoring justice *and* soul to our civilisation. This is what is needed: integral Christian culture. Not Theological, Social or Economic Liberalism. Not the Alt-Right either. The way back to a healthy, natural organic culture isn't skin-colour, or pitting race against race! It's a world ordered to the mercy and truth of Christ. Christendom, not Corporate Libertarianism. That's what Belloc and Chesterton knew...

At that moment, it happened again! Once more, Belloc was in

the mirror—and Chesterton too! They were standing on each side of the Gentle Traditionalist, Belloc to his right, Chesterton to his left. Chesterton smiled at me, while Belloc nodded. He didn't look as fierce, this time.

"Renewing Christendom might seem a tall order," the old man was saying, "but *you are not alone.*" Then he turned to his seat and the mirror turned to normal...

"And Christendom is necessary. The world is turning manic, mad," he said. "Today's mental anguish is beyond anything humanity has ever suffered. Anna sees this..."

"Y-yes," she said.

"You must not despair, dear Anna. The Lord would not reveal His Cross to you like this, were you not *strong* enough to bear it. Geoffrey will help you bear this Cross now. Others will help, too. There is too much at stake, too much terrible suffering, to allow a world ordered to secular materialism. A new Christendom—a world ordered to Christ—is the only answer. The Emperor and his knights fight day and night to restore Christian mercy and truth. Mercy to the unborn, mercy to the poor, mercy to nature, mercy to those in physical and mental agony, without hope, without meaning in their lives."

"But where do I start?" I said.

GT: One starts where one finds oneself. You, my good man, find yourself in Ireland! Let's start there. But what I say about Ireland applies elsewhere too. Because Catholic culture still exists in Ireland, as it does elsewhere. It's no longer the dominant culture it was. But it persists as a *subculture.* The same is true in places like America, where it was always a subculture. In any case, the question remains the same: How to make that subculture living, vital. And *visible.*

Geoffrey: Yes, because Catholicism is completely off the secular radar screen. People like LightShadow have no idea we even exist!

GT: Indeed. That is why the internet, used prayerfully, offers undreamt-of possibilities. However, Catholics should go beyond "preaching to the choir." Alas, on the internet, the faithful easily end up in Catholic "echo chambers." It's necessary to reach out beyond their own community—so people locked in the secular echo chamber can see the Faith. At least see it!

There is something else. France offers a clue…

Geoffrey: France?

GT: France. Where the Counter-Revolution was born…[1]

Anna: I understand. I saw that living in France. The Counter-Revolution is *visible* there, as you say. Like the *Manif Pour Tous* demonstrations against "gay marriage."

GT: Indeed. By some estimates up to a million people poured out to protest. Nothing remotely like that existed in the Anglosphere. But *prayerful* demonstration makes a difference. (Look what St John Paul II achieved in Poland via peaceful, pious demonstration!) They make the resistance visible. In France, everyone realises that a certain chunk of the population always resisted secularisation. Because there's always been *a visible counter-revolutionary subculture.*

Visibility like that creates the palpable sense that different cultural options exist. That palpable sense must exist in Ireland, too. Throughout the Anglosphere! Secular tyranny must be challenged by *making Catholicism visible.*

The Gentle Traditionalist paused, hoping, I think, his words might truly sink in. "This simple visibility," the old man said at last, "is critical. But there is something else."

"The Mass, the Eucharist," Anna said.

"Yes. It is so easy to get sucked down in our modern, unnatural world. More than ever, *supernature is needed to balance anti-nature.* Frequent Communion, daily if possible, will bring the Knights Christic mercy, purity and potency. Remember that."

"I will."

"Good man," GT said, "avail yourselves, then, of supernature. Go to the Holy Mass—daily, if at all possible! Go to Confession. Go to Eucharistic Adoration. Fortify yourself with the Rosary. Not only work is necessary, but prayer. *Ora et labora*—that is the

---

[1] See Buck, *Cor Jesu Sacratissimum*, 343–80, for a lengthy discussion of France and her Counter-Revolution.

key. The New World Order is shakier than it seems. There is hope! But you must pray and work. God's will be done on Earth—means *done through you*. You know what St Teresa of Avila said":

> Christ has no body now but yours. No hands, no feet on earth but yours. Yours are the eyes through which He looks compassion on this world. Yours are the feet with which He walks to do good. Yours are the hands through which He blesses all the world. Yours are the hands, yours are the feet, yours are the eyes, you are His body. Christ has no body now on earth but yours.

XXIX

Angels, Saints and Knights

ANNA stared at the floor. Unlike me, she had not seen Belloc and Chesterton in the mirror. She had not felt the surge from the Emperor's sword. She did not feel the living fire I felt. Nor could she shake how easily Brigid had succumbed to the idea of killing her baby. Nor how Ireland might succumb in the referendum, only months away now. Ireland, of all places… Then there was that dream that GT re-awakened: the sight of the Church destroyed, replaced by triumphant, uniform sterility.

Only now, I understood what GT meant, that Anna was strong enough to carry the Cross. Again, I saw, to my shame, I had shirked it.

Now, as the world judges these things, LightShadow was strong. He was magnetic and forceful. But he was impervious to reality. He barricaded himself in fantasy. He was, moreover, a mass of contradictions, lacking integrity. Anna wasn't any of those things. Consistently, she faced the world, even while the world broke her. St. Paul's second letter to the Corinthians flashed through my mind: "Whenever I am weak, then I am strong…"

I looked at my wife. She appeared so weighed down. But that, I saw, was because her heart wasn't barricaded. *It was pierced.*

"We seem so few…" Anna said.

"You seem! That is how it *appears* to you. This is an illusion. Great forces stand beside you!" GT said. "Today, Geoffrey sees that. He feels the fire of the Emperor. He knows he is not alone. But I realise, dear Anna, you require more before I leave." Rising from his chair, he removed his ring and handed it to her.

"You're giving me your ring?!"

"Only for a few moments. But such is all you need."

Anna stared down at the ring in the palm of her hand. It was pulsating…

Immediately, the sense shot through her that everything that day pointed to a message as simple as it was profound: however bad things looked, she was *not* alone!

Slowly, she started sensing worlds within worlds. Boundless, immeasurable worlds, worlds utterly unlike the sterile, clinical white of her dream, worlds filled with *colour*. All at once, Anna's vision was flooded with vivid, luminous hues, beyond anything this earth could offer. The most glorious sunset she ever saw was nothing compared to this delicate splendour. And now, the colours were resolving into forms. She discerned *beings*.

Immediately, Anna knew these were Hierarchies of Angels, the hosts of Heaven, and they were *vast*. From the Seraphim and Cherubim to the Thrones, Dominions, Virtues, Powers and Principalities to the Angels and Archangels, countless beings served Christ and His Blessed Mother, working day and night. The Hitlerism, Stalinism, Arianism, Jansenism Anna witnessed earlier would not have been defeated without Angels interceding on humanity's behalf. Similarly, the sickness in the cultural revolution could only be healed by the help of Angels. Christ was Lord of All, but that hardly meant the Angelic Hierarchies were there for nothing! No, Christ worked through His Angels. Without their intense, unceasing efforts, the world would be lost.

Intense effort, intense colour and now another intensity! It appeared before her like an immense sea of tears. Tears of grief, as well as joy. Was this emotional intensity? Not in a human sense, because ordinary human emotion remained agitated, volatile, violent. While these waters were deeper than the ocean, more silent and more still than the starry sky above.

Yet Angels were *not* detached; they *felt* everything, good and evil. They felt the shriek of babies killed in the womb. They felt that awesome tenderness of a hundred million mothers cradling their newborns. They felt a thousand hidden things we humans never notice. The sheer courage of a terrified man standing up to a mob, while his insides turned to jelly. The sacrifice of the last pennies of an old widow placed in a church collection box. The silent pious prayers offered up to Heaven. The lifetime's bitterness of a violated woman dissolving into forgiveness. The beauty of the poets, the clarity of the philosophers, the mercy of the saints... All these they felt and more.

Humanity inspired them. Humanity wounded them. But it *never enraged* them. And it never caused them to surrender hope. They would work with Christ till the end of time to overcome the Fall.

Yet this was not all! Anna discerned other beings: the Saints in Heaven. While lesser than the Angels, they, too, remain critical to God's plan. Indeed, they understood things the Angels could not comprehend. For once these Saints were tender flesh and blood: subject to earthly temptations Angels never knew. Unlike Angels, they had experienced, first hand, this petty, greasy, fallen world. While the messengers of Heaven only recognise God's will, Saints recall a world where His will is rarely done.

Now, these Saints included those who were holy men on Earth. Anna perceived distinctly here St Francis of Assisi and St Teresa of Avila. But they also included countless lesser souls who never achieved holiness during their earthly lifetimes. Within these latter souls, she now discerned a distinct group: *the Knights of Christ*. These Knights never attained the heights of a St Francis. But their work, too, was crucial. Often, they were laymen in society, more worldly, more subject to temptation.

With that, Anna started plummeting downwards. The luminous heights were lost, as she descended into dirt and darkness. Was it hell that she approached? Not quite—it was a wintry night in London long ago.

There, Anna saw a little pub, near the great gothic Houses of Parliament, beside Big Ben. She not only saw the pub, she smelled it: beer, pipes, a warm fire blazing in the corner. There, downing pints of ale, were Chesterton and Belloc. The two men were hardly Saints like Francis and Theresa! But still they *sweated*, day and night, for Christ and his Church. She glimpsed them, also, in the small London office of *G. K.'s Weekly*, battling the "fake news" of their day.

She then saw Belloc as a member of parliament, elected in 1905. He would soon see, in genuine horror, that the government was a sham. Then, as now, politicians were running scared of big money, media power and secret elites behind it all. She observed, too, Belloc at Mass each morning, preparing to "keep his head in hell": to *confront* the grim realities he saw.

Few saints could have survived that London atmosphere, choked with soot, grime and graft. But Heaven sent the Chesterbelloc into the heart of the British Empire, the most powerful city of its time. The two Knights did necessary work there, work which still helps souls today, a hundred years later.

Anna sensed, too, that the two warriors had been knighted by the Emperor—just like thousands of others in days of past, present and future yet to come. Did this mean Chesterton and Belloc beheld that same mystic sword descending from a cloud?

No. For the most part, the Knights of Christ met the Emperor in the unconscious, during those mysterious hours while we sleep. What happened to me, then, was extremely unusual: being knighted in full consciousness. Anna could not comprehend *why* my case was special. Clearly, it entailed nothing special on my part. Many other Catholic laymen, far greater than I, were knighted without knowing it.

Here, then, was how hell on earth was combatted: a collaboration of Angels, Saints and Knights fighting for Christ. Here was how hell on earth was overcome. For men and Angels kept their heads in hell, combatting the real human agony caused by Capitalism, Socialism, Liberalism, abortion, carbon poisoning of the atmosphere, a thousand other scourges of modernity.

Once more, a sweeping panorama of history unfolded before Anna's vision: *combat over centuries*. Again, she beheld the great fourth-century tower of Arianism. This time, though, she glimpsed more than before. She saw St Athanasius and St Anthony the Great, who mounted the challenge to Arianism. And she saw, too, they were not alone! Mighty Angels stood behind them, as they, in turn, stood behind lesser men of the day, including long forgotten Catholic Knights of old.

Only through cooperation between men and Angels, Heaven and earth, did the Arian tower come crumbling down.

The fifth century came. Rome fell before barbarian incursions. While Constantinople continued in the East, the Western Empire collapsed. The Dark Ages descended. But St Benedict, the "father of Western monasticism," wrote a rule and founded a way of life which once more saved the Faith.

And, at the very edge of the old empire, a wondrous, providential work unfurled. In cold Hibernia, Patricius lit a fire. While a continent burned, a golden age of Christianity now flourished on that sheltered "Isle of Saints and Scholars." Angels guarded scribes and monks there, copying ancient manuscripts, elsewhere consumed in flames. Later, Angels protected the Irish missionaries, who carried the torch of Christ back across the darkened face of Europe. And, again, Christian Knights defended the travelling saints and scholars.

Anna saw the mighty fruit of all this vast effort. *Europe was reborn.* And on Christmas day in the year 800, Pope Leo III crowned Charlemagne Emperor of Christendom...

Yet no matter how much men and Angels collaborated, Fallen Angels never ceased tempting humanity. By the tenth century, the Vatican was dominated by sex. Anna recalled that some even call this era the pornocracy or "rule of harlots."

Yet again, iniquity was checked. The Church was renewed. The High Middle Ages started their ascent, inspired by Angels working through Saints, including now Pope St Gregory VII, St Francis and St Dominic.

Again, time flashed forward. Anna watched the catastrophe of the Avignon papacy. The pope was removed from Rome to France, his throne contested by one and even two antipopes. But St. Catherine of Siena heard a voice from Heaven: "The Keys of this Blood will always belong to Peter and all his successors." And by one woman's courage and grace angelic, the pope returned to Rome.

Then: the Reformation! Across Northern Europe, Catholicism was all but extinguished. In Ireland, Anna witnessed hundreds of monasteries crushed by the forces unleashed by King Henry VIII. A century later, she saw the Irish genocide as Oliver Cromwell's armies massacred a quarter of the island's Catholic population. The Mass went underground, said in secret by terrified priests.

But Reformation led to Counter-Reformation. Hierarchies of Angels inspired great saints, such as St Ignatius of Loyola and St

Francis de Sales. The Catholic Church rebounded, renewed from within. Instead of falling away, a mighty fire of interior renewal now carried the Catholic Mystery to the ends of the earth. While all the time, pundits proudly predicted the Church's demise. Anna sensed them now: *Wrong*, again and again.

She saw, too, how Ireland continuously played a mysterious providential role. After the terrible famine of the 1840s, the Irish emigrated to North America and Australia, introducing Catholicism to those English Protestant matrices. A few Catholics had been present in those lands beforehand, particularly America. But the Irish bishops *forged* the American Church, and supported by the Irish faithful, they built churches across a continent. Yes, for fifteen hundred years, Ireland carried the Christic Mystery to the ends of the earth. It formed a special torch for the world, a torch forces long tried to extinguish. Until now, they never could...

Anna shot forward to the late twentieth century. She saw the Church in chaos, not unlike today. But a mighty pope from Poland rose up in the late Seventies. With Cardinal Ratzinger at his side, St John Paul II started, at least started, reining in the bedlam.

Yet the post-Vatican II catastrophe was so immense, demanding action on so many fronts at once, that some accused the pope of not doing enough.

Anna saw deeper. In 1978, the Church teetered on the brink of the abyss, just like today. Then, as now, the media cheered the Church's liberalization. How dismayed it was by the Karol Wojtyła surprise as he started steering the Church back from the edge! That media mocked him as a hidebound "restorationist." But a *genuinely* progressive pope it would never mock like that.

Certainly, Wojtyła made mistakes, including serious ones. Anna saw these. But she also saw the tremendous, unprecedented pressure on the papacy in the modern age. Any fallible human being, faced with this, was bound to fail at times. Still, Joseph Ratzinger recognised Wojtyła's greatness. When he became Pope Benedict XVI, he *consolidated* his mighty predecessor's feat. For thirty-five years, from 1978 to 2013, Wojtyła and Ratzinger worked to save the Church. A certain convalescence began, if not complete healing. Now, their combined efforts were steadily being undone.

Yet Anna saw that the present chaos could not last. The collaboration of Saints and Angels was never-ceasing. Dimly, Anna sensed the future. Great saints were coming to assist the Church, aided, as ever, by Angelic Hierarchies. Knights were coming too. Through the alliance of Angels, Saints and Knights, the remnants of Christendom would be gathered up, protected, strengthened. Catholicism was no longer the culture of the West, yet *little islands of subculture* remained. These fragments of Christendom would be nourished by men and Angels to come. The flame would be rekindled, as it always had been before.

But in these pale premonitions, Anna knew defeats could not be avoided. Catholicism in Ireland, as elsewhere, was too often like a limp fish carried along by the tide. That was why the abortion referendum might be lost. The Church had done too little, too late. But whatever happened, things were *not* over. Catholicism would regain its fire, swimming against the tide like a mighty salmon, rather than a minnow swept downstream...

For that recovery, though, reverent, sacred liturgy was crucial. Anna saw that the zany cartoon liturgy, prevailing in so many churches, would end. A true liturgy that summoned the faithful to genuine worship, just as it summoned Angels, was returning.

With it, Maximum Commitment Spirituality would return to Christianity as well. With it, the Church would regain the fire to fight for the unborn, fight for true marriage, fight the New Secular Religion and the New Age Religion. It would regain the courage to withstand the cultural revolution.

For all this, Angels fought. But never alone: Saints and Knights fought too. That His will be done on earth. That, eventually, His Kingdom come.

With that, Anna's attention slowly returned to the fading light of our small lounge, Brigid's head cradled in her lap, a saint seated opposite her.

"You see now," GT's voice startled her, "why you must never despair. Yes, hell exists. Yes, it erupts on earth. But Heaven is mightier, mightier than you mortals can ever possibly know. That is what I came to say today."

"Y-yes" was all she could say in her overwhelmed state. I took her hand in mine, sensing something extraordinary had happened.

"Now, I must take my leave of you," the Gentle Traditionalist said, rising from his chair. "Why don't you show me out, Geoffrey? Anna needs time to come round."

And with his handkerchief, GT wiped the tears from Anna's eyes. Then, he traced the sign of the cross on her forehead and Brigid's too. "You will be all right," he said, "this lunkhead you married finally got the message."

And with that, the old man and the lunkhead walked to the door. He put on his hat and, stepping outside, raised his umbrella. For some moments, he stood there, peering at me in silence, through the raindrops pattering down on his tattered umbrella.

I stammered inadequate gratitude for showers of grace. But he uttered not a word. Instead, he put a finger to his pursed lips. Then, he made one last, slow, silent sign of the Cross.

As he did, profound peace descended, bringing all my enlivened, astonished, stupefied emotions to a halt.

There were no more words to say. That did not mean there was no final message. The stillness itself was the message. As I stood there, *drinking* that silence, I saw how much I needed it: precious, prayerful silence to digest all that had happened.

Then that ancient figure winked, tipped his hat and walked off into the Irish rain.

XXX

Donegal Postscript

IT would be highly tempting to end the book there, with those last precious moments with the Gentle Traditionalist.

But I can't. The story isn't finished. Because three months later, Ireland voted to repeal its protection of the unborn child. Anna and I put our all into the fight to save babies, praying, fasting, debating, campaigning, offering everything up.

But we lost. We lost big. The pain is searing.

It is time to face how much has happened to the younger, globalised Irish generations, stripped of everything their culture once held dear. (Indeed, one Irish politician described the result as a "youth-quake.") The Church cannot be exonerated in this. Catholicism in Ireland, as elsewhere, has become feeble, a limp fish that just "goes with the flow."

I write these words from County Donegal. Anna and I have rented a cottage by the sea. Brigid is with us. She's expecting her baby in three months. (LightShadow left for California, where he now has a television contract.)

Now, Donegal, if you don't know, is pristine, wild, windswept land, lying in the most remote, northerly part of Ireland. Donegal is also home to one of the few remaining parts of the country where people still speak the original Gaelic language. And here, even more than the Cork mountains, we can still feel it: *The Real Ireland*. Not globalised Ireland. Not the Ireland awash in money and propaganda from the former Protestant Anglosphere, which never ceases protesting Catholic principles. Of course, the aim is no longer converting Ireland to Protestantism. It is promoting the "New Secular Religion" or the "New Age Religion"—under the pretext that these aren't religions at all.

No, here in Donegal, the last remnants of Catholic Ireland can still be felt. Donegal was the only county in Ireland to vote "no" to repealing the old anti-abortion legislation, "no" to butchering the unborn. And here we talk to the pious, praying Catholics we see every day at Mass. Many are broken-hearted by what has happened to their country.

Here in remote, northwest Ireland, I think of that northwest corner of another land in another time: Spain in A.D. 712. The Iberian peninsula had been overrun by Islam. But in that small, far-away corner of the country, Christianity held on. From there, the *Reconquista* began. No one in the eighth century would have expected it to succeed. But succeed it did. It took seven hundred years, but eventually Christianity was restored throughout the land. And Spaniards had the Universal Remedy again: His Body, His Blood.

In Ireland, it may take seven hundred years. It may take seventy. All I know is I'm not giving up.

People need the gold of Christ—not plastic.

The fight goes on. I wallow no longer. I stay true to my vow: "With God at my side, I will work, with all my might, to defend Christ's Church and Christendom."

Wherever you are in the world, I pray you join me.

Afterword

Occultism and the
Easternization of the Anglosphere

THIS Afterword's title represents a protest.

That protest is directed towards Colin Campbell, a British Sociology professor and author of *The Easternization of the West*. According to that remarkable book, revolutionary change has occurred since the 1960s, whereby "beliefs, values, and attitudes more typical of the East than the West"[1] now dominate the Occident. Indeed, Campbell goes as far as to say: "The cultural change in question is so dramatic as to suggest that the West is now no longer 'the West' as it has been constituted for most of its history."[2]

Whilst this claim may sound extraordinary, Campbell marshals formidable arguments that sweeping Easternization is happening under our noses. He is pointing to something fairly elusive, just as the Gentle Traditionalist does in the foregoing novel, when he says:

> Part of the problem is people don't see the essence here. They think Eastern means practicing yoga or Zen. But we're talking about something more subtle.
>
> Today, for instance, the Christian quest for salvation is increasingly replaced by the quest for enlightenment, mindfulness or self-knowledge. Christian understanding of evil and sin is replaced by the Eastern notion of error and ignorance. And Christian love is replaced by monism, oneness...
>
> There's also a growing belief reality is illusory, like the Eastern concept of Maya. Syncretism is likewise more Eastern than Western.
>
> It's these *ideas*, non-Christian ideas, indeed *pre-Christian*

---

[1] Colin Campbell, *The Easternization of the West: A Thematic Account of Cultural Change in the Modern Era* (Boulder, CO: Paradigm Publishers, 2007), vii.

[2] Ibid., 3.

ideas, that most concern me. The practices are less common. Most Westerners aren't about to start chanting the likes of Hare Krishna! Little do they realise their spirituality increasingly resembles the Orient's...

GT and Colin Campbell agree, then. Nevertheless, I cannot help but feel Campbell's case suffers, inasmuch as his sociological data remain overwhelmingly British and American in origin. Indeed, he even admits this, noting that "almost all the material is . . . drawn from Anglo-American sources."[3] Alas, Campbell, like so many, has little problem conflating important terms. For him, the Anglosphere all too frequently equals the West, whilst the West equals the Anglosphere. Here my protest starts. For Anglo-American culture certainly dominates the West, but the two should not be considered identical. Moreover, my years living outside the Anglosphere, in France, Spain, Germany and Switzerland, along with continued attention to these cultures since then (above all, France), tell me a different tale: Easternization is nowhere near as pronounced elsewhere in the West, as it is in Britain and America.

If, however, Anglo-American society now suffers profound Easternization, there is no reason to think the process will stop there! Given this realm's cultural hegemony over the world, it no doubt spreads beyond it. Just as the Protestantization of the Anglosphere prodigiously affected the whole world, so, too, will its Easternization. Here is why I write about Eastern invasion, or as my Geoffrey character comes to realize:

> With the New Age, something utterly alien to Western culture had landed in the Anglosphere. But it was not from outer space. It was from the East.

Commenting on one's own work like this is unusual for a novelist. The notion prevails that fiction ought to speak for itself. A skilled artist should need nothing else to convey his meaning.

However, I have no pretensions this novel is art! Truly, it seems more a "comic book without pictures" to me, albeit one with

---

[3] Ibid., 376. And again: "almost all of the data discussed in the chapters that follow actually do come from just two societies" (15).

serious themes. Now, some of these—the enormous power of media or the massacre of the unborn—require no elaboration. With the New Age it is different. It is the main agent of a sweeping Easternization, which is not sufficiently seen, let alone understood. Too many people are blind to a corrosive phenomenon eating away at Christianity, decade after decade.

For even though New Age books sell millions of copies, topping bestseller lists for years on end, even though this phenomenon seemingly mushroomed from nowhere, being non-existent a few short decades ago, and even though opinion polls reveal sharp rises of belief in things like astrology or reincarnation, the New Age remains "below the cultural radar" for most Catholics. As Marilyn Ferguson, a New Ager herself and author of the tellingly entitled *The Aquarian Conspiracy*, says:

> People hear this New Age stuff and think nothing but tofu and meditation cushions, or crystals and trance mediums. What they don't understand is that they're talking about their next-door neighbour.[4]

Or as my Geoffrey character realizes:

> Catholics and New Agers are like ships in the night. For people like LightShadow, we Catholics are irrelevant, "dinosaurs" from a past "Age of Pisces," whom they rarely—if ever!—encounter. Yet if, by chance, they *do* run into us, they can scarcely believe we exist. We are "neanderthals," who actually consider Western civilization worth preserving! On the other hand, Catholics scarcely see New Agers, at least not in all their untold hordes. Nor do we realize the powerful influence of New Age ideas. Because countless people may not consider themselves New Agers, but are nonetheless deeply affected by New Age thinking, as it ripples out through movies, music, internet and other media.

This ripple effect is tremendous. Obvious examples include American blockbusters like *The Matrix* films or Oprah Winfrey's media empire. Yet arguably the less obvious specimens are the more insidious, as New Age thinking subtly creeps into a legion

[4] Quoted in Campbell, *Easternization of the West*, 115.

of sitcoms, talkshows, pop music, novels, etc. Vast sums of money are likewise pumped in to promote it—a phenomenon we will return to. For now, suffice it to say Mel Gibson had to self-finance *The Passion of the Christ*, but there is no shortage of funds for movies with major stars like the *Da Vinci Code*...

Yes, close examination of Anglo-American popular culture suggests Campbell is right that "beliefs, values, and attitudes more typical of the East than the West" have taken hold more than is commonly appreciated. The sheer scale of this pains me, though, I am sure, not nearly enough. Like Geoffrey, I fear I remain insufficiently awake to what this *truly means* for real flesh and blood suffering *people*.

This I declare as a convert from the New Age to the Catholic faith. That is to say: someone who realized unutterably profound treasure was *absent* from New Age-ism. (Even though I was ensured this "holistic" spirituality was universal and thus—by definition—there could be nothing missing from it!)

With all this in mind, I recounted my extensive New Age experience in a semi-autobiographical book *Cor Jesu Sacratissimum*. Yet reactions to that book only highlight how few Catholics truly register this massive phenomenon. And in prayer, I felt the need to do more, go further.

This novel is the result. At one level, it recaps key themes from the earlier book in a hopefully more popular, accessible version. Hence, I hope LightShadow illustrates how New Agers espouse Eastern spirituality far more than they generally realize. I hope, too, that his personal mix of England and California suggests how peculiarly Anglo-American the phenomenon truly is and perhaps American above all. (As Jesuit Father Mitch Pacwa says, in a nutshell, the New Age is "a highly Americanized form of Hinduism."[5] As nutshells go, this is not bad...)

A Hidden Calculated System to Replace the Cross?
I mean to do more, though, than simply recap and this book is more

---

[5] Mitch Pacwa, *Catholics and the New Age: How Good People Are Being Drawn into Jungian Psychology, the Enneagram, and the Age of Aquarius* (Ann Arbor, MI: Servant Publications, 1992), 39.

explicit about the "Aquarian conspiracy" and its undergirding occultism. For like the Gentle Traditionalist, I am serious regarding:

> A hidden, calculated system... to replace the Cross. Of course, most are completely unaware of the occult agenda behind all this.

GT alludes to Theosophy—an Eastern system of esoteric thinking first developed by the Russian Helena Petrovna Blavatsky and later Alice Bailey. And he even refers to:

> An English-Eastern condominium [in] the political sense of the world: *joint rulership*. That's what Blavatsky, Bailey and their masters were aiming for, at any rate.

Now, I am painfully aware many eyeballs will severely rotate in their sockets seeing such material. Surely, there is no need for "conspiracy theory" when other, more mundane hypotheses can explain the Anglosphere's newfangled "universalism"!

For example, no book could contend better with my novel's apparently ludicrous imagery of occult condominiums and spaceships than the aforementioned *Easternization of the West*. With nary an occult cabal in sight, Campbell argues that "essential primary assumptions concerning reality and truth, time and history, the cosmos, and the nature of humankind... in the West"[6] resemble oriental philosophy as never before. And, certainly, this owes to globalization and the 1960s popularity of Eastern thought in the counterculture which led to today's New Age movement. But there is more, Campbell says. Other processes—independent of the East—have long been at work transforming Western thought.

In other words, *already existent trends* in the Occident facilitated acceptance of Eastern philosophy, but were not contingent on it. Such trends include a shift from belief in a personal Creator God to an impersonal life-force, a receding of Christian notions involving evil, sin and hell, and a rejection of dualism, associated with Christianity and Cartesianism alike, that favored Eastern monism. And Campbell's case has impressive breadth! He addresses developments as varied as quantum physics, the liberal

---

[6] Campbell, *Easternization of the West*, 363.

theology of Bultmann and Tillich that substituted immanentism for a transcendent God and the New Left's Freudo-Marxism, which replaced economic oppression with psychic oppression—taking the Left in a more psychic, subjectivist and less materialistic direction.

In short, Campbell demonstrates Western thinking was *already coming apart at the seams* before the East entered. Campbell sees, too, the role of Protestantization here and he amplifies a key idea in my novel, namely that the New Age represents

> the culmination of a process that began with the Protestant Reformation. For by rejecting priestly guidance, Luther effectively inaugurated the tradition whereby individuals have to decide for themselves on matters of doctrine, with only the Bible and the inspiration provided by the Holy Spirit to guide them. . . . One could say that this revolution *remained incomplete*, for although ultimate authority for the determination of religious truth now rested with the individual, this principle only really operated within the framework of one cultural tradition, that of Christianity, which was still assumed to be the only valid religion. Clearly there was *one more step to be taken* before it could be said that the principle that asserts that the individual is the sole authority qualified to determine the nature of religious truth had been fully realized. This was to allow the individual to decide the nature of religious truth not merely as it might be formulated within the confines of one tradition, but also as it might be found within any of the world's religions. It is *this final step in the process of implementing in full the principle of epistemological individualism that is clearly realized in the New Age movement*. For in this worldview there is no presumption that any one religious tradition should function as the taken-for-granted context within which individual seekers after truth ought to conduct their inquiry. Instead it is effectively *all of the world religions*, both those extant and those extinct, together with a myriad of minor faiths, cults, sects, and occult groups, that serve as the framework.[7]

---

[7] Ibid., 352; italics mine.

All this, I might add, comes from a perspective very different to my own: Campbell sees nothing tragic here. For him, the Reformation is a necessary stage in an Easternization process that he apparently salutes, though perhaps with occasional qualifications:

> The traditional Western worldview, in both its religious and secular forms, has been demoted from its previous position of preeminence and has been largely replaced by an Eastern one. For now it is only a minority of people in the West who hold to traditional Christian teachings, these having largely been replaced by belief in a diffuse spirituality, one that centers on the self and nature. More specifically the belief in sin has been replaced by the idea of ignorance and error, whilst the striving for salvation has been succeeded by a search for self-knowledge and enlightenment. At the same time, the traditional Western sense of the importance of history, most obviously evident in the belief in progress, has been abandoned . . . the former positive valuation of rational thought and analysis (together with an Enlightenment faith in science) has been cast aside in favor of intuition and mysticism . . . the traditional dualisms have been rejected, whether that of God and mankind, mankind and nature, mind and body. . . .[8]

Truly, Campbell's thesis is a stunning performance, which apparently makes a mockery of my "naive conspiracy theories."

Yet serious problems remain. We have, still, the conflation of Anglosphere and West. For whilst it is true his inclusion of German Protestants like Tillich and Bultmann might seem to belie this notion, Campbell is only concerned with their impact in Britain and America, where, by his own admission, he has drawn almost all his data. Moreover, I, for one, am clear that thinkers like Tillich or Bultmann never received the same attention in Catholic cultures like Spain or Ireland. And, having lived in such cultures, I cannot shake the feeling that Campbell, like so many others, does not truly see Catholic culture or even fully include it in the West. For him, the West remains firmly skewed to the Protestant Anglosphere.

[8] Ibid., 141–42.

But the book remains problematic at deeper levels. Most importantly, there is Campbell's bias: *he considers Christianity's collapse inevitable*, based on what he regards as its inherent flaws and our contemporary intellectual "progress." We will return to this bias. However, he also misses certain matters—murkier, messier, occult—which remain inadmissible to materialistically biased academia. Forty years of personal experience point me to critical but esoteric dimensions in the New Age Easternization process that remain entirely absent from Campbell's groundbreaking work. (And so my protest continues...)

Entering such territory, however, is profoundly uncomfortable for me. I neither enjoy being a controversialist, nor looking like a nut. Still, I point in directions Campbell fails to see and which will strike many as absurd.

Pointers, Only Pointers

Point, I stress. For, at this juncture of my life, I am unable to do much more than that. I offer no incontrovertible proofs to substantiate my "simplistic ideas." I will not convince the skeptical. However, in lieu of unfailing evidence, certain pointers may be fruitful for unknown friends and fellow researchers who sense how much is conspicuously lacking with Campbell. What follows, then, is an attempt both to amplify my strange assertions— if only a little—and supply more substance than was possible in the novel (without turning said novel into a treatise). Again, if only a little...

Here I return to my intensive participation in the "Aquarian conspiracy," which gives me a rare perspective amongst critical commentaries on the movement. At least, I have spent years studying innumerable analyses of the New Age, both scholarly and non-scholarly, and I see no one writing about it with my background.

For I am, as I say, a convert to the Faith, who was once steeped in all things New Age. My interest started as a teenager in the late 1970s, growing up on the American West Coast. Later in the '80s, I spent the best part of three years living at the Findhorn community in Scotland—a seminal site for the movement. As the Vatican document, *Jesus Christ: The Bearer of the Water of Life*, tells us:

The two centers which were the initial power-houses of the New Age, and to a certain extent still are, were the Garden community at Findhorn in North-East Scotland, and the Center for the development of human potential at Esalen in Big Sur, California, in the United States of America.[9]

Moreover, Father Malachi Martin suggests there are

only a handful of places New Agers can call their own. They do mark a *single site* as the New Age center of the world: Findhorn Bay in the north Scotch county of Moray, where the Findhorn River empties into the Moray Firth. Their community at Findhorn was to New Agers what the Vatican is to Roman Catholics.[10]

Some will think Martin overblown. Certainly, comparing Findhorn to the Vatican is an imperfect analogy, given that the New Age is hardly centrally organized like the Church. Analogies, though, are imperfect by definition and personal experience tells me Martin is closer to the mark than is readily seen. Be that as it may, any analysis of the New Age that omits Findhorn's enormous, often hidden influence goes seriously astray.

Now, in *Cor Jesu Sacratissimum*, I speak of Findhorn spreading Aquarian ideology via *ambassadors* to mainstream society.[11] For many thousands of people stream into Findhorn, but, more importantly, stream *back out of* Findhorn. There, I suggest they are conditioned by a strange, de-traditionalised spirituality, heavily indebted to the Theosophy of Alice Bailey. This, as we shall see, subtly obscures Christianity, deceptively working against it.

My point, though, is that I became a serious ambassador indeed for the "Aquarian conspiracy," pouring my lifeblood into it. For I left Findhorn in 1988 and spent most of the next decade as a paid New Age activist, running a New Age center in Cambridge, England, publishing New Age literature and arranging talks by key figures in the movement, such as Peter Russell,

---

[9] *Jesus Christ the Bearer of Life*, 2.3.2. Perhaps it is worth highlighting the wider locations here: California and Britain. Both are English-speaking and both are amongst the most progressive places in the Anglosphere.

[10] Martin, *Keys of This Blood*, 308; italics mine.

[11] Buck, *Cor Jesu Sacratissimum*, 135.

Jill Purce, Rupert Sheldrake, Caroline Myss and Sir George Trevelyan.

All this is elaborated in my earlier book and hardly need detain us now. One point must be stressed, though. I differed from many at Findhorn, inasmuch as I was an earnest student of the community's esoteric roots. When Anna speaks of her life at Findhorn, she voices my own experience:

> Most New Agers don't see their debt to Theosophy. Hardly anyone at Findhorn read Bailey and Blavatsky. But, although it was tough going, I actually did read them. To me, it's obvious their ideas completely shaped Findhorn.

Or as I write in my *Cor Jesu Sacratissimum*:

> By the 1980s, when I arrived, most Findhorn folk were clearly not pursuing esoteric studies. Whilst in former times, community members avidly devoured Theosophical literature, things had changed. Generally speaking, people were more engaged—sincerely and movingly—with each other's emotional experience than abstruse esoteric books. But, for myself, at least, another Findhorn existed. And during my years there, my orientation was different from that of many of my fellows. For more than most, I felt drawn to old archives regarding Findhorn's origins. And so I "dusted off" old lectures once held at the community, but now little read. From these, it was clear Findhorn's pioneers had been heavily influenced by earlier streams of Anglophone esotericism. And for long years after leaving the community, I continued pondering Findhorn's roots as an enthusiastic devotee.

The Anglophone esotericism I refer to is, again, Theosophy. I steeped myself in it, studying it intensively, practicing its methods. For me, the result was de-humanizing, a theme I explored in my earlier book and return to later.

Another way to say all this is that not only was I variously a participant, activist and apologist of the New Age movement for something like twenty years, but I was, I believe, *unusually cognizant of its origins* and seriously committed to them.

That twenty-year period has been followed by another two

decades, whilst I disengaged from the movement, converted to Catholicism and grew in my faith. Yet my past haunts me. For I have grown ever more disturbed by the abyss between Christianity and my old New Age "universalism," which supposedly included my new faith, but which, I now realized, subtly, continuously subverted it.

Writing these words in 2019, then, I bring forty years of experience and study to the table. Four decades have passed consuming many thousands of pages pertaining to the New Age, ranging from historical sources like Blavatsky, Bailey, Krishnamurti, Jung, Rudolf Steiner, Helen Schucman to contemporary writers like David Spangler, Ken Wilber, Caroline Myss, Eckhart Tolle, Dan Brown and more. To this may be added scholarly surveys, including the aforementioned Campbell, Pacwa and others we will turn to shortly. But the more I read, the more disquieted I became by the bizarre New Age bubble that Geoffrey comes to see:

> That bit about a bubble wasn't bad, I thought. Still, it didn't go far enough. The edges of a soap bubble were too soft, too clear, *too normal* to describe the sheer oddness of the New Age. No, another image was needed: something more rigid, opaque—most definitely not normal. Something outlandish. I turned it all over in my mind. And, as I did, the round image of the bubble transformed into a round flying saucer in my mind.
>
> It was almost as if some strange alien craft had landed in the West, filled with beings *who cared absolutely nothing* for the culture beyond. Out-landish indeed.
>
> "No, not a bubble," I exclaimed, "it's like this freakish UFO filled with ideas *completely alien* to Western civilization. And not only do the aliens reject everything the West has to offer, whether it's Christianity or rational thought—it's all 'left-brain' head-tripping to them—they turn around and say they universally embrace every perspective. What's more, they actually *believe* it!"

H. P. B.

The above is obviously a metaphor. The reader may rest assured I do not believe in literal invasion by extra-terrestrials! Still, my entire adult life points me to a less literal, if not necessarily less disturbing form of invasion. Infiltration is perhaps the best word and it commences with Helena Petrovna Blavatsky's arrival in New York City in 1873, founding her Theosophical Society there two years later. Blavatsky's American-rooted enterprise was later augmented extensively by the Englishwoman Alice Bailey who, in 1907, likewise arrived in America, following a sojourn in India.

But we begin with the Russian Blavatsky, often referred to as simply HPB. Here, at least, I am hardly alone regarding her colossal impact. As Gary Lachman, author of numerous studies on the esoteric (not to mention an original member of the rock group Blondie) writes:

> Although she died more than a century ago, Blavatsky's name still turns up in serious discussions about "ancient Wisdom," "secret teachings," and "inner knowledge," and it is generally agreed that her Theosophical Society . . . was more or less the official starting point of the modern spiritual revival. By "modern spiritual revival," I mean our contemporary widespread interest in a direct, immediate knowledge and experience of spiritual reality, and in a more profound relationship to the cosmos than traditional religions . . . can provide.[12]

Let us note some things. First, the "modern spiritual revival" here is nothing other than the Anglo-American New Age-ism critiqued in my novel—with all its dogmatic certainty that it offers more "direct . . . profound" routes to truth than any religious tradition. (Or, as Lachman confidently adds, "a sense of meaning and purpose that the official organs can no longer supply."[13]) Whilst Lachman's breezy dismissiveness is all too characteristic of the New Age—as I try to show with LightShadow—his assessment of Blavatsky's legacy remains invaluable. That legacy is so enormous, Lachman suggests, that:

---

[12] Gary Lachman, *Madame Blavatsky: The Mother of Modern Spirituality* (New York: Jeremy P. Tarcher/Penguin, 2012), ix.

[13] Ibid.

it can easily be overlooked, in the way that some prominent feature of the landscape can be overlooked—that is to say, taken for granted. Yet if Blavatsky's offering to our modern spiritual consciousness was to be suddenly removed, it would drag along with it *practically everything we associate with the very notion of modern spirituality. . . .* To press my point: Anyone who meditates . . . or is interested in reincarnation, or has thought about karma, or pursues "higher consciousness," or has wondered about Atlantis, or thinks the ancients might have known a few things that we don't, or reads about esotericism, or who frequents an "alternative" health center or food shop, would be aware of it if modern spirituality somehow became "HPB free." And this, of course, would include quite a few people *who never heard of Blavatsky, or who have only the vaguest idea of what Theosophy is* or of its place in the history of Western consciousness. Which is to say most people. . . . It's been said that all of modern Russian literature emerged from Nikolai Gogol's short story "The Overcoat." It can equally be said that practically all modern occultism and esotericism emerged from the ample bosom of his younger countrywoman and contemporary, HPB.[14]

Lachman, moreover, documents a surprising number of figures inspired by Blavatsky, including Gandhi, Nehru, Kandinsky, Yeats, Einstein, Thomas Edison, L. Frank Baum and even the purported inventor of Baseball, Abner Doubleday, once president of the American branch of the Theosophical Society. All this can be found in his *Madame Blavatsky: The Mother of Modern Spirituality.* The reader may wonder, then, if the author is merely a starry-eyed hagiographer, composing a paean to his heroine.

Reading his book suggests otherwise. Lachman is not uncritical of Blavatsky and, by his own account, remained uninterested in her for many years. Yet, repeatedly, his extensive studies of esotericism pointed to her legacy, until finally, he saw virtually all modern esoteric routes lead back to HPB and particularly her three-volume epic *The Secret Doctrine.*

---

[14] Ibid., x–xi; italics mine.

Still, Lachman is hardly impartial. His sympathies remain very much New Age (what he calls "modern spirituality," of course). The same cannot be said for J. Gordon Melton, a professor of American religious history who has published extensively on American cults and new religious movements. Melton is also a Methodist minister. He might, then, seem to represent Lachman's opposite pole. His work, though, strikes me as descriptive and objective, rather than prescriptive and polemical. Here, at any rate, is his estimate of Blavatsky's prodigy:

> No single organization or movement has contributed so many components to the New Age movement as the Theosophical Society. . . . The Society passed the occult tradition to more than one hundred separate organizations in North America and many more in Europe.[15]

Elsewhere, Melton adds:

> Madame Blavatsky, or simply HPB, stands out as the fountainhead of modern occult thought and was either the originator and/or popularizer of the many ideas and terms which have a century later been assembled within the New Age movement. The Theosophical Society, which she cofounded, has been the major advocate of occult philosophy in the West and the single most important avenue of Eastern teaching to the West.[16]

Finally, we append the views of Christopher Bamford. Bamford is both a scholar and an Anthroposophist—meaning he shares Rudolf Steiner's rejection of Theosophy (of which more below). Nonetheless, he recognizes:

> With Theosophy something quite new and revolutionary entered European consciousness and world evolution. . . .

---

[15] J. Gordon Melton, Jerome Clark, and Aidan A. Kelly, *New Age Encyclopedia: A Guide to the Beliefs, Concepts, Terms, People, and Organizations That Make up the New Global Movement toward Spiritual Development, Health and Healing, Higher Consciousness, and Related Subjects* (Detroit, MI: Gale Research, 1990), 458.

[16] Ibid., 71.

For although Madame Blavatsky is not yet counted with Marx, Freud, and Nietzsche among the "creators" of the twentieth century, that surely is her place despite her wild eccentricity.... Certainly there is no "alternative thinker" of our time, in no matter what field, whose accomplishment does not at some level rest on her strenuous effort. Behind the "New Age"—whether we think of Rudolf Steiner, Gurdjieff/Ouspensky, Peter Deunov, Schwaller de Lubicz, Krishnamurti or a host of other and apparently unrelated "spiritual" streams, from the "perennialism" of René Guénon to the magic traditions, the renewal of Pythagoreanism, Hermetism, and the Kabbalah, or the search for a synthesis between science and mysticism exemplified by such as Fritjof Capra, Rupert Sheldrake, Lyall Watson and others—behind all this lies Madame Blavatsky. This is not to mention such exoteric, cultural impulses as the present world movement for ecumenical and interreligious dialog and the attempt to create a non-Eurocentric theory of world evolution as an evolution of consciousness—for this, too, Madame Blavatsky's stubborn, independent, open-minded exploration, breaking open the prisonhouse of the aging secret societies, opened the way.

Her "revelation" thus not only changed the outer course of Western materialistic culture, but also transformed the premises of the established Western spiritual, occult, and esoteric traditions. It did so by... proposing a universal synthesis, a total view of the universe—divine, natural, and human [which was] at once a philosophy, a cosmogony, and a religion.[17]

What more to say? I have not researched these things as thoroughly as Bamford and Melton, but four decades of personal experience point me to the same conclusions. Yet whilst Colin Campbell explores the New Age in depth, he scarcely refers to Blavatsky at all! And he mentions Alice Bailey only once...

---

[17] C.G. Harrison, Christopher Bamford, *The Transcendental Universe—Six Lectures on Occult Science, Theosophy, and the Catholic Faith: Delivered before the Berean Society* (London: Temple Lodge, 1993), 8–9.

Alice Bailey

It is time, then, we turn to this obscure Englishwoman, who remained in America from 1907 till her death in 1949. There she married Foster Bailey, a 32nd-degree American Mason,[18] further developing HPB's "philosophy, cosmogony, religion" with his passionate, unflagging support. Personally, I wonder if Foster Bailey's Masonic inspiration transformed Theosophy more than is generally admitted. At any rate, Alice Bailey added staggering sociopolitical goals to Theosophy, not present in Blavatsky. For in her books, talk of a New Age, a New World Order and even a New World Religion emerges, which goes far beyond Blavatsky. (For such reasons, the Bailey material is sometimes referred to as neo-Theosophy.)

Now, Bailey's legacy is less obvious than Blavatsky's. HPB burst on the stage of the nineteenth century as a fiery comet: wild, provocative, flamboyant. By comparison, Bailey appears a quiet, humble figure, stolidly working away in the background. What can I say? Lenin may have been less original than Marx, but all the world sees his colossal influence. Alice Bailey was less original, less startling, than her predecessor, and few, very few, truly appreciate her gargantuan legacy. Many hardly see the New Age debt to Blavatsky, let alone Bailey! Alas, it is obvious Marxist-Leninism is the very root of Communism, yet it is hardly obvious at all the same is true of Blavatskyite-Baileyism and the New Age.

Happily, there are notable exceptions to this ignorance. For if the English sociologist Campbell scarcely notices Bailey, one of his colleagues in British academia, Steven Sutcliffe—a senior lecturer in religion at Edinburgh University—sees clearly here. Bailey, he writes, is the New Age's "chief theorist,"[19] adding that "Alice Bailey's discourse became the dominant model for 'New Age' activists in the second half of the twentieth century."[20]

---

[18] Foster Bailey, *The Spirit of Masonry* (New York: Lucis Publishing Company, 1957), 135.

[19] Steven Sutcliffe, *Children of the New Age: A History of Alternative Spirituality* (London: Routledge, 2003), 14.

[20] Ibid., 53.

Still, Bailey remains too little recognized. Part of the problem is that few have ever studied either Bailey or Blavatsky. For New Agers this material is "tough going" indeed (as Anna says). And for non-New Agers, including skeptical academics, there is little call to engage it. For such folk, Theosophy's key texts, most of which are said to be channelled from exotic Eastern Masters, will likely appear as nothing more than eccentric whimsy—much like the vast majority of New Age pablum.

Having studied it, this is not my perspective. Unlike the drivel of other "channelled" material, the Blavatsky-Bailey corpus is different. Whatever it is, it is hardly stupid. Nor does it elicit the "oohs" and "ahs" of credulous thrill seekers, who consume popular "holistic" books like airport thrillers, here today, gone tomorrow. No, the material is deliberately non-popular, difficult, demanding, immensely elaborate and sophisticated. It appeals to few New Agers. Yet it potently influenced many of the movement's pioneers. Some of these are obvious, such as David Spangler and Sir George Trevelyan. But many remain obscure background figures, who nevertheless *devote their lifeblood* to intensively studying—and intensively implementing—the Blavatsky-Bailey directives.

In my life, I have met numerous Theosophists like that: highly intelligent, intensely determined. In my youth, I worked seriously for their agendas. And I might be working in my maturity for these same agendas still—and even more seriously—had Christic grace not rescued me. Yes, I know these serious people, because I aspired to be one of them. I know, too, that such people sometimes exist in high, unexpected places, such as the deceased Dr Robert Muller, former Assistant Secretary-General of the United Nations, of whom more below...

But, as I say, New Agers themselves are likely to remain entirely unaware of their debt to these dogged souls. For example, I recently returned to Findhorn for the first time in a quarter century. There I encountered New Agers who appeared even less conscious of the Theosophical legacy than the ones I knew in the 1980s. Yet everywhere I went, I could "smell" the footprint of Theosophy, above all the Bailey footprint. This I believe would be obvious to *anyone who truly studied Alice Bailey*. Given time, I suppose I could compile an extensive (and extraordinarily dull) treatise of hundreds of correspondences between Findhorn culture and neo-Theosophy. Still, the correspondences would often seem circumstantial, less than convincing. But to *those initiated into Alice Bailey*, what I say is as plain as plain can be; to the uninitiated any number of connections may well remain unpersuasive.

All I can do is *point*. Once I knew a Christian minister who started to seriously engage New Agers. Something surprised him—how many of these respected "the Christ" or thought themselves followers of "the Christ"—even though they were definitely not Christian! This orientation to "the Christ" is familiar to anyone who knows the New Age well. Whence does it stem?

My answer lies, above all, in neo-Theosophy. For although Bailey is in continuity with Blavatsky on most points, differences exist. Perhaps the major one is between Blavatsky's overt anti-Christianity—which denies the historical Jesus—and Bailey's perspective. Because with Bailey *something called "the Christ" now assumes centre stage*. Indeed, "the Christ" becomes head of a "planetary hierarchy" of hidden masters now "externalizing" to usher in the Age of Aquarius. Moreover, this "Christ" is nothing other than the Maitreya Bodhisattva or the next Buddha awaited by the East! And for Bailey this "Christ" overshadowed both "the Master Jesus" and Krishnamurti.

Rather than attack Christianity full-on, as Blavatsky did, a more subtle, subversive tactic emerges with Bailey, one where Theosophy even appears somewhat Western. Bailey also quotes the Bible frequently. In other words, more familiar Christian terminology and cultural references were inserted into neo-Theosophy. Many are deceived. For I have even encountered intelligent New Agers who consider Bailey part of the Western Mystery tradition! And then there are hardline Blavatsky purists who object that Bailey is "too Christian"!

At any rate, if we concur with Lachman, Bamford and Merton that the New Age is shot through with HPB's "philosophy, cosmogony, religion," AND we also note that her *overt* anti-Christianity is mysteriously missing from the mix, we may sense that neo-Theosophy is more influential than many suppose. Likewise, we may better understand countless New Agers who honor "the Christ"—with little inkling their "Christ" has more to do with Alice Bailey than anything else. Likewise, there is LightShadow's esteem of "the Christ consciousness" in my novel—a popular term in New Age circles that also goes back to Bailey.[21]

Such is only some of the strange fruit of neo-Theosophy. For Alice Bailey worked herself to death, penning twenty-four dense books (some of which span from around 800 to 1400 pages) whilst also initiating related activities and organizations, with names like the Arcane School, Lucis Trust, World Goodwill. All this, as we shall see, finds curious support at the United Nations. Earlier, I described her global religious, social and political agendas as "staggering." That word may not go far enough. At any rate, I doubt anyone who does not know Bailey well can truly appreciate how far-reaching her ambitions were. Still, a certain sense can be had, listening to Bailey on the "New World Religion":

> The day is dawning when all religions will be regarded as emanating from one great spiritual source; all will be seen as unitedly providing the one root out of which the universal world religion will inevitably emerge.[22]

And moreover:

> in the *new world order*, spirituality will supersede theology; living experience will take the place of theological acceptances. The spiritual realities will emerge with increasing clarity and the form aspect will recede into the background; dynamic, expressive truth will be the key-note of the new world religion. The living Christ will assume his rightful place in human consciousness and see the fruition of his plans, sacrifice, and service, but *the hold of the ecclesiastical orders will weaken and disappear.* Only those will remain as

[21] It is not impossible it goes back even earlier to the Theosophy of Charles Leadbeater and Annie Besant. But I think its current usage, broadcast around the world by the likes of Oprah, among others, is indebted above all to Alice Bailey.

[22] Alice A. Bailey, *Problems of Humanity* (New York: Lucis Publishing Company, 1947), 140.

guides and leaders of the human spirit who speak from living experience, and who know no creedal barriers; they will recognize the onward march of revelation and the new emerging truths. These truths will be founded on the ancient realities but will be adapted to modern need and will manifest progressively the revelation of the divine nature and quality.[23]

Lest all this sound merely abstract or theoretical, let us note neo-Theosophy is replete with concrete recommendations, strategies, practices and predictions, as to how this *one world religion* should manifest. There are prayers and mantras (most notably *The Great Invocation*), recommendations for world festivals oriented to the full moon, including Easter and Wesak (the Buddha's birthday) and much else in those densely-packed pages.

Bailey's ambitions did not stop with a one-world religion, though. Long before George H.W. Bush, she called for a New World Order, with an astounding host of detailed social, political and economic proposals. Nonetheless, her mammoth, multifaceted project would have failed, were it not for followers who popularized her often near-incomprehensible theory. Another British academic Nicholas Campion illumines this, including Findhorn's potent role here:

> There were a number of enthusiastic New Age evangelists in the 1970s, all of whom were *deeply influenced by Alice Bailey.* The first was David Spangler.... From a background in childhood clairvoyance, Spangler discovered the New Age through reading Bailey in 1959, settled at the New Age community at Findhorn in Scotland and, after around 1970, became the most prolific author in the field. It was Spangler's books, *Festivals in the New Age*, published in 1975, and *Revelation: The Birth of a New Age*, which appeared in 1977, which brought the term New Age into a wider usage, efforts which were reinforced by his colleague and collaborator Sir George Trevelyan (1906–1966), who contributed the foreword to *Revelation*. George Trevelyan was *likewise a Baileyite*

---

[23] Alice A. Bailey, *The Externalisation of the Hierarchy* (New York: Lucis Publishing Company, 1957), 202; italics mine.

and was to be influential through the lectures he organized through the Wrekin Trust, which he set up in 1971.[24]

We note, too, that Spangler's work at Findhorn included "transmissions"—a word he preferred to channeling—from Theosophy's hidden hierarchy of masters, including the "Master Rakoczi" as well as the Maitreya Bodhisattva whom Alice Bailey identified with Christ.[25] He even formed a folk band, who set Alice Bailey's *Great Invocation* to music. (This is in line with Bailey's directive that the Invocation should be disseminated as widely as possible. According to her, it possessed a magic, mantric power to *invoke*…)

Here I would stress a point from my previous book: that, more than anyone else, David Spangler has long seemed to me the uncredited creator of what Findhorn is today. For although Findhorn was founded by other Alice Bailey acolytes, above all Peter Caddy, innovations by Spangler and his followers after 1970 changed the place almost beyond recognition.[26]

I will add I was at least passingly acquainted with Peter Caddy at Findhorn and somewhat more with his ex-wife Eileen. The same is true for Trevelyan and Spangler later on. I organized talks with the former and spent several days during workshops with the latter, whose writings I also devoured. But if I knew none of these people well, I was closely associated with those who did. Looking back, I near-idolized Spangler in particular, and the

---

[24] Nicholas Campion, *The New Age in the Modern West: Counterculture, Utopia and Prophecy from the Late Eighteenth Century to the Present Day* (New York, NY: Bloomsbury Academic, 2017), 126; italics mine. In terms of the Californian side to the New Age, Campion also cites Bailey apostle Dane Rudhyar as another key popularizer during this time (127).

[25] The transcripts of these were available to be read by community members. They have never been published officially, although an extract from the communication attributed to the Maitreya was included in David Spangler, *Links from Space* (Forres, Scotland: Findhorn Publications, 1971), 21–23. Peter Caddy's autobiography also contains numerous references to the Theosophical "Master Rakoczi" both in relation to Spangler and himself. See Peter Caddy, *In Perfect Timing: Memoirs of a Man for the New Millennium* (Findhorn, Forres, Scotland: Findhorn Press, 1996).

[26] Buck, *Cor Jesu Sacratissimum*, 137.

same goes for other people, too. Such folk might not be his official followers, but they nevertheless doggedly, methodically pur-
sued agendas he pioneered. Spangler, I would like to say, still
strikes me today as a sincere, genuinely kind man, with many
admirable qualities.

Be that as it may, all manner of unofficial agendas exist, unrec-
ognized by academic studies of the New Age. One picks such
things up in the New Age: grapes from the grapevine. And one
picks still more grapes when *one owes one's livelihood* to the movement. For that was my uncommon situation over a dozen years,
including full immersion at what is possibly the epicenter (or
"Vatican") of the movement and later, full-time paid activist.
Moreover, there is such a thing as New Age *shoptalk*. If one is literally in the business of arranging seminars with New Age leaders, one inevitably hears things that those only attending the
seminars do *not* hear. And my "conspiracy theory" would be significantly stronger were I justified in reporting details of intimate
conversations with these figures.[27]

New Age Networks

This unusual vantage point informs the present thesis: that powerful, unofficial New Age networks—profoundly indebted to
Blavatskyite-Baileyism—exist. And these networks proceed with
careful, sophisticated effort to replace traditional Christianity
with Eastern concepts.

For a commonplace notion prevails of New Agers as superficial
eccentrics, pottering away in a harmless little world of their own.
The truth is otherwise. And Alice Bailey's utopian dreams—better, *stratagems*—were not simply crackpot reveries with the eph-
emeral "here today, gone tomorrow" appeal that characterizes
the truly crackpot. Rather, seventy years after her death, they continue to attract serious people, with serious funding, even, as we
shall see, in the highest echelons of the United Nations.

Now, such things *have* been recognized by certain Christian
fundamentalists. Indeed, something of a cottage industry of

---

[27] See Buck, *Cor Jesu Sacratissimum*, 141–42, for a small bit more in this direction.

evangelical books has sprouted as a result, starting with Constance Cumbey's *The Hidden Dangers of the Rainbow.* Alas, these well-meaning books often seem overwrought to me, scarcely understanding Theosophy and misquoting its authors, mangling their meaning. Still, such Protestants are frequently far more awake than Catholics to the continuing New Age corrosion of Christianity. One may be grateful for that, whilst still regretting how little serious work is done by sober, informed and intelligent Catholics in this regard.

There is, however, one outstanding exception: an immensely researched treatise by Eastern Catholic Lee Penn: *False Dawn: The United Religions Initiative, Globalism, and the Quest for a One-World Religion.*[28] Ostensibly, Penn's primary focus is not Theosophy, but the URI of the first item in his subtitle. This is an extraordinarily ambitious global "interfaith" project, with all kinds of connections to people in high places. I say ostensibly, however, because Penn's book concerns far more than simply the URI. And, as we will shortly see, it has *everything* to do with his subtitle's final item: the *one-world religion* Alice Bailey dreamed of.

Still, a brief detour into the URI is not amiss at this point. For as Penn makes clear, the URI is not so much invested in friendly ecumenical dialogue as in serious agendas to replace traditional religions with a globalist religious ideology that mocks them. But let us hear Penn himself:

> The introduction to the URI Charter sets out the movement's planetary ambitions: "Working on all continents and across continents, people from different religions, spiritual expressions and indigenous traditions are creating unprecedented levels of enduring global cooperation. . . . The URI, in time, aspires to have the visibility and stature of the United Nations."
>
> Unfortunately, the URI has a grandiose agenda that goes far beyond its principal, publicly stated aim of promoting peace, tolerance, and non-violence among all religions and spiritual movements. As shown by the repeated, public speeches and writings of URI leaders and activists since the

[28] Hillsdale, NY: Sophia Perennis, 2004.

movement began in 1995, the URI and its allies propose the following:

- Squelching Christian evangelism, in the name of promoting inter-religious peace.
- Marginalizing orthodox Christians as "intolerant" and "fundamentalist."
- Preparing the way for a new, global spirituality that can accommodate domesticated forms of all current religions and spiritual movements.
- Promoting a new, collectivist "global ethic."
- The idea that the main goal of religion is social reform, rather than service to God.
- The idea that all religions and spiritual movements are equally true, and equally efficacious as ways to attain communion with God.
- Population control—especially in Third World countries.
- Providing a global podium and respectability for cultism, occultism, witchcraft, Theosophy, and other spiritually harmful religious movements.

This agenda isn't written directly into the Charter of the URI. However, it is plainly evident in the public statements and actions of URI leaders and their allies.[29]

Moreover, formidable, thrusting force surges here! As Penn details, the URI attracts millions of dollars of funding, as well as support from notables like George Soros and Ted Turner of CNN. By 2004 (when Penn wrote the book) it had:

grown from a California-based movement of 55 people in the mid-1990s to a global movement of over 26,000 activists in 56 countries, with backing from prominent foundations and from Federal officials.[30]

On top of that:

the URI is building an ever-closer relationship with the UN and its agencies.[31]

[29] Ibid., 6.
[30] Ibid.
[31] Ibid.

Alice Bailey would be impressed. The URI strongly resembles her plans for a New World Religion on the back of a New World Order. Penn, I think, would agree with this assessment. For his exhaustive research into the URI's background repeatedly pointed him back to Theosophy and *particularly the Alice Bailey variant thereof*. (This is evident from reading the book, but even a quick glance at the index confirms the Bailey references are more plentiful than Blavatsky's.)

This is why *False Dawn* concerns far more than just the URI. Rather, the URI is Penn's point of departure to explore networks of groups and individuals indebted to Theosophy who are ideologically affiliated with (or identical to) those I worked with in the 1980s and '90s. Alas, scope prevents exploring this in depth. A few salient indicators must suffice.

For example, Penn repeatedly references the aforementioned Dr Robert Muller, Alice Bailey disciple and former Assistant Secretary-General of the United Nations. Muller speaks of the URI as follows:

> The role and responsibility of the new United Religions Organization and of the World Parliament of Religions . . . will be no less than to give humanity *a new spiritual, planetary, cosmic ideology* to follow the demise of Communism and Capitalism.[32]

Likewise, Penn cites Muller *speaking at Findhorn* in praise of Mikhail Gorbachev's initiatives. As for Gorbachev himself, Muller considers him

> the prophet of a united human family, and the *global architect* who will give the world *his vision, plan and proposals* how the Earth and humanity can become the ultimate cosmic success of the universe and of God.[33]

Now, as we will see, Gorbachev's communist roots-cum-"global architecture" may have more links to Theosophy than might be supposed. Moreover, Muller is simply one example among numerous figures, connecting Alice Bailey, the New Age and the

---

[32] Ibid., 134; italics mine.
[33] Ibid., 372; italics mine.

United Nations (here we note that both Findhorn and World Goodwill—an Alice Bailey initiative—are NGOs at the UN).

Gorbachev and the UN aside, Penn also documents odd links between leading New Agers and US politics. For example, there is the matter of Jean Houston as Hillary Clinton's "spiritual advisor," as well as Barbara Marx Hubbard, a Findhorn Fellow (and Bailey ideologue) whose

> name was placed in nomination for the vice presidency of the United States with her campaign for a positive future.[34]

Indeed, I recall Hubbard talking of this at Findhorn. For in 1984, the Democrats sought a female candidate—Geraldine Ferraro was eventually chosen—and Hubbard regaled us with how close she came to being nominated at the Democratic convention that year (to the astonishment of Edward Kennedy and other leading politicians of the time).

Penn's book, then, exposes the networks I knew as a New Age "ambassador" from Findhorn. Close study of its well-documented text (over 3000 footnotes!) reveals an amazing number of New Agers (including the aforementioned Houston, Hubbard and Spangler, as well as Neale Donald Walsch, Joanna Macy, Gordon Davidson, Marianne Williamson) who form a web of connections thoroughly indebted to Alice Bailey. (Or as Muller has it, "a new spiritual, planetary, cosmic ideology"...) Of course, not all these people are intimately acquainted with Bailey arcana. However, cognoscenti exist who *are* very well acquainted indeed. And Penn reveals the deep kinship, respect and ideological affiliation that cognoscenti enjoys with those who, I imagine, are incognoscenti (e.g., Marianne Williamson and Matthew Fox may not know Alice Bailey well, but they salute Spangler).

Alas, we cannot tarry with Penn, but I recommend his book to anyone who doubts GT's apparently absurd notions regarding "piggyback globalists":

> Malachi Martin [saw that] New Agers . . . meant to rule the world. And he was right: a breathtaking agenda for a new syncretistic, decidedly non-Christian, "planetary culture" is

---

[34] Ibid., 326.

evident throughout New Age literature, going straight back to Theosophy.

"Planetary culture, global synthesis," Anna interjected, "those terms are through and through the New Age. And you're right, there's an almost political agenda there to remake the entire world."

"Globalism by another name," GT said, "And most definitely political, even if that fact is often hidden and even if, obviously, New Age leaders lack governmental power to dominate the West. That's why they ride on the backs of those who do."

What else can I say? Having studied Theosophy over many years, the thorough, monumental agenda Penn charts is transparent to me. It would likewise be transparent to other Christians if they would only take time to:

1) Study the *serious key texts of Theosophy* (rather than standard New Age drivel) and look to the immense socio-religio-political agendas therein.

2) Look to the contemporary New Age milieu to see how much of it confirms the outworking of those agendas. Here Lee Penn can help them admirably.

Valentin Tomberg

It is tempting to end here. But beyond these two avenues of exploration, I now take a third track that may appear even stranger than the foregoing. For further personal experience points to *plans* to re-make the West in the image of the East. And so I return to a more autobiographical vein, hoping the sympathetic reader may bear with me.

For I owe an immense debt to the great Catholic convert Valentin Tomberg. Once steeped in the Anthroposophy of Rudolf Steiner, he later penned the masterpiece *Meditations on the Tarot.*[35] That book, I hasten to add, has nothing whatsoever to do with

---

[35] For an acute discussion of Tomberg from a Catholic perspective, see Michael Martin, *The Submerged Reality: Sophiology and the Turn to a Poetic Metaphysics* (Kettering, OH: Angelico Press, 2015), 189–202.

divination or reading Tarot card spreads. Rather, it is a profound 600-page discourse on the Catholic Mystery, which *liberated* me.

Now, in *Cor Jesu Sacratissimum*, I divulge an intimate experience in 1997 that led to my Christian baptism. This experience was the greatest liberation of all. However, Tomberg was the key figure who effected my transformation from New Ager to not only Catholic, but indeed the traditional Catholic I am now. For after that interior revolution of 1997, I was baptized an Anglican—and an exceedingly New-Agey, liberal Anglican, at that. Without Tomberg, I might still be that same New Age Anglican today!

What can I say? After twenty years' immersion, New Age dogma gets *entrenched*. Only Tomberg's *Meditations* could divest me of my Theosophical trappings. For Tomberg showed me how these hardly constituted the inclusive "modern spirituality" I supposed—as, alas, millions now suppose, including former members of Blondie and how many more media stars? Yes, Gary Lachman's "modern spirituality" can never include real Christianity. But only Tomberg could show me that.

There is the matter, too, of the "de-humanizing effects," alluded to earlier. Because Theosophy spawned attitudes in me completely different from Christianity—attitudes of remote detachment, control, power-seeking and grandiosity. As I elaborate in *Cor Jesu Sacratissimum*, an aloof, even inhuman, orientation was overtaking my soul. Alice Bailey celebrated the bomb being dropped on Japan as the greatest event in several millennia? Well, then, I celebrated it, too! Alice Bailey preached rigid control of the astral [emotional] body? Well, by jing, I would rigidly control my astral body! And LightShadow's impervious arrogance certainly draws on my own inflated bearing at the time.

Tomberg deconstructed my Theosophy. He led me to the holy sacraments of the Church, of which he spoke with the highest reverence: "There is nothing in the physical world more holy— more healing in the deepest sense of that word—than the bread of Communion Service."[36] This was said before Tomberg's con-

---

[36] Valentin Tomberg, *Anthroposophical Studies of the New Testament* (Spring Valley, NY: Candeur Manuscripts, 1985), 99.

version and draws perhaps on a repeated profound experience that he later described to Bernard Martin: "The transformation in the Mass deeply shakes him [Tomberg] every time in his innermost being."[37] Together, the holy sacraments and Tomberg's guidance undid the impersonal Eastern orientation of my youth. For this Russian sage realized that living Christianity was warm, human, humble. It brings, he says, the "gift of tears," whereas, by contrast: "An advanced pupil of yoga or Vedanta will forever have dry eyes."[38]

Close reading of *Meditations on the Tarot* reveals further warnings like the above, many of which are brief, subtle or easily missed. The following, however, is plain and particularly relevant here:

> Continuity—or tradition and life—implies faithfulness to the cause that is espoused, to the direction taken, to the ideal that one has as a guide . . . for the sake of the continuity of life. This is what is stated by the seventh commandment: *Thou shalt not commit adultery.* There is carnal adultery, psychic adultery and spiritual adultery. The Biblical prophets spoke of this in relation to the unfaithfulness to the alliance of Sinai on the part of the kings and people of Israel, who on many occasions gave themselves up to cults of Canaanite divinities. This is today also the case when one embraces, for example, the Vedanta or Buddhism, whilst having been baptized and sufficiently instructed in order to have access—given good will—to experience of the sublime Christian mysteries. [In] the case where one changes faith, i.e., where one substitutes the ideal of liberation for that of love, an impersonal God for the personal God, return to the state of potentiality (or nirvana) for the kingdom of God, a wise instructor for the Savior, and so on. . . . Spiritual adultery is therefore the exchange of a higher moral and spiritual

[37] Private correspondence quoted in Elisabeth Heckmann and Michael Frensch, *Valentin Tomberg: Leben, Werk, Wirkung*, vol. 1.2 (Schaffhausen: Novalis, 2001), 48.

[38] Anonymous [Valentin Tomberg], *Meditations on the Tarot: A Journey into Christian Hermeticism* (Amity [i.e., Warwick], NY: Amity House, 1985), 36.

value for a lower moral and spiritual value. It is, for example, the exchange of: the living God for an impersonal divinity; Christ crucified and resurrected for a sage deep in meditation; the Holy Virgin-Mother for Nature in evolution. . . .[39]

It is not hard to see how all this relates to the Easternization of society (and anyone who truly knows Theosophy will readily see that "Nature in evolution" evokes not only Darwin, but Blavatsky, as well). Yes, Tomberg was awake to the spiritual adultery of the West. He wept, he wrote and he warned. In my own bumbling fashion, I try to follow him.

Now, occasionally, *Meditations on the Tarot* points very specifically to Theosophy. One salient reference occurs during a long discourse on the lure of spiritual power with its attendant danger of psychological inflation. For Tomberg warns of the temptation for certain "spiritual initiates" to seek their own glory, rather than Jesus Christ. And here he invokes Blavatsky's Eastern Masters, which may sound strange to those inured to Enlightenment rationalism, as Tomberg hardly rules out the fantastic phenomena Blavatsky and other Theosophists reported. (And why should Catholics rule out such phenomena, when we believe in both the preternatural and the supernatural? Unless the Enlightenment has corrupted the Catholic mind considerably and "superstitious" medieval Christians frequently knew better than we do...?)

Be that as it may, Tomberg contrasts the glory of the Lord with the quest for spiritual power:

> The possibility of the other "glory," i.e., the manifestation of mastership in one's own name, also exists. The words of the Master at the head of this Letter—"I have come in my Father's name, and you do not receive me; if another comes in his own name, him you will receive" (John v, 43)—state it clearly. Experience in the domain of Occult, Esoteric, Hermetic, Cabbalistic, Gnostic, Magical, Martinist, Theosophi-

---

[39] Ibid., 298–99.

cal, Anthroposophical, Rosicrucian, Templar, Masonic, Sufi,
Yogistic movements, and other contemporary spiritual
movements, supplies us with ample proof that the words of
the Master have in no way lost their actuality. . . .

Because *for what other reason* do the Theosophists, for
example, prefer the Himalayan mahatmas, whose astral
bodies through projection appear from a great distance (or
who "precipitate" letters written in blue or red crayon), to
the Master, who has never ceased to teach, inspire, illumine
and heal, amongst us and near to us—in France, Italy, Germany, Spain, to name only the countries where there have
been well-established cases of meetings with him—and
who himself said: "I am with you always, to the end of
time" (Matthew xxviii, 20)?

For what other reason does one seek a guru amongst the
Hindu yogis or Tibetan lamas without giving oneself half a
chance to seek for a teacher illumined through spiritual
experience in our monasteries or spiritual orders, or
amongst lay brothers and sisters who practice the Master's
teaching and perhaps are quite near at hand? [40]

Let us add that Tomberg was not only concerned with "Himalayan mahatmas, . . . Hindu yogis or Tibetan lamas" replacing
Christ, but likewise Western Masonry. Thus, he continues:

And why do members of secret societies or orders of the
Masonic type consider the Sacrament of Flesh and Blood of
the Lord insufficient for the work of building the new-man,
and why do they seek special rituals to supplement it or
even to replace it? [41]

And he concludes:

All these questions fall under the heading of the words of
the Master: "I have come in my Father's name, and you do
not receive me; if another comes in his own name, him you
will receive." Why? Because for some *the superman has more
attraction than the Son of Man*, and because he promises

[40] Ibid., 151; italics mine.
[41] Ibid.

them a career of increasing power, whilst the Son of Man offers only a career of "foot washing."[42]

All this, I believe, hints at a bigger picture, one that includes the strange way Western Masonry (rooted above all in the Anglo-sphere) intertwined with Eastern Theosophy. (As mentioned, Foster Bailey was a high degree Mason and Blavatsky, too, was initiated into an American Masonic lodge—an extremely unusual "privilege" for a woman of that era.) But whilst *Meditations on the Tarot* hints *publicly* at such things, we also have testimony to the *private* Tomberg in this matter. For Martin Kriele—whom Tomberg regarded as his "spiritual son" and to whom he entrusted his literary estate—reports:

> [Tomberg] took very seriously the occultism without Christ that based itself on the Theosophy of Blavatsky and worked out of the Indo-Tibetan region. It was very influential from the background. It was, for example, partly instrumental in the spread of Bolshevism, in the benevolent neutrality toward it, in the threatening east-west polarization, but also in the "esoteric" *youth movement* of the "New Age" which began to flourish at the time.[43]

Yes, careful study of Tomberg's life and writings convince me he saw the New Age temptation to "manifestation of mastership in one's own name," i.e., *personal power* stemming from Indo-Tibetan Theosophy. To counter it, he advocated fidelity to the

---

[42] Ibid. It should be noted this passage is followed by what may seem a qualification. Tomberg asks the reader to interpret his words neither in terms of lacking respect for the Indian mahatmas, nor in terms of opposition or hostility to the esoteric groupings he invokes. It has sometimes been suggested this negates Tomberg's serious warning above. I tend to think that this reflects a desperate—often very desperate!—need to make Tomberg into something of a "New Age universalist," which he was not. Close reading of his book reveals he went to extraordinary efforts to be gentle, refusing polemic towards any party. This is another example of the same. Tomberg clearly sees in Theosophy a preference for the superman to the Son of Man. The whole passage bears out a very grave warning in terms of both Theosophy and Masonry, even if he sincerely wishes to not antagonize.

[43] Martin Kriele, *Anthroposophie und Kirche: Erfahrungen eines Grenzgängers* (Freiburg-im-Breisgau/Basel/Wien: Herder, 1996), 156; italics mine.

Holy Church—admonishing esotericists or "Hermeticists [who] behave as pontiffs, without the sacraments and the discipline that this entails."[44] And he likewise wrote a "manual of liberation" for those embroiled in esotericism—whether Eastern or Western— separated from the Church. With me, his efforts succeeded. For his *Meditations on the Tarot* liberated the young man I was from the Eastern Occultism without Christ that permeates New Age youth. It is doing the same for many more.

A Small Aside on Bolshevism

Yes, the New Age is young and naive, purposively rooted, I think, in a younger culture than Europe's, one historically less permeated by the sacraments. But now we briefly turn to different questions that may surface in reader's minds, after absorbing Kriele's words above. Namely, what has Marxist-Leninism to do with the Age of Aquarius? Why did Tomberg make the curious links we have just invoked?

My answer entails more layers than one. There is a fairly obvious stratum, unsurprising to anyone with deeper knowledge of Theosophy. For Blavatsky's life testifies to her own linkage between the Indo-Tibetan region she loved and the Russia she remained loyal to—even volunteering for Russian espionage, after becoming a naturalized American![45] And there is the curious fact that, whilst Alice Bailey consistently condemned German Fascism, she always appeared more forgiving to Russian Communism. This, I think, struck me even as a New Ager. For example, Bailey goes so far as to say:

> The Greek Orthodox Church reached such a high stage of corruption, graft, greed and sexual evil that, temporarily and under the Russian Revolution, it was abolished. This was a wise, needed and right action. . . . The refusal of the revolutionary party in Russia to recognize this corrupt church was wise and salutary. . . .[46]

Likewise, Bailey's curious sympathy for Communism extended

---

[44] Anonymous (Valentin Tomberg), *Meditations on the Tarot*, 190.

[45] Lachman, *Madame Blavatsky*, 171.

[46] Bailey, *Problems of Humanity*, 131.

to her widowed husband, Foster, who years after her death doggedly carried on her work, whilst praising Maoism:

> The cultural revolution in China was begun a few short
> years ago. This also is an hierarchical project.[47]

This means to say: guided by Alice Bailey's occult hierarchy of
Masters led by "the Christ." And Foster Bailey adds:

> The change for the better in the life of the common people
> in China in the last few years is more than amazing. . . .
> Today under Mao the mass of the people receive the great-
> est attention. . . .[48]

What we have here is nothing less than the New Age's "chief
theorist" (as Sutcliffe has it) and her husband endorsing the most
murderous regimes in human history. Indeed, there is a "means
justify the end" mentality in much of Theosophy and its New
Age successors. Spangler, for example, speaks of being informed
by spiritual entities who regard human tragedy and trauma as
"grist for the mill, if at the end of a thousand years, we emerge
wiser with a culture that is more holistic."[49] All this ties in with
the strange heartlessness of key New Age texts mentioned in the
novel section of this book.

There is also the matter of the Agni Yoga books of Helena
Roerich, which were introduced to me at Findhorn. Roerich was
another follower of Blavatsky, who, like Bailey, claimed inspiration from the same Indo-Tibetan masters. Indeed, Helena Roerich travelled those remote regions extensively in the 1920s and 30s
alongside her husband Nicholas, a painter known for his exotic
canvases of the vast, lonely expanse of central Asia.

Limitations of space prevent detailing these strange matters.
Still, a curious letter the Himalayan Mahatmas allegedly gave the
Roerichs to take to Russia speaks volumes in itself. The following
lines were addressed to the Soviet government in 1926:

---

[47] Foster Bailey, *Running God's Plan* (New York: Lucis Publishing Company
1972), 12.

[48] Ibid., 166.

[49] David Spangler, *Facing the Future* (Everett, WA: Lorian Press, 2010), 79.

We are sending the earth for the grave of our brother *Mahatma Lenin.* . . . In the Himalayas we know what you have accomplished. You have abolished the Church, which had become the breeding-ground of falsehood and superstition. You have wiped out the bourgeoisie, the source of prejudice. You have destroyed the prison of education. . . . You have crushed the spiders of profiteering. . . . You have recognized that religion is the teaching of the all-embracing nature of matter. You have recognized the insignificance of personal property. . . . You have bowed down before Beauty. You have brought children the full might of the cosmos. . . . We . . . send you our help, thus affirming the *Oneness of Asia.*[50]

The Roerichs' expedition on their masters' behest was not unappreciated by Moscow. The Russian security agency of that time, forerunner to the KGB, was assigned to the Roerichs to protect their mission to carry Himalayan soil to Lenin's grave.[51]

Whilst geopolitics is beyond our scope, a final allusion to another side to the Roerichs' work is not amiss. For they had access to the American as well as Soviet administration. Thus, Henry A. Wallace, 33rd Vice President of the U.S. under Franklin Delano Roosevelt, was a devotee of the Roerichs. And there are reports from credible sources[52] that the appearance of the Great Seal's esoteric imagery of the truncated pyramid on the American dollar bill, during the Roosevelt administration, was suggested by Nicholas Roerich.

Unsurprisingly, Alice Bailey supported the Roerichs from the beginning. Indeed, her Lucis Trust promotes Agni Yoga to this day. All this, I believe, is relevant to the links Lee Penn documents between Gorbachev and today's neo-Theosophists.

Such matters hardly surprise anyone well-versed in Theosophy. It is likely Tomberg knew these things. However, he may have had

---

[50] Quoted in Sergei O. Prokofieff, *The East in the Light of the West* (Forest Row: Temple Lodge, 2009), 55; italics mine.

[51] Ibid., 54.

[52] Karl E. Meyer, "The Editorial Notebook; The Two Roerichs Are One," *The New York Times*, 22 January 1988 (available at www.nytimes.com/1988/01/22/opinion/the-editorial-notebook-the-two-roerichs-are-one.html).

further reasons to link Indo-Tibetan occultism to Bolshevism, "east-west polarization" and the like. For Tomberg had a unique vantage point of the Soviet sphere. He was, first of all, a Russian who witnessed the 1917 revolution and spent half his life in Russia or adjacent Estonia. Moreover, much later on, in England, this cultural background offered him an unusual livelihood:

> I am working for the BBC as "Monitor," i.e., as part of the "ear" of the country. Whilst the work in itself is interesting as well as objectively necessary, I nevertheless experience myself in it as if in an inferno. It is infernal inasmuch as I am employed for the Russian and Estonian language—and this means that I have to listen almost exclusively to Moscow and have to digest what I hear. A stream of lies and hatred is pouring through my ears and my head—for eight hours daily.[53]

Rudolf Steiner

Yes, Tomberg experienced diverse things few Westerners ever do, including long years of careful, paid full-time work "to digest" the Soviet mentality. Does this, alongside his knowledge of Theosophy, *completely* explain the peculiar links he made between Eastern Occultism without Christ, Eastern Communism and esoteric initiatives with the young?

No. Still another factor exists here: the Anthroposophy of Tomberg's youth, prior to his conversion. Here we approach strange matters, gingerly. For much in Anthroposophy bears out everything I am driving at. Yet some may question my invoking a system of thought markedly hostile to the Church. I hesitate for another reason also—the problem of identifying Tomberg with something he later explicitly rejected and renounced. For as he wrote to an Anthroposophical admirer in 1970:

> Nothing lies further from me today or would be more tiring than to see the ashes of the Anthroposophical past raised up. . . . Shield me from discussions about [my Anthropo-

---

[53] Private letter, quoted in Heckmann and Frensch, *Valentin Tomberg: Leben, Werk, Wirkung*, 180.

sophical work] and similar things, which are now *totally alien* to me.[54]

Moreover, Tomberg requested these "totally alien" works never be re-published. Unfortunately, his wishes were not respected. His early works are in print again and many confuse the mature Catholic Tomberg with the Anthroposophical Tomberg of his youth. This grave confusion, I think, is precisely what he meant to avoid. I have no wish to add to it.

After these caveats, however, and prayer, I proceed. First, though, Anthroposophy bears explaining for those unfamiliar with it. Such is no easy task in a short space! Still, in crude, broad strokes, Anthroposophy refers to Rudolf Steiner's so-called "esoteric Christianity," which is, alas, at odds with the Church on countless points. This Christian esotericism was Steiner's attempt to redress the catastrophe of Theosophy. For Steiner was once a leading Theosophist, even whilst he regretted Blavatsky's hostility to Christ and sought—sincerely, I believe—to Christianize her legacy. Around 1912, Steiner gave up this fruitless task. Instead, he established an esoteric schooling that profoundly rejected the Church, but nonetheless revered the Crucifixion on Calvary as the turning point of cosmic history. This Steiner called the *Mystery of Golgotha*, a hallowed phrase in Anthroposophy to which we will return.

What can I say? I have no wish to defend Anthroposophy which, among other things, suffers from the colossal inflation of which Tomberg warned. Whatever one makes of Steiner, though, he saw and venerated the cosmic Mystery of Calvary in ways far beyond anything Blavatsky and Bailey could ever comprehend. And alas, also far beyond the comprehension of countless liberal theologians today! He deserves this justice, at least.

Be that as it may, the youthful Tomberg worked for this Anthroposophy. Eventually, though, he renounced it, declaring:

> Christianity . . . is one and indivisible. One should not—one cannot!—separate from so-called "exoteric" Christianity its gnosis and mysticism, or so-called "esoteric" Christianity.

[54] Quoted in Sergei O. Prokofieff, *Valentin Tomberg and Anthroposophy: A Problematic Relationship* (Forest Row: Temple Lodge, 2005), 3–4; italics mine.

Esoteric Christianity is entirely within exoteric Christianity;
it does not exist—and cannot exist—separately from it.[55]

Tomberg, then, moved on. The same is true of myself. I studied much Anthroposophy in my past and even if, like Tomberg, it is now alien to me, it hardly follows *ipso facto* that everything I ever read from Steiner is worthless. No, certain Anthroposophists, and not just Steiner, have *acutely sharpened* my awareness of what lies behind the New Age.

For example, there was the fanatically anti-Catholic Russian Anthroposophist Sergei Prokofieff. Do I profit from Prokofieff's rabid condemnation of the Church (and indeed of Tomberg as a renegade to Anthroposophy)? No. Have I profited from his extensive investigation into Blavatsky's progeny? Yes. For example, his Russian background allowed him to better document the strange things cited earlier regarding the Roerichs, things little understood outside Eurasia.

Hesitantly, then, we turn to the fact that Steiner (and Prokofieff after him) spoke to *ambitious Theosophical agendas to flood Russia and the West with an alien spirituality*. Steiner, I believe, possessed profound insight in these matters. But even those skeptical of his gifts may yet give him credence here, inasmuch as he once occupied the highest echelons of the Theosophical Society, being head of its German section. In short, *the man was in a position to know.*

We commence, then, with comments from Steiner's lectures in 1915, three years after his break from Theosophy. Steiner now speaks with unprecedented explicitness about his former ties. By this point, he felt free to declare that Theosophy was rooted in the work of

> *Indian occultists* . . . whose prime interest it was to turn the occultism which could be given to the world through H. P. Blavatsky in a direction where it could influence the world in line with their special aims.[56]

These special aims, Steiner suggests, were varied. They entailed *political goals to link Russia to Asia*, paralleling the connections

---

[55] Anonymous [Valentin Tomberg], *Meditations on the Tarot*, 590.

[56] Rudolf Steiner, *The Occult Movement in the Nineteenth Century and Its Relation to Modern Culture* (London: Rudolf Steiner Press, 1973), 35; italics mine.

Tomberg made between Indo-Tibetan occultism and Bolshevism. What is most apposite, though, is Steiner's assertion of *calculated plans to de-Christianise the West*. Theosophy, he says, meant to rob the world not only of Jesus Christ, but also, as we shall see, Jehovah (rendered Jahve in much of what follows).

> The Indian occultists [influencing Blavatsky] had no other aim than the promotion of their own special interests— Indian interests. They had in mind *to establish all over the Earth* a system of wisdom from which Christ, and Jahve too, were excluded. Therefore something whereby Christ and Jahve were eliminated would have to be interpolated.
>
> The following method was then adopted. It was said: Lucifer is in truth the great benefactor of mankind . . . Lucifer brings to men everything they have gained through the head: science, art, in short, all progress. He is the true Spirit of Light; it is to him that men must adhere. . . . Hence the statement in *The Secret Doctrine* that men *should not adhere to Jahve* for he is only the Lord of materiality, of all the lower, earthly impulses; the true benefactor of mankind is Lucifer. This shimmers through the whole of *The Secret Doctrine*, and is, moreover, clearly stated there. And so for occult reasons H. P. Blavatsky was prepared in such a way as to become a hater of Christ and Jahve.[57]

Thus it was, Steiner says, that Blavatsky gave "vent in *The Secret Doctrine* to a volley of abuse on the subjects of Judaism and Christianity, interwoven with certain teaching about the nature of Jehovah."[58] One year later in 1916, Steiner elaborated:

> Blavatsky was misled by certain beings who had an interest in guiding her into putting Lucifer in the place of Christ, and this was to be achieved . . . by maligning [Jehovah], representing him merely as the god of the lower nature. Thus did those cosmic powers who desired to advance materialism work even through what was called "theosophy."[59]

[57] Ibid., 93–94; italics mine.

[58] Ibid., 67.

[59] Rudolf Steiner, *The Karma of Vocation* (Spring Valley, NY: Anthroposophic Press, 1984), 118.

And years later in 1923, Steiner asserted that Blavatsky

> fell under outside influence, namely of eastern esoteric
> teachers propelled by . . . the desire to create a kind of
> *sphere of influence—first of a spiritual nature, but then in a more
> general sense—of the East over the West*, by providing the
> West's spirituality, or lack of it if you like, with eastern
> wisdom. . . . Various factors were at work, including the
> wish to link India with Asia in order to create an Indo-Asian
> sphere of influence with the help of the Russian Empire.[60]

For those who know little of Theosophy—including the vast
majority of academics—these appear strange, fantastic allega-
tions. Reluctantly, I include them, because, from my vantage
point, so different to theirs, Steiner's claims are entirely consis-
tent with thousands of pages of Theosophy consumed in my
youth. No, more: reading Steiner has eerily illumined what I read
back then and his above remarks find *ample* corroboration there.
Much is "hidden, in plain sight." It would be more widely recognised, if only intelligent researchers would properly read Bailey's
work particularly, which, alas, only its intelligent devotees ever
really read. Likewise, Steiner has illumined my experience with
Findhorn and the networks Lee Penn documents.

Here is why I cite Steiner. For if there is any truth at all to his
notion that *Blavatsky was guided to "putting Lucifer in the place of
Christ"* and if, as I argue, the New Age is largely an outgrowth of
Theosophy, a wider public deserves to know.

The Struggle with the False Christ

And so we proceed further along strange byways. For there is
Steiner's talk, scattered in lectures across the years, of the
attempt to erect a False Christ in the West.

Now, so far we have quoted Steiner after his decisive break with
Theosophy in 1912. But prior to the final rupture, Steiner, already
in conflict with his colleagues, was speaking out, albeit not so
explicitly. We turn to his 1911 lectures on the Gospel of St. Mark,

---

[60] Rudolf Steiner, *The Anthroposophic Movement: Eight Lectures Given in Dor-
nach, 10–17 June 1923* (Bristol: Rudolf Steiner Press, 1993), 74.

where he discusses Islam and Buddhism in relation to Christianity. Steiner reminds his audience how the West absorbed Islam's scientific culture during the Middle Ages. (Our present-day numerals, for example, stem from Arabia.) He then predicts that, in an analogous fashion, certain *externals* from Buddhism will enter the West. According to him, these externals, like Arabic science, possess value. But Steiner is categorical that it is *only a matter of externals*, because the East understands *nothing* of the Mystery of Golgotha that transformed the world. Grave danger attends us if we believe the East can offer Christ.

To this end, Steiner invokes St. Mark's Gospel: "False Christs and false prophets will appear . . . when men say to you: 'Lo, here is the Christ, lo, there—believe them not!'" He continues immediately afterwards:

> There is another [stream] claiming to be better informed than Western [Christian esotericism] about the nature of Christ. This other stream *will introduce* all kinds of ideas and dogmas which will develop quite naturally out of . . . oriental Buddhism. But Western souls would be showing the worst kind of feebleness if they failed to understand that the Buddha . . . stream has as little light to throw on the direct development of the Christ-idea as Arabism had in its time.[61]

As noted, Steiner speaks less explicitly here than he would later. The context, though, leaves little doubt that his talk of a "stream" that "will introduce . . . dogmas" about Christ means Theosophy. And the same is true of *this*:

> The attempt might be made to transplant *this* as a fixed and unalterable system into Europe and to *produce out of it an idea, a conception, of Christ.*[62]

In other words: a false Christ. But according to Steiner and Catholics alike: "That would be as absurd as if the Arabians . . .

---

[61] Rudolf Steiner, *Background to the Gospel of Saint Mark* (London: Rudolf Steiner Press, 1968), 155–56; italics mine.

[62] Ibid., 156; italics mine.

had set about giving Europe a true idea of Christ."[63] And six years later, in 1917, Steiner warned of

> *the aim of leading human beings away from Christ*, Who passed through the Mystery of Golgotha, and of securing the ruler-ship of the earth for another individuality. It is a *real struggle, not just something that I know of as abstract concepts* or what-ever but a real struggle. It is a real struggle that concerns itself with placing another being in place of the Christ. . . . It will be the task of a healthy, honest spiritual development *to eradicate such strivings*, which are in the true sense of the word anti-Christian, *to remove them, to annihilate them*. This can be achieved, however, only through clear insight. This other being whom the brotherhood wishes to substitute as ruler they will call "Christ"; *they will actually designate him as the "Christ."*[64]

What can I say? These are strange matters indeed. Let us note, however, that Steiner said all this *before* Alice Bailey's "Christian-ization" of Theosophy, with "Christ" as the Maitreya Bodhisattva (which "Christ," moreover, will soon incarnate as part of the "Externalization of the Hierarchy"—or public emergence of "masters" ushering in her New Age). And, of course, Steiner also said it long before Spangler channelled that same "Christ" at Findhorn.[65] And even longer before Oprah Winfrey started pop-ularizing terms like "Christ consciousness"…[66]

I am well aware how ludicrous all this sounds to my Catholic readers! Rightly so. Alas, a "Christ" spouting Eastern New Age-isms hardly sounds ludicrous to the millions reading New Age books and watching New Age talkshows. This situation did not

[63] Ibid., 154.

[64] Rudolf Steiner, *The Reappearance of Christ in the Etheric: Selected Lectures from the Work of Rudolf Steiner* (Spring Valley, NY: Anthroposophic Press, 1983), 153; italics mine.

[65] See note 48. Also in 1980, Spangler was still suggesting that "Christ" could re-appear in physical form in the "first part" of the twenty-first century. What is clearly meant here is the Maitreya, given all that Spangler said previously. See David Spangler, *Conversations with John* (Middleton, WI: Lorian Press, 1980), 4.

[66] An internet search I just did for "Oprah Winfrey" and "Christ conscious-ness" turned up 19,100 results.

exist in Steiner's time. In his comments above, he speaks of a "real struggle" that he knows from personal experience, not simply abstract theory. Is it possible that, however strange it may seem, the man was perfectly sincere in this—as well as *prophetic*, given all that has happened since 1917?

Now, some caveats. There is a danger of decontextualization here. The above quotes are fragments, scattered through lectures given over many years, which often appear obscure, even contradictory.[67] Moreover, Steiner's language is comprised of esoteric jargon alien to Catholicism and likely to confuse. Quoting more would have risked greater confusion and I have already somewhat simplified what I quote with ellipses. Nonetheless, these shortened quotes remain faithful to Steiner's meaning, as well as I can grasp it.

Amidst these caveats, one thing merits particular attention. What Steiner means by Lucifer is not precisely the same as the Catholic understanding, though it certainly relates to it. For Steiner treated Lucifer as one form of evil, amidst other forms. Detailed scrutiny of Anthroposophical theories of evil need not detain us (although we note that later Tomberg specifically critiqued it).[68] Suffice it to say, Steiner's Lucifer refers to *seduction*. He described demons working to entice human beings into extravagant fantasy and false ecstasy, divesting them of earthly responsibility and morality. This, for Steiner, was Luciferic evil. And his claim Blavatsky sought to substitute Lucifer for Christ takes on all the more meaning, when we understand the dark bewitching grandiosity Steiner specifically ascribed to this Fallen Angel. Steiner saw the Theosophists as Luciferic and would undoubtedly regard many New Agers in a similar light, were he alive today.

What can I say? All my New Age experience leads me to see what Steiner was "getting at." Whilst Tomberg no doubt rejected

---

[67] Here I note that the last comments, regarding a being who will be designated Christ, do not appear to be directed to Theosophists. Rather, Steiner seems to point towards Masonic orders working in the Anglo-American world. Whilst this may seem to contradict the earlier extracts, Steiner repeatedly pointed to cooperation between Western and Eastern occultism. I point to the same throughout this book.

[68] Anonymous [Valentin Tomberg], *Meditations on the Tarot*, 402.

Anthroposophical "categories of evil" with good reason, the effect of New Age spirituality on my own soul was Luciferic, much the way Steiner suggests. Earlier I spoke of being de-humanized. I could also say I succumbed to *the escapist temptation to circumvent my humanity.* The autobiographical sections of my earlier book demonstrate this, I hope. Likewise, the haughty LightShadow who prefers his own fantastic revelations to tradition draws on the man I used to be. And so I echo Steiner's warnings regarding a spirituality that is Luciferic rather than Christian. For millions, it seems to me, are now *seduced* like I was.

A Deliberate By-Pass?

Still more might be quoted from Steiner, were it not for the aforementioned problems. Whilst I do not recommend Anthroposophy, some researchers may yet profit from further scattered references Steiner made to Theosophy. Of particular note are various allusions to an attempt to *by-pass* the Mystery of Golgotha. For Steiner believed there was an Eastern agenda to preserve certain *later* elements of Western culture—e.g., modern science—whilst *hollowing out the core of that culture*: the Christic Transfiguration of the world on Calvary (for which no words can ever suffice…).

This "leaping-over" Christ is transparently obvious to me. For in this matter, Steiner's thoughts *converge* with so much else from my life. I know the staggering agendas in those dense books from Alice Bailey that no one reads except serious devotees. I know what certain self-proclaimed initiates and New Age leaders told me in confidence. I know what scholars like Sutcliffe, Campion and Penn report. All this and more converges with Steiner's mysterious thoughts on a deliberate, calculated *by-pass*.

This convergence led me, in my last book, to represent my thesis of the New Age in a simple formula. Although, as I said before, that formula "runs the risk of being crudely simplistic," I re-present it here, slightly modified:

> New Age-ism equals: Anglo-American Synthesis of Pre-Christian world religion (absent Judaism, and chiefly Eastern).

Plus: Twentieth-Century Imports from Secularism, Liberalism, Psychotherapy, Ecology—and the Esoteric.
Minus: Twenty centuries of Christian Theology and Tradition (particularly Catholic).[69]

In other words, there is a *leap* here—or by-pass—from the time
before Christ to recent developments in the modern West…

An Incomplete Conclusion

This afterword has been no easy task. The New Age movement
entails vast sprawling territory. It is no isolated phenomenon
with a few eccentrics frolicking away in a small corner of our culture. On closer examination, one sees its links to everything from
Hollywood blockbusters and television talkshows to geopolitics
and the United Nations. One sees, too, serious people exerting
serious effort, backed by serious money, to replace the Christian
foundations of the West with crypto-orientalism: Eastern spirituality disguised as universal.

To return to where we started, Colin Campbell amply demonstrates his claim: "the New Age . . . provide[s] an emergent meaning system [that is] in essence, Eastern." And although Campbell
excessively conflates the West and the Anglosphere, Christians
should heed his words:

> Modern Western civilization is increasingly dominated by a
> worldview that is essentially Eastern in character, the tradi-
> tional Western values and beliefs having been demoted to a
> secondary position.[70]

He understands, too, the New Age movement as a main agent
of this transformation. Inadequate as it is, his book features one
of the best treatments of New Age-ism I know.

"Inadequate as it is"—because, alas, Campbell misses a *lot*.
Whilst he acutely analyses *contemporary* New Age phenomena,
his treatment of its *origins* remains lacking. There is no evidence
he understands Alice Bailey's mammoth influence at all. There is

---

[69] Cf. Buck, *Cor Jesu Sacratissimum*, 130.
[70] Campbell, *The Easternization of the West*, 319.

only scant acknowledgment of Blavatsky's "maternity." Findhorn *does* receive attention, yet without recognizing *its enormous debt to Bailey's "Christianized," politicized Theosophy!* Likewise the URI is absent too—not to mention the millions of dollars pouring into it, along with other New Age initiatives connected to the UN. What my novel intimates about things like the money behind Oprah Winfrey's media empire and the like hardly seem important to Campbell either.

This is not surprising. As much as I critique Campbell, I imagine he would critique me. Ideas like Blavatsky deliberately replacing Christ with Lucifer and my other "conspiracy theories" would most likely appear ludicrous to him.

At any rate, Campbell has no need for such. As mentioned earlier, he considers the collapse of Western Christianity inevitable. Why he thinks that is beyond our scope. Still, to my mind, he overly interprets history in terms of intellectual and material "progress." Campbell pays profound attention, then, to ideological pressures generated by the clash of ideas and evolving perceptions of reality. Likewise, he addresses economic realities (e.g., what rising disposable income meant for the 1960s counterculture youth). In such domains, his discourse is frequently stunning. What he says of the evolution of Marxism or Protestant individualism leading to the New Age merits close attention.

Alas, all this appears like nothing more than inexorable processes of change to Campbell: natural, necessary, even organic. He has neither need, nor room for anything else. Obviously, my perspective is different. The ongoing deliberate destruction of Christianity is not inevitable! And to my mind, Campbell resides in the lofty ivory tower of positivist academia—with insufficient reference to all the messy human passion, power and politics lurking behind our present Easternization—and, needless to say, the super- and preternatural.

Lee Penn understands this much better than Campbell. But then Penn tackles a very different kind of research: investigating nitty-gritty reality in terms of the networks, Realpolitik and sheer, staggering *money* behind the Easternization of the Anglosphere. Penn is also awake to the far-reaching power of Theosophy in ways that elude Campbell. Yes, Penn's *False Dawn* is the single best book I see on the New Age. But Campbell's remains a runner-up. Both books can be profitably studied together.

Here is why I stress two masterly works devoted to different sorts of research. Still, such research is not enough to substantiate all I see from my decades with the "Aquarian conspiracy." In other words, forty years of encounters with New Age pundits, occultists, magicians, healers, Theosophists, Anthroposophists, Freemasons and the like, participation in countless New Age meditations and seminars, rituals and workshops and determined effort to penetrate the literature behind all this, lead me to the personal conviction that Lee Penn's thorough research merely scratches the surface of a reality that is hidden, deliberately deceptive—in a word: occult.

What Tomberg said privately to Kriele, I now declare openly: there *is* Eastern Occultism without Christ. My entire life points to this, from the moment I first arrived at Findhorn, aged sixteen. This oriental esotericism seems to stem from an Indo-Tibetan context, just as Tomberg suggested and just as Blavatsky, Bailey and Roerich always said it did. Kriele says Tomberg took this "very seriously" for it was "very influential from the background." I would like to say I share Tomberg's grave concern. But, instead, I will now be very frank: I fear I do not share it enough.

Like Geoffrey in my novel, I fear I have been asleep, dithering for far too long.

For I write from Ireland, weeping as the country is overtaken by a Liberalism imported, above all, from the Anglo-American world. The New Age/SBNR movement is the spiritual component of this Liberalism: the progressive party at prayer. Predominantly Anglo-American globalization has changed *everything*. In Ireland we see the astonishing fact that 1,600 years of Catholic Christianity can almost *evaporate* in just fifty years. Above all, the culprit here is the liberal *progeny*—theological, social, economic—of the revolution introduced into the Anglosphere by Henry VIII. What took five centuries in England—the transition from Catholicism to liberal, capitalist Secularism—has now (almost) happened in Ireland in five decades…

Five decades, I might add, is also the time Ireland took to follow Britain into killing the unborn. As I hope I have shown, the

Social Liberalism that massacres babies is supported by the Spiritual Liberalism of the New Age. (Here I note the "abortion ritual" described in the novel is based on a true story known to me. One Catholic reader of my manuscript thought it sounded "far-fetched." Alas, it is not. Again: "ships in the night"...)

A final thought regarding these British Isles now comes to me. Just as I finish this afterword, a beloved friend from my English New Age past has died. This is not the place to pay tribute to her generous soul. But I reel from the unconsciously Eastern tributes paid to her. They are filled with New Age certainties that she is now liberated from "personal identity" and no longer need suffer in this veil of illusion...

I do not know the authors of these sureties, but they are unlikely to be conscious practitioners of Eastern religion. No, they most likely identify with "modern spirituality"—whilst rejecting the older term "New Age"—and having no idea whatsoever that their minds have been colonized by Lachman's "mother of modern spirituality": HPB. Or as GT says, they are EBNC—Eastern But Not Conscious of it.

With mental colonization like this, there would seem no need to pray for my friend's soul! How many more of our dead are *robbed* of prayer, because of unconsciously-held Eastern conceptions of the afterlife...? It is one more reminder of the tragedy unfolding in England and spreading to Ireland, of why I write this book and why I came to feel that my last book did not go far enough. This book proceeds further, even if I am still groping my way towards things I cannot sufficiently document. Still, I addressed the same realities in *Cor Jesu Sacratissimum* and the interested reader will find much more there to supplement this awkward, piecemeal afterword.

That is just about it. I close as I began, awkward, uncomfortable. I did not like invoking Anthroposophy. Yet Steiner called for a "real struggle" to "annihilate" a false conception of the Christ that could, in time, *dominate the West.*

Sceptics, including Catholics, may snicker at this. Such snickering is even fashionable. What if the sceptics are wrong? What if "real struggle" is required by Christians everywhere, precisely because sceptics like Campbell are wrong? There is no "inevitable decay of Christianity" easily explained by cultural "progress." But there *is* effort towards destroying Christian faith on a large scale, systematic effort that is cunning, covert, forever denied, yet mightily organised, networked and financed.[71] For my part, I fear Rudolf Steiner saw more in these matters, a hundred years ago, than the vast majority of Catholics do now. Even whilst today New Age talk of "Christ consciousness" spreads everywhere…

I close saying, again, these are pointers, only pointers. I pray they may be helpful, at least for certain Christians who care about the fate of the West and are willing to look beyond an academy constrained by Enlightenment rationalism, postmodernism and worse.

★ ★ ★

A "Stop Press" Postscript

After completing this manuscript, I learned Marianne Williamson became an official candidate for president in the US Democratic primaries for 2020. There is scarcely time to comment as this book heads to the typesetter, but even a terse note seems in order. Here is a development inconceivable in the America I grew up in. The candidate's books have sold over three million copies. According to her website, she is

> author of four #1 *New York Times* bestselling books. She has been one of America's most well known public voices for more than three decades [as] a popular guest on television programs such as Oprah, Good Morning America, and Bill Maher.[72]

Williamson's overriding inspiration has been *A Course in Miracles*, a book by the American Helen Schucman, allegedly dictated by Jesus. In it, "Jesus" repeatedly denies the very fundamentals of Christianity, saying his message was misheard by the Apostles.

---

[71] I might add that great Popes once warned about Masonic, if not Eastern occult, endeavour towards this goal, but it has become fashionable to snicker at them, too. Cf. Leo XIII's encyclical letter *Humanum Genus* from 1884.

[72] "Marianne's Bio," accessed December 3, 2019, https://marianne.com/about.

Also for me, the links, ideological and more, between William-son and Findhorn's David Spangler (with all his inheritance from Alice Bailey—the New Age's "chief theorist," to reiterate Sut-cliffe) are apparent. They will be obvious to many others, but are, in any event, readily confirmed by internet searching.

Now, a final very personal comment. I have spoken at length about the *subtle* de-humanizing effects I experienced with New Age spirituality, which certainly drew on *A Course in Miracles*. And on page 91 of this book, the Gentle Traditionalist remarks:

> *A Course in Miracles* discounts all human suffering as unreal. Likewise, Alice Bailey celebrates dropping the bomb on Hiroshima—as the greatest event in untold millennia (greater, apparently, than Christ's coming).

At the same juncture, GT also references Neale Donald Walsch's claim that Hitler never hurt anyone. Such attitudes are directly related to the de-humanization I experienced. However, I could *only* consciously register that de-humanization (which, again, was subdued and not obvious) via tasting, at long last, a *different* spirituality—one which I found to be more elevated and more *human*.

But the present Williamson phenomenon only demonstrates the extent to which that very human Christian spirituality is being surrendered. Valentin Tomberg's words, quoted above, resound in my ears:

> Spiritual adultery is . . . the exchange of a higher moral and spiritual value for a lower moral and spiritual value.

The spiritual adultery of the Anglosphere, replacing Christianity with either secularism or the strange, subtly aloof spirituality promoted by Williamson, Schucman, Spangler, Bailey, Walsch, Tolle, et al., carries immense human cost. In Ireland, as else-where, that cost now includes the lives of the unborn. But the cost is hardly limited to such slaughter, appalling though that be.

Feast of St. Francis Xavier,
Jesuit Apostle of the East
3rd December 2019

ROGER BUCK is a Catholic convert who once resided at Findhorn, Scotland—probably the most renowned New Age community in the world. He was a full time New Age activist for many years. Then, a profound conversion experience changed his life forever (as described in his book *Cor Jesu Sacratissimum*). He lives in the rural northwest of Ireland, an endless source of inspiration for all his writing, as well as YouTube videos.